GRAHAM KERR'S
KITCHEN

OTHER BOOKS BY GRAHAM KERR

Graham Kerr's Minimax™ Cookbook
Graham Kerr's Smart Cooking
Graham Kerr's Creative Choices Cookbook

GRAHAM KERR'S KITCHEN

G. P. PUTNAM'S SONS
NEW YORK

G. P. Putnam's Sons
Publishers Since 1838
200 Madison Avenue
New York, NY 10016

Book design by H. Roberts

Library of Congress Cataloging-in-Publication Data
Kerr, Graham. Graham Kerr's kitchen.
p.   cm.
A collection of recipes to be presented on the PBS program Graham Kerr's kitchen.
Includes index.
ISBN 0-399-13989-3 (acid-free)
1. Cookery. 2. Low-fat diet—Recipes. 3. Low-cholesterol diet—Recipes.
I. Graham Kerr's kitchen (Television program) II. Title.
TX714.K479   1994   94-21013   CIP
641.5'63—dc20

Printed in the United States of America
1 2 3 4 5 6 7 8 9 10

This book is printed on acid-free paper.
∞

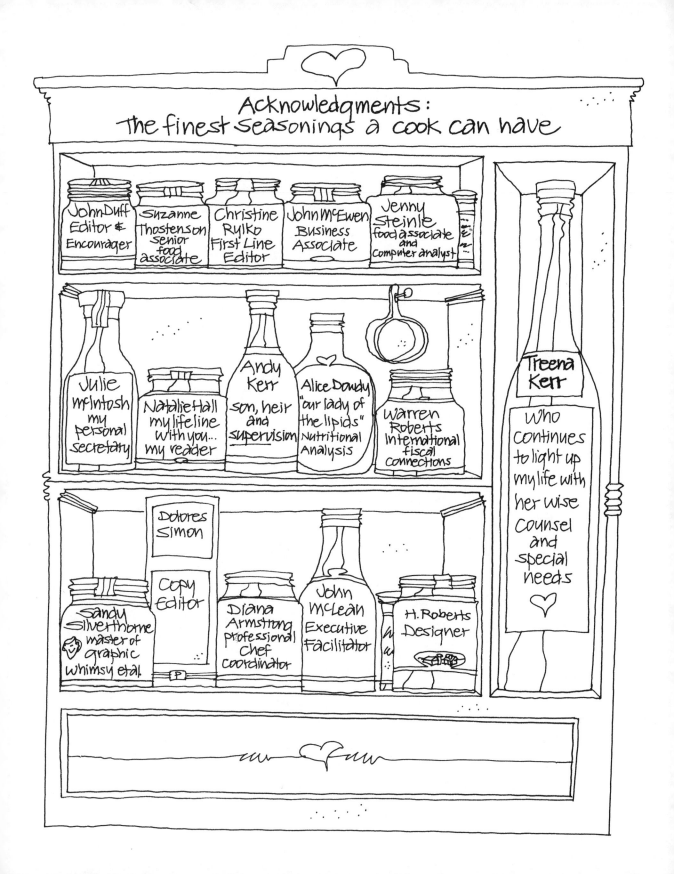

Contents

Preface

Do Yourself a Flavor:
Read How to Use This Book

On the following pages, you'll find a description of all the recipes in this book, laid out in menu fashion, from appetizer to main dish to dessert, just the way you'd read the menu in a good restaurant. Instead of the price, you'll find the page number of that dish's recipe. So if you have a chicken breast defrosting in the refrigerator, check the menu under Main Dishes, Poultry, and you'll find all our suggestions.

But this brings me to the ultimate purpose of this book and its companion television series. Until recently, the whole idea behind cookbooks was to provide dozens, if not hundreds, of recipes from which you could select one or two that somehow took your fancy. However, this book is not organized by recipe. Instead it's divided into 26 chapters, with each chapter highlighting one basic cooking technique that reduces fat and increases flavor, with the recipes used as examples for that technique. Yes, you still have more than 100 complete recipes at your fingertips. But I think even more importantly, you also have basic cooking techniques that can be applied to *all* your cooking.

By technique, I mean "a way of handling food." In this book, and all my books since *The New Seasoning*, published in 1975, I have searched for techniques that reduce risk while at the same time enhancing the aromatic, colorful, and textural pleasures of food. I continue to look for core techniques that can be used wherever I find excessive use of fats, sodium, refined carbohydrates, and large portions of flesh protein. In this book, I have concentrated upon 26 techniques that are spaced through the book like telephone poles linked together to carry one message:

We can make creative healthy changes that last, provided we own the solution.

By ownership I mean that you consider each core technique as a maypole upon which you attach your favorite foods, like ribbons that are woven into a meal. I want the techniques to provide you with tools to easily create your very own recipes with your favorite ingredients that meet both your physical and emotional needs.

For instance, after reading the Macaroni and Cheese recipe in this book, you can choose to prepare it exactly as is with the suggested sweet potato sauce. But if you don't like sweet potatoes, you could still use the technique of replacing high-fat white sauces with smooth vegetable purées and substitute another vegetable, like white beans or parsnips. The creative possibilities for all your favorite dishes are endless.

spinach

beans

poultry

potatoes

jicama

rice

oranges

Maypole

When you exercise your right to substitute your own favorite foods into my techniques, it means that you really do own the creative result. In this way, the healthy recipes you choose will give you the dishes that enable you to make permanent diet changes because you have a diet that's matched identically to you.

The techniques start with methods of cooking various kinds of sauces, go on to main dish techniques, and end with techniques for desserts. Each chapter opens with a one-page discussion of that technique, with my most basic information and tips. I think you'll find these interesting and of great help in understanding the versatility of the technique.

This is followed by a recipe I created with that technique for my television show, by springboarding with one of my television viewers. Springboarding is the process by which we use someone else's recipe or health needs as a diving board to dive into a new recipe.

Also in the recipe, look for the symbol ⚑, which means if you make that recipe in double or triple portions, you can freeze it and have it on hand for a quick and easy extra meal. The extra-meal recipe is the next part of the chapter. Then we've introduced another television viewer, with whom I've springboarded to create a recipe, and finally, we've included a culinary professional with whom I've springboarded for the final dish of each chapter.

After a brief read through the chapters that appeal to you most, you will quickly see how you too can wrap your own favorite flavorings around one or more of my techniques and develop your own recipes.

A great help to me in personalizing recipes is the Food Preference List that you will find on page 6. Please find a photocopier and make a copy of this survey for each person in your family, plus one. Then, when completed, make up a master sheet with a red dot beside every food that is disliked with that individual's initials by its side, and keep it handy.

You can now experiment with using a little less meat, less salt for anyone with high blood pressure, less sugar, and quite a bit less fat and oil. In each case that you shrink the risk, please increase the whole grains, vegetables, and seasonings that feature as "well liked" on the Food Preference Lists. Chances are you'll start to develop a whole new way of eating that will actually last because you made the recipe fit the relationship.

I'm delighted with this cooperative, creative cookbook relationship. Won't you join me?

*Substitute your
favorite foods*

The Menu

APPETIZERS

Bean Tereena
Colorful layers of sweet red bell peppers, creamy garbanzo bean cheese, roasted garlic, and spicy pesto for dipping and spreading.
(Beans) 116

Chinese Dolma
Fried rice with Canadian bacon and vegetables rolled in tender collard green leaves and served with salsa. (*Bao Syang*) 86

Jumbo Potstickers
Bundles of chopped shrimp, shiitake mushrooms, and ginger wrapped in dough and dipped in lime and green onion sauce.
(Étouffée) 190

SOUPS

Beautiful Soup
A medley of grains, wheat berries, brown rice, wild rice, pearl barley, and quinoa is the basis for a soup with onion, garlic, tomato, carrots, fresh thyme, cloves, parsley, kidney beans, and Swiss chard. (Whole Grains) 102

Corn Chowder
Golden puréed corn is the sweet creamy base for this chowder with onions, zucchini, Canadian bacon, and whole corn kernels.
(Smooth Vegetable Sauces) 69

Creamy French Onion Soup
This lightened version of the classic is filled with sweet onions in a rich broth, topped with crispy croutons and cheese.
(Brown Onion Sauces) 45

Oxtail and Barley Soup
Both aromatic and satisfying, beefy roasted oxtails are teamed with shiitake mushrooms and pearl barley. (Meat in the Minor Key) 166

Potsticker Soup
Dumplinglike bundles of shrimp, shiitake mushrooms, and ginger in spicy hot and sour Thai broth. (Étouffée) 192

Turkey Tomato Soup
Home-style heartiness from turkey, rice, and tomato soup. (Ground Meats) 176

Wao Bao Chicken Soup
Chicken, rice, and vegetable soup with lemon, lime, ginger, and garlic. (*Bao Syang*) 87

MAIN DISHES

Beef

Beef Pilaf with Cilantro and Allspice
Professional chef Peter Kump marinates steak in red wine, allspice, and cilantro and presents it with a rice pilaf colorful with zucchini, red bell pepper, and onions. (Rice) 112

Cottage Pie
Great for the crowd—pair the stew of your choice with an easy and delicious crust of light whipped potatoes. (Meat in the Minor Key) 168

Dungaree Pie
Hearty ground-beef chili with kidney beans, green peppers, and tomatoes is baked in a crunchy rice–Parmesan cheese crust.
(Rice and Cheese Crusts) 135

Monterey Casserole
Fiesta family fare—easy layered casserole of ground beef, refried beans, corn, zucchini, olives, and corn tortillas.
(Meat in the Minor Key) 169

Steak and Peppers
Tender strips of flank steak are tossed with red and green bell peppers and served over fettuccine noodles in a hot paprika sauce.
(Sauce Thickeners) 29

Lamb and Game

Afghan Lamb *Palow*
Lamb stew spiced with cinnamon, cumin, and cloves, studded with carrots, raisins, and almonds, and served with rice pilaf.   (Rice) .108

Braised Duck with Pineapple and Peppers
A tropical stew with tender chunks of duck, green bell peppers, and pineapple, served over rice.   (Poultry Skin On) 200

Lime, Lamb, and Barley
Chef Jerri Fifer Broyles marinates lamb in garlic, rosemary, curry, lime, and wine, then tosses it with pearl barley, mushrooms, tomatoes, yellow squash, green onions, red currant jelly, and parsley.   (Whole Grains) 104

Stir-Fried Duck and Lychees
Sweet crispy lychee nuts are an irresistible texture with stir-fried duck, sweet red bell peppers, and snow peas.   (Poultry Skin On) 198

Venison with Crunchy Cabbage
Marinated venison in a rich brown onion sauce is delightfully contrasted by Chef Michel Bouit's crunchy, minty cabbage studded with hazelnuts. (Brown Onion Sauce) 46

Pork

Chinese Dolma
Fried rice with Canadian bacon and vegetables rolled in tender collard green leaves and served with salsa.   (*Bao Syang*) 86

Fried Rice
Seasoned rice and wheat berries tossed with Canadian bacon, sun-dried tomatoes, green onions, and eggs.   (*Bao Syang*) 84

Roast Pork with Apple Gravy
Well-seasoned roast pork is served with golden potatoes and Brussels sprouts in a rich apple-orange gravy.   (Roast Meats and Gravies) . . .50

Roast Smoked Pork Loin
Professional chef Tom Douglas roasts a boneless pork loin with potatoes and ladles it with a rich, caramelized shallot and carrot gravy. (Roast Meats and Gravies) 54

Roast Pork Stir-Fry
Roast pork with garlic and ginger is stir-fried with sweet snow peas and crisp jicama and moistened with apple juice.   (Roast Meats and Gravies) .52

Smoked Pork and Apple Tiddy Oggy
Innovative low-fat pastry crust tops this savory meat pie filled with a stew of smoked pork chop, sweet potatoes, and apples. (Pastry Crusts) 124

Sweet and Sour Surprise Meatballs
Ground pork and rice meatballs are filled with a juicy pineapple surprise, topped with sweet pineapple and tomato sauce, and served over noodles.   (Ground Meats) 177

Wild Bill's Nearly Famous Pork Tenderloin
The baking juices of the pork tenderloin form the base of a low-fat sauce with onion, garlic, mushrooms, wine, thyme, and sage. (Sauce Thickeners) 26

Poultry

Bangers and Mash
Smoked chicken sausage is teamed with creamy mashed potatoes in a hearty brown onion sauce for a springboarded version of England's favorite comfort food.   (Brown Onion Sauces) 42

Breast of Chicken in Sweet Pepper Sauce
Juicy braised chicken breasts in an easy sauce of red, green, and yellow bell peppers, wine, mushrooms, and cilantro.   (Strained Yogurt) 58

Chicken Breasts with Cabernet, Orange and Ginger Sauce
Chef David Day presents tender boneless chicken breasts with pears in a lovely red wine, orange, and ginger sauce.   (Poultry Skin On) 202

Chile, Cheese, and Chicken Enchiladas
Chicken breast, mild chile peppers, onion, and cheese are wrapped in tortillas and topped with two simple red and green reduced sauces. (Reductions) 16

Chinese Chicken Salad
Boneless chicken breasts, marinated in sweet hoisin sauce and wine, are tossed in an oriental vinaigrette with bean thread noodles, Chinese cabbage, green onions, and cilantro. (Vinaigrette Broths and Sauces) 78

Chunky Chicken Curry
Marinated chunks of boneless chicken breast in a curry sauce with pineapple, zucchini, and carrots are served with butternut squash and rice. (Étouffée) 192

Creamy Garam Masala Chicken
A creamy white curry with ginger-marinated chicken chunks and a sweet yogurt sauce of ground almonds, cardamom, and coriander by Chef Gerri Gilliland. (White Sauces) 38

Creole Chicken
Warm chile peppers and spices heat up this very quick and easy dish of chicken, Canadian bacon, green bell pepper, and tomatoes. (The Maillard Reaction) 185

David's Chicken Piccata
Enjoy Chef David Glynn's version of boneless chicken breasts and wild mushrooms in a red pepper purée, wine, and caper sauce over linguine. (Meat in the Minor Key) 170

Oven-Fried Chicken
Chicken breasts are simply coated with yogurt and mustard, rolled in bread crumbs, and baked to perfection. Served with buttermilk and parsley-spiced mashed potatoes. (Strained Yogurt) 61

Potpie
A delicious low-fat pastry crust tops a savory meat pie made with any of your favorite meat stews. (Pastry Crusts) 126

Peruvian Chicken
Quick and easy, chicken cooked with onions, tomatoes, mushrooms, and potatoes in red wine sauce. (The Maillard Reaction) 182

Roast Chicken with Cranberry Gravy
Roast chicken with tender sweet potatoes and crisp green broccoli is served with a rich cranberry gravy. (Roast Meats and Gravies) 53

Rosemary Chicken with Butternut Sauce
Chicken breasts stuffed with rosemary and parsley are ladled by Chef Martin Frost with a fresh cilantro and butternut squash sauce and pungent ginger-infused quick couscous. (Smooth Vegetable Sauces) 70

Smoked Turkey–Stuffed Peppers
Sweet red bell peppers stuffed with smoked turkey, crispy jicama, hot jalapeño peppers, cumin, kidney beans, and rice, served with a creamy cilantro and Parmesan cheese sauce. (Stack 'n Steam) 150

Stuffed Swiss Chard Leaves
Quick and easy—Swiss chard leaves are rolled around ground turkey, jicama, jalapeño pepper, cumin, kidney beans, and rice filling and baked in tomato-vegetable juice. (Stack 'n Steam) .152

Turkey Meatballs and Mushrooms
Grape jelly and tomatoes combine in the sweet and spicy sauce that coats these ground turkey meatballs and mushrooms. (Ground Meats) 174

Turkey Pastrami Paprikash
Tender golden potatoes are ladled with creamy white-onion sauce, spicy turkey pastrami, and crunchy cabbage. (White Sauces) 34

Seafood

Ahi Burger with Mustard Ice Cream
Bursting with ginger and horseradish, this ground tuna burger is served with mustard "ice cream" by Chef Jean Pierre Lemanissier. (Ground Meats) 178

Clams with Black Bean Sauce
Chef John Rowley features a zesty sauce of black beans, ginger, garlic, and red chile that clings to each clam. (*Bao Syang*) 88

Grilled Halibut in Apple Cider Vinaigrette
An apple cider vinaigrette is the base for culinary professional Joy Delf's marinated and grilled halibut with ginger, lime, orange juice, cumin, and garlic. (Vinaigrette Broths and Sauces) 80

Grilled Salmon with Garlic Cucumber Relish
Chef Mary Sue Milliken mixes garlic and crunchy pickling cucumbers with yogurt to complement grilled salmon and marinated roasted red, green, and yellow bell peppers. (Strained Yogurt) .62

Mahimahi with Cockles and Mussels
Chef Rick Moonen's pan-seared mahimahi fish is teamed with cockles, mussels, carrot, zucchini, chives, dill, tarragon, and a burst of lemon. (Étouffée) 194

Orange Roughy Poached in Vinaigrette
Orange roughy is poached in a citrus-infused vinaigrette and served with fresh pineapple, hot red pepper, and fresh mint. (Vinaigrette Broths and Sauces) 77

Russian Salmon Pie
Fresh with lemon and dill, colorful layers of tender pink salmon, asparagus, and mushrooms are presented by Chef Suzanne Thostenson in a crunchy rice and cheese crust. (Rice and Cheese Crusts) 136

Smoked Chilean Sea Bass with Thai Vinaigrette
Earl Grey tea and cloves are the basis to smoke sea bass with a vinaigrette sauce of gingerroot, lemon grass, lime, cilantro, mint, and couscous. (Vinaigrette Broths and Sauces) 74

Striped Sea Bass with Roasted Vegetables
Chef Matt Stein presents sea bass with roasted potatoes, carrots, squash, and leeks in a spicy paprika sauce. (Roasted and Broiled Vegetables) 162

Twin Fillets of Orange Roughy and Salmon
Tender fillets of orange roughy and salmon are wrapped in Swiss chard by culinary professional Diana Armstrong, steamed to perfection, and served with a white wine, rosemary, and cumin sauce. (Stack 'n Steam) 154

The Peacemaker
Oysters and Canadian bacon in a creamy horseradish sauce are presented in a hot, crusty French bread loaf. (Bread Crusts) 140

Vegetarian

Bean Enchiladas
Spicy, cheesy Bean Tereena is spooned into tortillas and topped with cheese. (Beans) 118

Black Beans and Rice
Black beans, red and green bell peppers fragrant with lime and cilantro, served with seasoned brown rice and fruit salad. (Beans) 119

Black Bean Burritos
Quick dinner fare: black beans, cilantro, and chile peppers in a reduced red sauce and wrapped in flour tortillas. (Reductions) 20

Broccoli and Cauliflower au Gratin
Crisp broccoli and cauliflower are baked in a sweet potato purée with Parmesan cheese. (Smooth Vegetable Sauces) 68

Champ
Buttermilk-mashed potatoes are filled with a low-fat golden-yellow "butter" sauce. (Brown Onion Sauces) 28

Creamy Peas
Delicate petit peas are delectable in a creamy white onion sauce, garnished with fresh mint. (White Sauces) 36

Nora's Spicy Black Beans
Chef Nora Pouillon creates a "vegetable rainbow" of sugar snap peas, corn, and Swiss chard and tops it with black beans spiced with orange and hot chile flavorings. (Beans) 120

Roasted Eggplant Curry

Chef Neela Paniz shares this quick and easy recipe for sweet roasted eggplant, onions, tomatoes, and potatoes bathed in spicy curry sauce. (The Maillard Reaction) 186

Roasted Vegetable Lasagne

A hearty lasagne dense with roasted red bell peppers, zucchini, eggplant, spinach, and mushrooms in tomato sauce. (Roasted and Broiled Vegetables) 160

Vegetables with Fennel and Thyme Sauce

Chef Thierry Rautureau combines fennel, thyme, cloves, and anise in an easy reduced sauce, delicious on crisp blanched vegetables and sprinkled with goat cheese. (Reductions) 22

Whole-Grain Island on a Parsnip Sea

An island of rice, wheat berries, pearl barley, and peas floats in a "sea" of sweet creamy parsnip purée, fragrant with rosemary. (Whole Grains) 100

Wild Mushroom Risotto

Earthy porcini mushrooms, sun-dried tomatoes, white wine, and Parmesan cheese are the base for this rich, creamy rice creation. (Rice) . .111

Pasta

Angel Hair Marinara

Delicate angel hair pasta in red marinara sauce becomes the base for your favorite garnish: clams, shrimp, green olives—it's your choice. (Pasta) 208

Angel Hair Pasta with Mushrooms, Escarole, and Clams

Chef Peter Pryor tosses clams, hearty green escarole, and mushrooms with angel hair pasta in a sauce of fish stock, tomatoes, and Parmesan cheese. (Pasta) .210

Creamy Pesto with Hot Pasta

Linguine is sauced with a low-fat version of the classic fresh basil, walnut, Parmesan cheese, garlic, and lemon juice pesto. (White Sauces) . .37

Latin American Pasta Shells Marinara

Jumbo pasta shells are stuffed with beans, mushrooms, and onions and ladled with a quick, easy marinara sauce. (Pasta) 206

Linguine with Scallops

Tender moist scallops and shrimp are tossed with linguine studded with sweet smoky roasted garlic, zucchini and red, green, and yellow bell peppers. (Roasted Vegetables) 158

Macaroni and Cheese

Macaroni cooked in a golden sweet potato purée with Parmesan cheese and minty peas. (Smooth Vegetable Sauces) 66

Rigatoni Cavafiori Patty

Tube-shaped rigatoni is bathed in a creamy cheese sauce and studded with sweet red bell peppers and mushrooms. (Pasta) 209

LUNCH/BRUNCH

Cornquichetador

A beautiful low-fat quiche of golden corn custard and sweet red bell peppers in a crunchy rice and Parmesan cheese crust. (Rice and Cheese Crusts) 132

Cornbread

This favorite golden bread is a low-fat winner: sweet with honey and savory with buttermilk. (Egg Substitutes) 95

Fruit Soufflé Omelet

A sweet fruit omelet topped with creamy orange sauce. (Egg Substitutes) 92

Ham and Cheese Sandwich

Graham's favorite sandwich has smoked ham, Swiss cheese, and sweet and smoky roasted red bell peppers. (Roasted and Broiled Vegetables) 160

Ham Sandwich Pie

Crunchy rice and Parmesan cheese crust is filled with Canadian bacon, French bread slices, roasted red peppers, and a corn custard. (Rice and Cheese Crusts) 134

Lamb Palow Pop-Ups

Lamb stew in toasted whole wheat pitas with sweet and spicy mango chutney.   (Rice) . . .110

Mushroom and Spinach Omelet

This mushroom and spinach–filled omelet is set off by fresh dill and Parmesan cheese.   (Egg Substitutes) 94

Paisano Sandwich

Slice your sandwich off a loaf of French bread slathered in cheese spread and filled with layers of Canadian bacon, spinach, and tomatoes. (Bread Crusts) 143

Potatoes Baked with Apples and Onion Sauce

Potatoes baked until tender with Canadian bacon, onions, and apples in a rich and hearty brown onion sauce.   (Brown Onion Sauces) 44

Rice-Filled Omelet

Chef Kweethai Chin Neill creates an egg dish dense with chicken, rice, pea pods, and red bell peppers.   (Egg Substitutes) 96

Torta Rustica

Layers of roasted eggplant, zucchini, bell peppers, Canadian bacon, and spinach are smothered in custard and baked by chef Jenny Steinle in a beautiful bread crust.   (Bread Crusts) . .144

DESSERTS

Carrot Cake

Layers of carrot, pineapple, and raisin-studded cake are filled with crunchy and creamy walnut-cheese filling.   (Cakes) 214

Cherry Cobbler

Sweet cherry filling topped with crumbly low-fat pastry cobbler topping.   (Pastry Crusts) 127

Chocolate Cookie Sandwiches

Low-fat ice cream or tea sandwiches: chocolate cookies are filled with raspberry jam and creamy strained vanilla yogurt.   (Cocoa) 224

Cocoa Cookies and "Cream"

Chocolate cookies are layered with raspberry purée and whipped "cream" for an elegant yet easy parfait presentation.   (Cocoa) 222

Cocoa Spice Cake

Rich and moist with prune and pear purée, this dark chocolaty cocoa cake has a creamy topping with fresh strawberries.   (Cakes) 218

Fresh Strawberry Pie

Chef Lizzie Burt's easy no-bake pie with a crust of walnuts, oatmeal, and raisins filled with fresh strawberries glistening in a simple berry sauce. (Sauce Thickeners) 30

Frozen Cocoa Soufflé with Warm Raspberry Sauce

Chef Vincent Guerithault creates an elegant iced cocoa soufflé drizzled with meltingly warm raspberry sauce.   (Cocoa) 226

New Black Bottom Cupcakes

Moist cocoa cupcakes are filled with banana cream and topped with chocolate chips. (Cocoa) 225

Pumpkin Bread

Fragrant nutmeg, cinnamon, and ginger flavor this sweet pumpkin-raisin bread. (Cakes) 217

Spiced Apple Pie

Chef Terri Berkey's rich cashew nut pastry crust is the base for this warmly spiced apple pie. (Pastry Crusts) 128

Steamed Apples Julie

Apples stuffed with cookies, toasted walnuts, and juicy raisins are steam-infused with cinnamon and allspice and topped with a creamy maple-sweet sauce.   (Stack 'n Steam) 153

Steamed Carrot Pudding

A steamed carrot pudding topped with creamy carrot and walnut sauce.   (Cakes) 216

Introduction

This is a book for those who want to change the way they eat. It's also about people who are already changing and those professional cooks who establish the food trends that help to change us all.

Like lint on a dark suit.

You know, other people's behavior has a way of attaching itself to us, like lint to a dark suit. We observe someone we know who is losing weight—I call them "a work in progress." They look and feel great. We ask them for their secret and hope they'll reveal a speedy magic bullet: a specific powder, or program, regimen, routine, even a recipe. Then we can rush off enthusiastically to eat 4 grapefruit and a large bowl of bran cereal a day.

Magic Bullet.

Give it a week or two and then the muttering will start: why did it work for them, but not for you?

What you missed was your friend's "sequence": the set of life events that culminated in resolve to make a permanent lifestyle change. What was the sequence of events that happened step-by-step until the weight was lost, the cholesterol lowered, or hypertension controlled with less medication? We long for a simple system that's just right for us and millions like us. But the fact is, there aren't millions "just like us" and there is no single system that is exactly right for everyone.

It really works!

However, I do believe that there is a common "sequence" to making a successful and permanent eating change.

Am I at Risk?

The sequence begins with something that gets your attention: an annual doctor's check-up, weight gain, cholesterol level increase, or your blood pressure up. Or it could be someone you love, and for whom you cook, who needs to change a habit that you *know* is harmful.

Are you at risk?

Our bodies all respond differently to the food we eat and the beverages we drink, but since we eat and drink several times a day, every day of our lives, what we do accumulates. A small but harmful indulgence on a daily basis can create significant medical risks, whereas a series of small positive changes can become an enormously important contributor to our future health.

Let's begin the sequence for you with a direct question: **Am I at risk?**

If you're the person who decides what to cook for other people, then you need to broaden the question to:

Not everyone's the same.

Is anyone I cook for at risk?

But let's start the sequence with you, since the knowledge of our own limits makes us better able to appreciate the limits of others.

Your Physician First

There is nobody better qualified than your personal physician (or health clinic) to make simple initial health assessments that are the beginning of your desire to make lifestyle changes involving your diet.

Doctor getting your attention.

Bring the following check-list to your doctor and make sure these issues are discussed:

Your personal medical history and your extended family's health history, to determine if you are particularly susceptible to any disease, genetically or through lifestyle.

Blood analysis, urine analysis, and blood pressure.

Are there any modifiable factors for you to work on through your diet, like high cholesterol or weight control?

I also suggest that your doctor show you a decade-by-decade prognosis for your future health. Using my weight as an example, in 1970 I weighed 187 pounds; in 1980, 190 pounds; and in 1990, 205 pounds. Over two decades I had gained 18

Projecting into the future.

pounds. Without changing my eating habits, I could continue to gain and therefore could pre-dict that by the year 2000, I could weigh between 215 and 220 pounds; by the year 2010, 225 to 230 pounds.

If this were to happen, I would be up to 50 pounds overweight, which is technically called obese. Therefore, I would be much more at risk for heart disease, high blood pressure, stroke, diabetes, cancers of the prostate and bowel, degenerative joint disorders, etc.

Of course, no prognosis is inevitable. What you're trying to discover from your doctor is whether you have the potential for health risks from your current lifestyle habits. We're often reluctant to get news that we need to change our lifestyle—our freedom of choice is somehow threatened. We worry about making a fuss about nothing. We feel fine and hate to be self-focused—isn't it selfish of us?

Can I turn the tables for you (and myself) for just one moment with some very personal ques-tions: Are you loved by anyone? If you become seriously ill, would anyone care? If you became disabled and needed help to get around, would this burden someone you love?

If the answer to any of these questions is yes, then you may suddenly realize that either prevention or intervention on your behalf, because of a known health-risk factor, may be a truly loving and unselfish gesture on your behalf.

The question posed above can then become an exclamation: **I am at risk!**

Do I Want to Change?

During my "Galloping Gourmet" days in the 1960s, a sequence started when I was told I had a 265 cholesterol count and a high uric acid level in my blood, pro-ducing gout and kidney stones—and I was only 35 years old. I didn't change right then because my physician didn't say that I was "at risk" (he certainly would today). Of course, since I

Galloping Gourmet days.

was also up to my neck cooking in clarified butter and good brandy, I probably wouldn't have batted an eyelid.

But let's move on to our modern enlightened times and assume that your doctor has told you that you are "at risk" unless you change one or more habits. It's here that another simple question continues the sequence: **Do I want to change?**

In my galloping days, I would have said no, and that, for a season, would have been that. But seasons change, and change, and change, until eventually we do too. In our younger years, the choice is usually up to us. But today, as I look carefully over my shoulder, I see at least three strong motivators.

The Children Are Watching

A recent study asked young adults who or what influenced them to adopt their present eating habits. Overwhelmingly they replied that what *their father* ate had the greatest impact. In follow-up interviews, it became clear that the chil-

The kids are watching . . .

dren saw their mothers go to all kinds of trouble to serve their fathers what they liked. This signaled that the fathers' food selections were "good," or at least "right."

My wife, Treena, and I are now grandparents five times over. While our immediate three children have grown away from our direct influence, our grandchildren have taken their place and seem all the more vulnerable to observing poor (but delicious) habits and judging them as good or right because "Grandpa or Grandma likes them."

Yes, the children are watching; and I for one, want to be the best example going. If it's rich ice cream or an apple for dessert, guess what I choose? I can hear the crunch from here, but it isn't from chocolate chunks in triple-chocolate-strength cream!

Combating the "Creep"

Creeping disorder.

Health risks from your diet can kind of creep up on you. It's so easy to say that the risk from a pat of butter on your toast is minimal; but let the pats accumulate over a whole day, joining with the fat in all the other foods you eat that day, and that pat of butter becomes part of a tangible health risk to the 40 million people in this country who suffer from diagnosed cardiovascular disease.

The good news is that little changes can easily combat this creep. Let's go back to that pat of butter. One tablespoon of butter has fully one third of the saturated fat you should consume in an entire day. Have a pat of butter at each meal and you're over the recommended ceiling for saturated fat for that day. Hope you haven't eaten any cheese, milk, or meat, which would put you way over the saturated fat limit.

But what if you changed that butter to my favorite substitute on bread: sweet and creamy strained yogurt (see page 234)? You go from consuming a third of your saturated fat limit to zero—no fat at all! Strained yogurt leaves you plenty of room to eat moderate amounts of cheese, milk, and fresh proteins. An entire chapter on strained yogurt in this book should give you the full scope of its culinary potential.

Another dramatic example comes from eggs. One egg has 71 percent of all the cholesterol the average person needs in one day. What happens if you replace eggs with liquid egg substitute? You go from 213 grams of cholesterol to zero—no cholesterol at all! A definite health advantage, not just for the obvious egg dishes but for all your baking, as well. See the chapter on Egg Substitutes in this book for some great recipes.

Environmental pollutants.

I've decided to choose a lifestyle that slowly benefits my future health. While some other environmental pollutant may assault me, at least I will not have deliberately selected the polluted path. My motive to avoid nutritional creeps is simple: as I grow older, I'm becoming wiser, and I choose to be a quiet influence toward the positive in life.

The Marriage Foxhole

Does K-ration stand for Kerr ration?

I call the last major motivator in the sequence toward change the marriage foxhole. It refers to my life with my wife, Treena. In marriage we committed ourselves "for better or worse, for richer or poorer, in sickness and in health." This put us in a foxhole, battling against inherited genetic tendencies. Treena's family history and genetic predisposition put her at high risk for heart disease, much higher than mine. My diet limits can include an occasional ice cream, egg, or small steak. But hers, frankly, cannot. My reason for not eating these personally permissible foods when she must exclude them is simple: I do not want her to be tempted to eat something that's forbidden fruit, just because it's on her husband's plate.

There is an old saying that applies here: "Do nothing that makes your brother stumble, offended, or weak." A good slogan to hang on the fridge door.

The Will to Change

The next step in the sequence of change is profound and should never be underestimated: **The will to change.**

I have found that it helps to reinforce this next step by looking at a mirror, saying the words aloud slowly and staring deliberately: **I will change**. Make a note of the date and time you make this declaration and put it where you won't lose it—even engrave it at the bottom or top of your mirror. The investment you'll be making in this declaration will be minimal when compared to the millions and millions of dollars that partially motivated people fork out each year for medication, operations, diet programs, health club memberships, and special equipment, even for books like this!

Recipes That Fit Your Unique Needs

Until this part of the sequence, you've concentrated upon motive and recording accurately your point of departure. Now you need to look at the best way to change your eating habits.

I'm constantly being written by people with personal diet needs, asking for recipes that suit their specific situation. I also receive many treasured family recipes that their owners want to be changed in order to come into more reasonable diet standards. All these people's special nutritional needs and letters asking for help became the inspiration for the recipes that you'll find throughout this book.

But before I could set about creating and changing recipes, I needed detailed input from these people, telling me their food likes and dislikes. I found it was best if they filled out a Food Preference List (see page 6). This gave me the basis to select ingredients and flavoring that would be most acceptable.

Then the sequence continued with something I call "springboarding."

Make Your Own Dive

Everyone who has joined me in this book is involved in springboarding. To some extent, we all springboard in many areas of our life—we observe, listen, learn, and then adapt each other's behavior to suit our own circumstances

In my field of creative change, a recipe or Food Preference List becomes a springboard, or platform. We bounce up and down on it to get the feel of it, then we experiment, maybe by just changing one or two ingredients. And the final recipe is, so to speak, a dive into a pool that represents our individual food preferences and special health needs.

For example, on page 222 you'll find a springboard chocolate cookie creation I did with Suma-Kotrba. She sent me a recipe for a chocolate dessert, hoping I could bring it into nutritional reason. She liked the changes I made, with the exception of the Grape Nuts cereal texture in the cookie (which I really loved). So Sharon and I both make our cookie, using each other's recipes as springboards to get a final result that exactly suits our own tastes.

Springboard   favorites   loved one   invent something

FOOD PREFERENCE LIST
Check what you like, cross out what you don't like.

1. Seasonings and Flavors
Allspice ☑ Almond Extract ☒ Anchovies ☑ Basil ☑ Bay Leaf ☑ Canadian Bacon ☒ Capers ☒ Caraway Seed ☑ Cardamom ☑ Cayenne Pepper ☑ Chili Powder ☑ Chives ☒ Cilantro ☑ Cinnamon ☑ Cloves ☑ Cocoa ☒ Coconut Essence ☑ Coriander ☑ Cumin ☑ Curry Powder ☑ Dijon Mustard ☑ Dill Weed/Seed ☒ Fish Sauce ☐ Flowers—Edible ☐ Garam Masala ☑ Garlic ☑ Gingerroot ☐ Juniper Berries ☐ Kaffir Lime Leaves ☑ Lemon Grass ☑ Maple Syrup ☑ Mint ☑ Molasses ☑ Nutmeg ☑ Nuts ☑ Oregano ☑ Paprika ☑ Parmesan Cheese ☑ Parsley ☑ Pepper ☑ Rosemary ☑ Saffron ☑ Sage ☑ Salt—Sea ☑ Savory ☑ Sesame Oil ☒ Shallots ☑ Soy Sauce ☒ Strained Yogurt ☑ Sun-dried Tomatoes ☑ Tarragon ☑ Thyme ☐ ☐ Turmeric ☐ Vanilla ☑ Vinegars ☑ Worcestershire Sauce ☑ Zests of Citrus

2. Vegetables
☐ Artichokes ☑ Asparagus ☑ Beans—dried ☑ Beans—fresh ☑ Beets ☒ Bok Choy ☑ Broccoli ☑ Brussels Sprouts ☑ Cabbage ☑ Carrots ☑ Cauliflower ☑ Celery ☑ Corn ☑ Cucumbers ☑ Eggplants ☑ Fennel ☑ Green Onions ☑ Greens—Salad ☒ Jicama ☒ Leeks ☑ Kale ☑ Mushrooms ☒ Okra ☐ Onions ☑ Parsnips ☑ Peas—Dried ☑ Peas—Green ☑ Peppers—Sweet Bell ☑ Peppers—Hot ☑ Potatoes ☑ Radishes ☒ Rutabagas ☑ Spinach ☑ Sprouts ☑ Squash—Summer ☑ Squash—Winter ☑ Sweet Potatoes ☑ Swiss Chard ☒ Tomatillos ☑ Tomatoes ☐ Turnips ☑ Water Chestnuts ☐ Other

3. Fruit
☑ Apples ☑ Apricots ☑ Avocados ☑ Bananas ☑ Berries ☑ Cherries ☑ Cranberries ☒ Dates ☑ Figs ☑ Grapefruit ☑ Grapes ☐ Kiwifruit ☑ Lemons ☑ Limes ☑ Mangoes ☑ Nectarines ☑ Oranges ☑ Papayas ☑ Peaches ☑ Pears ☒ Persimmons ☑ Plums ☑ Prunes ☑ Raisins ☑ Rhubarb ☑ Tangerines ☐ Other

4. Main Ingredients
☑ Bacon ☑ Beans ☑ Beef ☑ Chicken ☒ Duck ☑ Eggs ☒ Egg Substitute ☑ Fish ☒ Game ☒ Game Hen ☒ Goose ☑ Grains ☑ Ham ☒ Lamb ☑ Pasta ☑ Pork ☑ Rice ☑ Sausage ☑ Shellfish ☒ Tofu ☑ Turkey ☐ Other

5. Food Styles
☑ Asian ☐ British ☐ Caribbean ☑ Chinese ☐ French ☐ Greek ☐ Indian ☐ Italian ☑ Japanese ☐ Northern European ☐ South American ☑ Spanish ☐ Thai ☑ USA/Northeast ☑ USA/Northwest ☑ USA/Southern ☑ USA/Southwest ☐ Other

6. Cooking Techniques
☑ Bake ☑ Boil ☑ Braise ☑ Broil ☑ Casserole ☑ Deep-Fry ☐ Étoufée ☑ Grill/Barbecue ☑ Microwave ☐ Poach ☐ Pressure-Cook ☐ Reduce Liquids ☑ Shallow-Fry/Sauté ☑ Skewer ☑ Smoke ☑ Soup/Stew ☑ Steam ☑ Stir-Fry ☐ Wrap Cookery

Favorite Main Dishes and Desserts
Write in the space provided your three favorite main dishes and desserts

_____

_____

_____

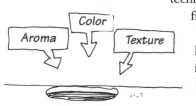

Tess Fields is another great example. She adored parsnips, but just couldn't find many recipes that featured them as a main ingredient. Using her preference for parsnips as the platform, I springboarded to create a silky parsnip cream sauce for whole grains or pasta. Now if you like the possibilities inherent in a puréed vegetable sauce, but don't like parsnips, it's your turn to springboard, using the puréed vegetable of your choice: sweet potatoes, butter beans, the list is endless.

As you can see, springboarding unlocks creativity and, most importantly, tailors *my recipes* to *your personal likes and needs.* When you springboard and modify something to fit you more exactly, you have taken an essential step to *lasting* diet change.

To help you start the process of springboarding, please think about the main dishes that you like the most. You will then notice that this book is divided into 26 basic cooking techniques. Your main dishes will match with one of these general categories. If you then turn to the chapter on that technique, you should find many ideas to help you reduce health risks and increase flavor in all your cooking.

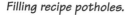

Filling recipe potholes.

How to Fill a Culinary Vacuum

Remember, whenever you use a cooking technique that reduces health risk by removing an ingredient (especially fat, oil, cream, eggs, cheese, fatty meats, and flesh proteins), you create a culinary vacuum that must be filled with healthier ingredients that enhance aroma, color, and texture. This is another key to making lasting diet change; otherwise your "healthy" food will be so bland-tasting that you will probably revert back to your previous eating habits.

I can't stress enough how much it will help to take the time to write down your own Food Preference List, both for yourself and the people for whom you cook. So turn to page 6 and do it now. May I strongly recommend that you photocopy the page and give one to each member of your household? Not only will you have a checklist of enjoyable foods that can be used to fill the vacuum created by the reduction of fats,

salts, sugars, and large amounts of flesh protein, you could trigger completely new ideas for the way you cook and season food.

One brief word of encouragement before you start the Food Preference List. One of the world's most popular and unique recipes is the Reuben sandwich: a thick layer of tender corned beef, melted Swiss cheese, juicy sauerkraut, and Russian dressing on fried rye bread. The ingredients make it obvious that Mr. Reuben must have worked in a delicatessen.

My word of encouragement is that just like Mr. Reuben, you, too, live in the midst of your own circumstances. You have a unique connection to many foods—both from the present time and through your memories. I'm not saying to cut off all of your connections, but to accentuate the positive while at the same time reducing (not eliminating) the negative, and to do it in a creative way that suits your individual taste. The new dishes you create are more a matter of your relationship to food than to recipes; and your day-to-day foods will be changed for the better and be more likely to remain changed because they are yours.

Now, please, do yourself a *flavor* and fill in the Food Preference List on page 6.

The Point of Creative Departure

At this point you have traveled a good way down the sequence of lasting diet change. Let's see what you may know about yourself and your family:

- You are willing to change your lifestyle to improve your health.
- An accurate technical evaluation of your present physical condition and an idea of your future health if your present direction is not changed
- A good idea of what you actually cook and eat
- A profile of foods you like and dislike

- A list of cooking techniques that can help to reduce risk in the foods you presently eat

We now come to what I think is one of the most exciting parts of the sequence and it is here that I must give you permission to be creative.

This book is full of people, just like you, who want to change, and having changed, to settle comfortably and enjoyably into their new positive lifestyles. Treena and I are just entering our 22nd year of food change. But note please that our change lasted because we created a new lifestyle out of the best of our past, not out of its wreckage.

In our 22 years of experience with change, we found that we needed two disciplines: a means of measuring our daily food and an accountability link to keep us on track.

How to Measure Moderation

"A little of what you fancy does you good." So goes the popular British saying, echoed by Julia Child's admonition, "You can eat anything if you eat it in moderation." I heartily agree, yet I must inquire, How does one measure moderation, since clearly what's good for the 30-pound goose isn't necessarily good for the 10-pound gander?

I am constantly amazed by the way some folk measure their food. Their diligence and accuracy are truly remarkable, and they deserve the kind of applause reserved for one-of-a-kind star performers. Of course, they truly are "one of a kind" because most of us find it impossible to count so assiduously!

Have you ever tried to keep an accurate

What's good for the goose . . .

Early attempt at "weighing with the eyes."

food diary, recording everything you eat and drink for just one week? Studies show that even when people attempt to be absolutely honest and record their food choices by weight and/or volume, their estimates were almost 50 percent understated from the reality. In other words, what they thought was an 1,800-calorie meal with 50 grams of fat turned out to be 3,600 calories with 100 grams of fat. If our efforts at measurement are in any way similar, is it any wonder that you and I throw up our hands and say dieting doesn't work? After all, in most cases it's not only *what* we eat but *how much* that really makes the difference.

Learn to Weigh with Your Eyes

I have several suggestions to aid you in marvelous measurements. First, purchase a good kitchen scale that will weigh up to 4 pounds (1.8 kg) in both ounces and grams. Select one full month and commit to weighing every single thing you eat in your normal portion size, including second helpings. Buy a good calorie and fat guide and use it to teach yourself what's in it for you, expressed by total calorie and fat grams. If you or any member of your family is hypertensive (high blood pressure), then also measure sodium (salt).

Now you can begin to learn to weigh with your eyes. As you actually pick up, weigh, and measure everything day after day, you'll come to remember instinctively a food's value. Think of equivalents in your mind. For instance, when the scale reads 3½ ounces, you'll see a steak the size of a deck of playing cards. This is a great visual reminder of the amount of steak from a choice-grade cut that has 172 calories and 10 grams of fat. Later, when you size up a steak on a plate,

just by looking at it you will have weighed with your eyes. Perform this task for 30 days and you will be well on the way to success. I know of no better way to grasp what food actually means to your body. I believe that the reason why 96 percent of people fail to make lasting changes in their diet is that they never learn how to make these visual measurements.

Another great aid to measuring moderation is the exact nutritional analysis in this book of each recipe, based on the University of Minnesota's computer software program called the Nutrition Data System. I have also incorporated the Percent Daily Value figure that was devised by the Food and Drug Administration and introduced on their new food label. This figure shows you what percent of that nutrient's daily limit you have consumed at that meal. So if you don't know how many grams of fat you must eat each day, just look at the Percent Daily Value column and you'll see where you stand. You should know that this figure is based on a healthy person who consumes 2,000 calories a day. Adjust your personal daily value accordingly.

More Than a Collection of Recipes

As I mentioned in the Preface, this book is organized into 26 chapters, each of which teaches you a basic cooking technique that lowers fat and increases flavor. Each chapter has 4 recipes that illustrate that chapter's cooking technique. The first and third recipes are collaborative springboards created by requests from viewers of my television shows: people who wrote me with special dietary needs or wanted favorite family recipes revised into more reasonable health terms.

The second recipe in each chapter is provided as an answer to one of my most repeated requests: Can you create something that's easy to make at the last moment for busy-people-on-the-go?

My astute food associate Jenny Steinle pointed out that almost every recipe has one element that could be executed in greater volume with little extra effort, packaged, frozen, and carefully thawed later. This is delicious, healthy, and convenient fast food! For instance, a slow-cooked pilaf that used brown and wild rice with wheat berries could be tripled. A good Italian marinara sauce (tomatoes, garlic, carrot, celery, and onion) could be made by the gallon and frozen in small containers. And there are no added packaging costs or chemical additives!

To aid you in spotting extra meals, look for this logo ⊠. You'll then see instructions for doubling or tripling some aspect of that recipe and freezing it for future use. This I can promise you: Follow the tips below for planning and freezing extra meals and you'll have hundreds of fast and creative recipes that will surprise you with their ability to meet your needs for convenience, health, and enjoyment.

Tips for Freezing Extra Meals

- Learn to spot the time-takers. Review every recipe for elements that you could double or triple now, saving you time and effort later. Maybe you could use a bright highlight pen.
- Don't overdo the extra-meal quantity. Your freezer can accept no more than 2 pounds (900 g) of food to be frozen per cubic foot of its capacity. Thus, a 3-cubic-foot deep freeze should not have more than 6 pounds (2.7 kg) of food at any one time.
- Cool food quickly before you freeze. Don't let the extra meal lie around before freezing. It will continue to cook, perhaps ruining a perfectly crisp texture. Put the extra meal in your freezing container, seal it, and then cool it in very cold water before freezing.
- Pack it flat. I use heavy-duty sealable plastic freezer bags. These can be cleaned and used again and again. Use a size that meets your needs, exhaust the air, seal, and then freeze so that it is flat.
- Note the date. Cooked food deteriorates faster than uncooked food, losing color, flavor, and texture. So please date each bag with a description and use within 6 months.
- Frozen menu. Keep an extra plastic bag, on which you just write down the names of what you freeze. Keep the pen in the bag with spare bags of various sizes. It will be your reminder of what you've got and when you need to use it.
- Some food doesn't freeze well. The higher the fat content, the shorter its storage potential. Raw tomatoes are terrible; salad vegetables, especially greens, go to mush. Milk and yogurt sauces will curdle.
- Defrost carefully. Frozen foods spoil faster than freshly cooked and cooled. Don't ever leave food out at room temperature for over 3 hours to thaw.
- Thaw overnight in the refrigerator. To be safe, I allow my extra-meal bags to gradually thaw in the refrigerator (think ahead!) or I

microwave them for 6 to 8 minutes for each 1 pound (450 g) of food at 30 power setting (the usual power used for the defrost cycle).

- Try for a perfect marriage! Remember that your extra meal is a preplanned leftover that will gradually lose its flavor over the 6-month freezing-period limit. Therefore, when you use it, marry it to fresh fruit, vegetables, pasta, and whole grains, seasoned with the very best condiments that will enhance aroma, color, and texture.

My Professional Friends

The last recipe of every chapter is a contribution from some very special culinary professionals. These are people who have earned not only my admiration for taking valuable private time to develop recipes that meet special needs, but also (I hope) your respect.

I think the 1990s will mark one of the most extraordinary decades of change ever witnessed in the professional kitchen. In fact, the best result should be a synergism in which the future is

seen through a knowledge of both complex classical cuisine and the extremely simple "foods of the people" that have effectively nourished different nationalities for hundreds of years.

I never expected to see famous chefs discussing new dishes with registered dietitians, blending their senses with this consultant's science for the consumer's good.

The truth is that neither the chef nor the dietitian has much, if anything, to *lose* because both have genuinely overlapping motives of pleasing and caring for those they serve.

It is my hope that you will see this synergism in creative action with their recipes and that you might go out of your way to visit their restaurants and send your compliments and mine to the chef.

TECHNIQUES
& RECIPES

1

REDUCTIONS

Cooking flavorful liquids, like chicken stock, fruit juices, or wines, reduces the volume and intensifies the taste, creating a base for sauces.

*I*f I had to reserve my ultimate enthusiasm for a single technique, reductions would be it: cooking flavorful liquids, like chicken stock or wine, to reduce their volume but intensify their taste, leaving you with a base for great sauces.

The key to all my work is to focus attention upon the aromas, colors, and textures that come from low-risk, nutrient-dense foods and seasonings. Whenever these "flavoring good guys" are assembled, they migrate and mingle with bland substances because there is a *liquid* present. It follows that a good result depends on good liquids.

This is especially so when fatty foods, which commonly are relied upon to carry flavor and provide "mouth feel," are minimized.

The best, most flavorful liquid of all is achieved from the reduction process. By reducing, I just mean heating the liquid so that it evaporates, decreasing in volume while increasing a thousandfold in flavor. This reduced liquid can be used as the base for many unforgettable sauces and zesty glazes.

Tips and Hints

- Try always to match the flavored liquid to the main ingredients, with the object being to enhance natural flavor without smothering it. I have a few suggestions for some main ingredients: for chicken breast, use chicken stock; for small steaks or dark stews, use beef stock and red wine; for fish and shellfish, fish bone stock and white wine; for pork chops, unsweetened apple or orange juice; for vegetables, a savory vegetable broth or citrus juice.
- Have liquids on hand for reductions by making stock in large quantities, reducing and freezing in small portions (see recipes, page 229-234).
- Aromas evaporate quickly in reductions. So, in the last moments of the reduction cooking process, revive the aroma by adding fresh herbs or spices. For example, a crumbled bay leaf, fresh lemon thyme, a couple of cloves, or a splash of dealcoholized wine.
- When using prepared commercial stocks, please check the label for sodium content if you or a loved one is hypertensive. Even something that says "low sodium" on the label may be over the top for this type of condition.

✠ Chile, Cheese, and Chicken Enchiladas

The sweet red tomato and the tart Mexican green tomatillo are the base for two very easy and quick sauces that are a lovely festive touch for these chicken enchiladas. They are prepared with the reduction process and are much lower in fat than the original recipe's white sauce, sent to me by Mary New. I also substituted strained yogurt and cottage cheese for the original recipe's 2 tablespoons of butter and 1½ cups of sour cream, and I reduced 2½ cups of cheese to only 1/2 cup of low-fat Monterey jack. Remember, the sauces will be spicy from the jalapeño seeds. If you like a milder sauce, remove the seeds.

Tomato sauce with onion, jalapeño, garlic, cumin, oregano
Brick red
(color, texture, aroma)

Tomatillo sauce with onion, garlic, jalapeño, cilantro
Pale green
(texture, color)

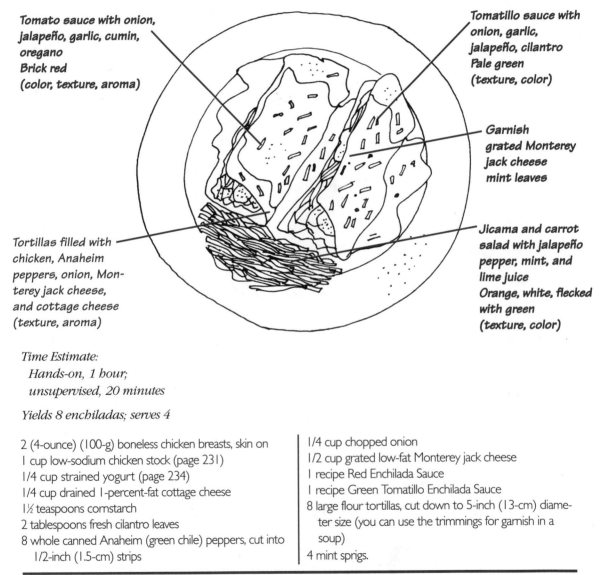

Garnish
grated Monterey jack cheese
mint leaves

Tortillas filled with chicken, Anaheim peppers, onion, Monterey jack cheese, and cottage cheese
(texture, aroma)

Jicama and carrot salad with jalapeño pepper, mint, and lime juice
Orange, white, flecked with green
(texture, color)

Time Estimate:
Hands-on, 1 hour;
unsupervised, 20 minutes

Yields 8 enchiladas; serves 4

2 (4-ounce) (100-g) boneless chicken breasts, skin on
1 cup low-sodium chicken stock (page 231)
1/4 cup strained yogurt (page 234)
1/4 cup drained 1-percent-fat cottage cheese
1½ teaspoons cornstarch
2 tablespoons fresh cilantro leaves
8 whole canned Anaheim (green chile) peppers, cut into 1/2-inch (1.5-cm) strips

1/4 cup chopped onion
1/2 cup grated low-fat Monterey jack cheese
1 recipe Red Enchilada Sauce
1 recipe Green Tomatillo Enchilada Sauce
8 large flour tortillas, cut down to 5-inch (13-cm) diameter size (you can use the trimmings for garnish in a soup)
4 mint sprigs.

Mary New says that cooking healthily has become the normal routine for her and her husband, son, and daughter. "My children don't even realize it's healthy, just that it tastes good." After years of cooking low-fat recipes, Mary has found that her body **prefers** this style of eating. "There are some things I just can't stand the taste of anymore, like pepperoni pizza, because they feel too rich and don't digest very well. My body has gotten used to not having fat and it's a way of life now."

Prepare the enchilada sauces (page 18).

Lay the chicken breasts skin side up in a hot skillet just large enough to hold them, about 9 inches in diameter. Cover with the chicken stock, bring to a slow boil, and simmer very gently for 20 minutes. Remove from the pan and, when cool enough to handle, discard the skin and slice the meat against the grain into thin pieces. Set aside.

In a small processor, combine the yogurt, cottage cheese, cornstarch, and cilantro, pulsing just to mix—don't overprocess until it becomes runny.

Preheat the oven to 350°F (180°C). Brush a 9 x 13-inch (23 x 33-cm) baking dish with light olive oil.

Put the red enchilada sauce and the green tomatillo enchilada sauce in two large bowls. Dip a tortilla into the red sauce and lay it flat on a plate. Spread 1 tablespoon of the cottage cheese–yogurt mixture down the center, sprinkle with 1 teaspoon of chopped onion, lay a few chicken strips on top, and finish with a few chile pieces. Roll it up tightly and place in the prepared baking dish. Continue stuffing and rolling the remaining tortillas, using the red sauce for 4 enchiladas and the green sauce for the others. Do not pack them too tightly in the pan. Spoon some of the red sauce over 4 of them and the green sauce over the remaining, but don't drown them or they will become soggy. Sprinkle with the grated cheese and bake for 20 minutes.

To serve: Place a green and red sauced enchilada on each dinner plate, with the jicama salad on the side, and garnish with the mint sprigs. Offer the extra sauce on the table.

Nutritional Profile per serving			
	Classic	**Springboard**	**Daily Value**
Calories	1,019	395	
Calories from fat	513	81	
Fat (gm)	57	9	14%
Saturated fat (gm)	32	3	15%
Sodium (mg)	1,373	382	16%
Cholesterol (mg)	207	32	11%
Carbohydrates (gm)	58	58	19%
Dietary fiber (gm)	9	9	36%
Classic compared: Chicken Enchiladas			

✖ RED ENCHILADA SAUCE

Time Estimate:
  Hands-on, 15 minutes;
  unsupervised, 20 minutes
Yields 1½ cups; serves 4

1 pound Roma tomatoes (450 gm), peeled and coarsely
  chopped
2 tablespoons chopped onion
1 jalapeño pepper with seeds, chopped
1 clove garlic, bashed, peeled, and chopped
1/2 teaspoon ground cumin
1/2 teaspoon dried oregano
1½ cups low-sodium chicken stock (page 231)

In a processor or blender, whiz the tomatoes, onion, garlic, jalapeño, cumin, and oregano for 3 minutes on low speed, gradually and slowly pouring in the stock. Transfer to a saucepan and boil over medium high heat to reduce and thicken, about 20 minutes.

✖ GREEN TOMATILLO ENCHILADA SAUCE

Time Estimate:
  Hands-on, 15 minutes;
  unsupervised, 20 minutes
Yields 1½ cups; serves 4

1 pound tomatillos (450 gm), husks removed
1/2 medium onion, peeled and chopped fine
2 cloves garlic, bashed, peeled, and chopped
1 jalapeño pepper with seeds, chopped fine
1 tablespoon chopped fresh cilantro
1½ cups low-sodium chicken stock (page 231)

Place the tomatillos in a small saucepan, cover with water, bring to a boil, and simmer for 10 minutes. Drain off the water and press the cooked tomatillos through a sieve and into a saucepan with a wooden sieve or spoon. Combine the tomatillo purée with the onion, garlic, jalapeño, and cilantro in a food processor or blender and whiz for 3 minutes. Pour into a saucepan, add the chicken stock, and boil to reduce volume and concentrate flavors on medium-high for 20 minutes.

☒ LOOKING AHEAD FOR AN EXTRA MEAL

Double or triple the recipe for the red enchilada sauce. You might not want to double or triple the jalapeño peppers, as they can get mighty powerful. The reduced sauce can be frozen in resealable freezer bags. Flatten the bags, expelling any air, label and date. The sauce can be frozen for up to 6 months. Break off bits of the frozen sauce to toss into dull soups and sauces, or use it in the Black Bean Burritos recipe that follows.

Freeze the reduced sauce

JICAMA SALAD

You can prepare this while the enchiladas are baking.

1/2 pound (225 g) jicama, peeled and cut into match-
    sticks
1 medium carrot, peeled and cut into matchsticks
6 large mint leaves, sliced very fine
1/2 jalapeño pepper, seeded and sliced very thin
1 teaspoon grated lime zest
1 tablespoon freshly squeezed lime juice

In a large bowl, toss all the ingredients and let marinate until the enchiladas are ready to serve.

Black Bean Burritos

This family favorite is extra quick when you use red enchilada sauce from the previous recipe, prepared in a double batch and frozen. But whether the red enchilada sauce is in your freezer or whipped up from scratch, with a can of black beans in the cupboard you're only an hour away from eating delicious and healthy "fast food."

Time Estimate:
Hands-on, 15 minutes;
unsupervised, 30 minutes
Serves 4

1 teaspoon light olive oil with a dash of toasted sesame oil
1 clove garlic, bashed, peeled, and chopped
2 serrano chile peppers, cored, seeded, and chopped
1 (15-ounce) (425-g) can low-sodium black beans
1/2 cup fresh cilantro leaves, chopped
1/4 teaspoon freshly ground sea salt
2 cups Red Enchilada Sauce (page 18)
8 small flour tortillas

Garnish
1/4 cup strained yogurt (page 234)
1/4 cup chopped fresh cilantro
Ground cumin to taste

Preheat the oven to 350°F (180°C). Pour the oil into a medium skillet on medium heat and fry the garlic and chopped chiles for 2 minutes. Add the beans and cook, mashing and stirring, for 3 minutes. Remove from the heat, add the cilantro and salt, and stir to mix well.

Heat the red enchilada sauce in a small saucepan. Spoon a little onto the bottom of an 8 x 8-inch (20 x 20-cm) baking pan. Spread about 2 tablespoons of the beans down the middle of each tortilla, roll them up, and lay them in the prepared pan. Cover lightly with the sauce and bake for 20 minutes.

To serve: Place 2 enchiladas on each serving plate and spoon the rest of the sauce over the top. Garnish with the strained yogurt, cilantro, and a sprinkle of ground cumin.

Nutritional Profile per Serving: Calories—363; calories from fat—54; fat (gm)—6 or 9% daily value; saturated fat (gm)—2; sodium (mg)—354; cholesterol (mg)—4; carbohydrates (gm)—66; dietary fiber (gm)—12

❊ BAKED APPLE SLICES WITH "CREAM"

I used the reduction technique in this dessert to create a fragrant apple-infused sauce that is a sweet adornment for baked apples. The recipe is based on the food preference list I received from Joan Kidd. She and her husband, Ron, are both retired nurses who spend a lot of time in their mini motor home, traveling all over the United States and Canada. Joan wrote me to say that she thought this recipe was "delicious!"

Time Estimate:
  Hands-on, 35 minutes;
  unsupervised, 80 minutes
Serves 6

6 apples, cored, peeled, and sliced thin, cores and peels
  reserved
1 1/2 quarts (1.4 l) water
1/4 teaspoon freshly grated nutmeg
2 whole cloves
1 2-inch (5-cm) piece cinnamon stick
1/4 cup packed brown sugar
1/4 cup apple butter
1 tablespoon arrowroot mixed with 2 tablespoons
  water (slurry)

"Cream"
6 tablespoons strained yogurt (page 234)
1/8 teaspoon ground cinnamon
3 tablespoons pure maple syrup

Garnish
6 mint sprigs

Pour the water into a medium saucepan, add the reserved apple cores and peels, and bring to a boil. Add the nutmeg, cloves, and cinnamon stick, reduce the heat, and simmer, uncovered, for 30 minutes. Strain, discarding solids, and return to the same saucepan. On medium high heat, boil until reduced to 1 cup. Stir in the brown sugar and the apple butter, remove from the heat, and set aside.

Preheat the oven to 350°F (180°C). Place the apple slices in a 9 x 13-inch (23 x 23-cm) baking dish. Pour in the apple butter mixture and toss until well coated. Bake, uncovered, for 30 minutes. Remove from the oven and let cool for 10 minutes.

While the apples are cooking, mix all the cream ingredients in a small bowl and set aside.

Tip the cooking juices from the baking dish into a medium saucepan. Bring to a boil, remove from the heat, stir in the arrowroot slurry, return to the heat, and stir until thickened and clear, about 30 seconds. Stir in the baked apples and coat well.

To serve: Spoon the apple slices and sauce into serving bowls, top with a mound of cream, and garnish with the mint sprigs.

Nutritional Profile per Serving: Calories—180; calories from fat—9; Fat (gm)—1 or 2% daily value; saturated fat (gm)—0.2; sodium (mg)—30; cholesterol (mg)—1; carbohydrates (gm)—44; dietary fiber (gm)—4

✛ BLANCHED VEGETABLES WITH A REDUCTION SAUCE OF FENNEL AND THYME

Diners at Rover's—Thierry Rautureau's restaurant in Seattle—call his meals works of art. Here he has created a special sauce using the reduction technique, blending fennel, anise, and thyme. It's a great candidate for making in double or triple batches and freezing. You'll be delighted by how it complements the barely cooked vegetables.

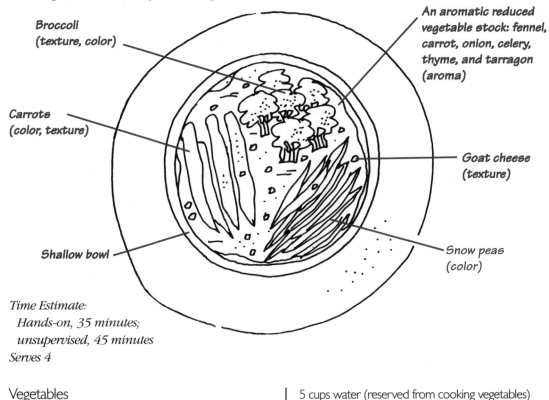

Broccoli
(texture, color)

An aromatic reduced
vegetable stock: fennel,
carrot, onion, celery,
thyme, and tarragon
(aroma)

Carrots
(color, texture)

Goat cheese
(texture)

Shallow bowl

Snow peas
(color)

Time Estimate:
Hands-on, 35 minutes;
unsupervised, 45 minutes
Serves 4

Vegetables
1 bunch of broccoli
4 carrots, peeled and julienned
1 cup snow peas, strings removed
Leaves from 3 stems basil, julienned

Sauce
1 tablespoon extra virgin olive oil
1 small onion, peeled and diced
1 small carrot, peeled and diced
1 small stalk celery, chopped
1 small fennel bulb, chopped

5 cups water (reserved from cooking vegetables)
3 bay leaves
2 thyme sprigs
5 whole black peppercorns
2 whole cloves
1 sprig tarragon
1 tablespoon fennel seeds
1 tablespoon anise seeds
8 parsley stems

Garnish
3 ounces (100 g) goat cheese

Thierry Rautureau, a much lauded chef, says the biggest recent success at his Rover's restaurant in Seattle is a five-course vegetarian dinner that showcases the freshest and best produce in season. When I asked Thierry about his attitude toward people who ask for lower-fat dishes, he surprised me with his intensity. "My restaurant dishes and my personal eating style at home and when eating out have changed. I look for a different outcome: fresh, organic, and flavorful are the three main keys. I also eat a lot more fish and vegetables than in the past."

I should tell you that Thierry has a wonderfully pragmatic French attitude toward life and the future. By the year 2000 he believes that "organic food will be grown in volume and be less seasonally concentrated." Then he added, "I hope I'm right."

So do we all, mon vieux!

The vegetables: Fill a large pot with enough water to cover the vegetables and bring to a boil. Remove the broccoli stems and separate the florets. Plunge the broccoli florets, carrots, and snow peas into the water, return to a boil, and cook for 1 minute. Drain, reserving the water and vegetables separately. Transfer the vegetables to a large bowl and toss with the basil.

The sauce: Heat the oil in the same large pot over medium heat and fry the onion, carrot, celery, and fennel until translucent, about 5 minutes. Add 5 cups of the reserved poaching water and bring to a boil. Skim off any impurities and then add the bay leaves, thyme, peppercorns, cloves, tarragon, fennel seeds, and anise seeds. Simmer, uncovered, for 45 minutes, or until reduced to 3/4 cup, and then strain through a fine sieve.

Place the reduced stock and the blanched vegetables in a large skillet and gently stir until the stock has come to a boil and the vegetables are heated through. Cover and keep warm until ready to serve. Divide the vegetable and sauce between four bowls and top with a little crumbled goat cheese.

Nutritional Profile per Serving

	Classic	Springboard	Daily Value
Calories	150	142	
Calories from fat	72	54	
Fat (gm)	12	6	9%
Saturated fat (gm)	5	3	15%
Sodium (mg)	95	190	8%
Cholesterol (gm)	21	10	3%
Carbohydrates (gm)	10	15	5%
Dietary fiber (gm)	4	5	20%

Classic compared: Vegetables Amandine

2 SAUCE THICKENERS

Using low-fat starches like arrowroot or cornstarch as a thickener, enjoy splendid sauces for meat, potatoes, and vegetables.

While natural thickening occurs through both reduction (page 15) and sieving or processing both vegetables and fruits (page 65), classic methods of thickening sauces use flour and fat—usually butter for its flavor. The French system cooks the flour and fat together in what is called a *roux*, or rubs them into a sandy texture called *beurre manié*. In this way the fat is held in suspension, distributed throughout the sauce, and doesn't show up in clear fat droplets. The so-called white or blond sauces cook quite quickly. The brown sauces take hours to clear their starch. My alternative to the flour/fat combination is to use the culinary technique of adding starches, like cornstarch or arrowroot, as a thickener for defatted cooking liquids.

If you have a passion for sauce-making and believe, as I do, that we should look at the future through the classics, then you could not do better than to search out a copy of *Sauces, Classical and Contemporary Sauce Making*, by James Peterson (Van Nostrand Reinhold).

Tips and Hints

- The general rule is to use 1 level tablespoon of starch for each 1 cup of liquid to be thickened. In a small bowl, make a paste (slurry) of the starch with double the amount of liquid, like water, wine, stock, or citrus juice. Remove the liquid to be thickened from the heat, stir in the slurry, return to the heat, and stir until thickened and clear.

"Sauce a little too thick again, Graham?"

  Arrowroot thickens almost immediately, but cornstarch requires boiling for at least 30 seconds to clear its starch taste.
- Thicken white or opaque sauces with cornstarch and rice starch.
- Use arrowroot to thicken if you want complete clarity or sparkle. Serve arrowroot-thickened sauces immediately and keep warm; otherwise the texture becomes slippery.
- Use cornstarch to thicken sauces with dairy products, like strained yogurt, and crisp stir-fried vegetable sauces.

Wild Bill's Nearly Famous Pork Tenderloin

Bill Hubbard wrote us under the pen name of Wild Bill. A couple of years ago the wild one had to endure open-heart surgery. Since the operation did nothing to change his love of cooking, he wanted me to "clean up" his nearly famous recipe, which called for a traditional flour-butter roux to thicken the sauce. Arrowroot in place of the roux helped that problem right away. But I was also concerned about the sodium levels. I substituted low-sodium beef stock for bouillon cubes, fresh celery for celery salt, fresh garlic for garlic salt, and I used only a third of the Worcestershire sauce. Now it's up to you *to make it famous.*

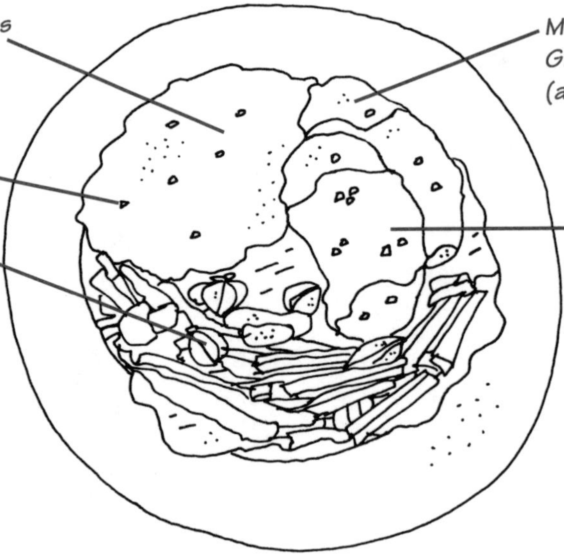

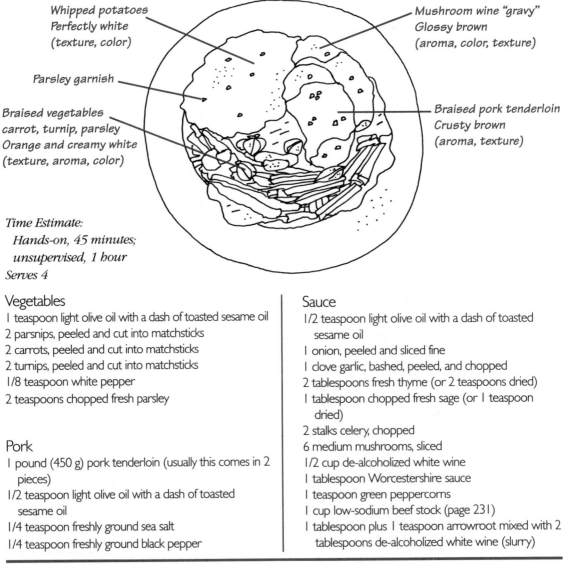

Whipped potatoes
Perfectly white
(texture, color)
Mushroom wine "gravy"
Glossy brown
(aroma, color, texture)
Parsley garnish
Braised pork tenderloin
Crusty brown
(aroma, texture)
Braised vegetables
carrot, turnip, parsley
Orange and creamy white
(texture, aroma, color)

Time Estimate:
Hands-on, 45 minutes;
unsupervised, 1 hour
Serves 4

Vegetables

1 teaspoon light olive oil with a dash of toasted sesame oil
2 parsnips, peeled and cut into matchsticks
2 carrots, peeled and cut into matchsticks
2 turnips, peeled and cut into matchsticks
1/8 teaspoon white pepper
2 teaspoons chopped fresh parsley

Pork

1 pound (450 g) pork tenderloin (usually this comes in 2 pieces)
1/2 teaspoon light olive oil with a dash of toasted sesame oil
1/4 teaspoon freshly ground sea salt
1/4 teaspoon freshly ground black pepper

Sauce

1/2 teaspoon light olive oil with a dash of toasted sesame oil
1 onion, peeled and sliced fine
1 clove garlic, bashed, peeled, and chopped
2 tablespoons fresh thyme (or 2 teaspoons dried)
1 tablespoon chopped fresh sage (or 1 teaspoon dried)
2 stalks celery, chopped
6 medium mushrooms, sliced
1/2 cup de-alcoholized white wine
1 tablespoon Worcestershire sauce
1 teaspoon green peppercorns
1 cup low-sodium beef stock (page 231)
1 tablespoon plus 1 teaspoon arrowroot mixed with 2 tablespoons de-alcoholized white wine (slurry)

Buttermilk Mashed Potatoes

While the pork is baking, prepare this side dish.

Serves 4

4 medium russet potatoes, peeled and quartered
3/4 cup 1-percent-fat buttermilk
1/4 teaspoon freshly ground sea salt
1/4 teaspoon freshly ground white pepper

In a large pot of boiling water, cook the potatoes for 30 minutes. Drain, return the potatoes to the pot, put a towel over the top, and let them sit on very low heat for 15 minutes to dry out. Transfer the potatoes to a warm bowl and whip them, together with the buttermilk, salt, and white pepper, using an electric beater, until mashed.

⋈ Extra Meal

Double the buttermilk mashed potatoes, using half with the baked pork and saving the other half in the refrigerator. Potatoes don't like to be frozen, so use them within 2 days. Reheat them in a microwave oven, double boiler, or in a bowl over a pan of hot water. Give them plenty of time to heat through if you're using the stovetop method, about 20 to 30 minutes. Add more milk if they seem thick. Following is an easy sauce to serve with your leftover mashed potatoes.

The vegetables: Preheat the oven to 350°F (180°C). Pour the oil into a medium skillet on high heat and fry the parsnips, carrots, and turnips to heat through, about 2 minutes. Spread the cooked vegetables out in an 8 x 8-inch (20 x 20-cm) baking pan and sprinkle with the white pepper. Set aside.

The pork: Trim away all the visible fat; cut each piece in half lengthwise, then in half crosswise. You should have 8 pieces about 3 to 4 inches long (8 to 10 cm). On medium heat, pour the oil into the same skillet and fry the cut-surface side of the pork until very brown. Sprinkle with the salt and pepper and lay the pieces, brown side up, on top of the cooked vegetables.

The sauce: In the same skillet, fry the onion, celery, and garlic in the oil on medium heat for 3 minutes. Add the mushrooms, sage, and thyme, then deglaze with the wine and beef stock. Stir in the peppercorns and Worcestershire sauce and remove from the heat.

Pour over the pork, cover with foil, seal the edges and bake for 1 hour.

Remove the cooked pork from the oven and transfer to a carving board. Strain the cooking liquids from the baking dish into a small saucepan. Bring the juices to a boil, skimming off any fat that rises to the surface. Remove from the heat, stir in the arrowroot slurry, return to the heat, bring back to a boil, and stir until thickened, about 30 seconds.

To serve: Distribute the pork and vegetables on individual serving plates. Ladle with the sauce and garnish with a sprinkle of parsley. This is terrific served with buttermilk mashed potatoes.

"Due to open heart surgery, an artery bypass, valve repairs, and a 'balloon job,' " **Bill Hubbard** says, "I have to eat right, I don't have a choice." But this active 74-year-old and his wife of 27 years, Anne, also love good food and want it to have good taste. Bill says that he looks for the fat in all his recipes and tries to eliminate it. He never uses a roux to thicken his sauces. While this dish was the first time he tried arrowroot, he often uses cornstarch and flour as a thickener. He's also purchased a good set of nonstick pans so that he only has to use a teaspoon of olive oil in his cooking, which really helps him to keep his fat way down.

Nutritional Profile per Serving			
	Classic	Springboard	Daily Value
Calories	494	438	
Calories from fat	171	81	
Fat (gm)	19	9	14%
Saturated fat (gm)	10	3	15%
Sodium (mg)	930	510	21%
Cholesterol (mg)	148	91	30%
Carbohydrates (gm)	29	51	17%
Dietary fiber (gm)	5	7	28%
Classic compared: Wild Bill's Nearly Famous Pork Tenderloin			

✖ CHAMP (BUTTERMILK MASHED POTATOES WITH BUTTER SAUCE)

Traditionally, mashed potatoes from my Scottish heritage (and many other ethnic heritages) are served in large snowy mounds with a well in the center filled to overflowing with rich butter sauce. These low-fat mashed potatoes have all the visual appeal of their traditional presentation, but the well is filled with a rich yellow sauce thickened to glistening perfection with arrowroot. It's also extra quick when you've made a double batch of the buttermilk mashed potatoes from the previous recipe and have them standing by in the refrigerator.

Time Estimate:
  Hands-on, 20 minutes;
  unsupervised, 10 minutes
Serves 4

1 Recipe Buttermilk Mashed Potatoes (page 27)

Sauce
2 cups low-sodium chicken or vegetable stock (page 233)
1/16 teaspoon powdered saffron or turmeric
1/4 teaspoon freshly ground sea salt
1 tablespoon arrowroot mixed with 2 tablespoons low-sodium chicken or vegetable stock (slurry)
4 teaspoons fresh chopped chives

Prepare the buttermilk mashed potatoes, or just heat a previously made and refrigerated recipe.

The sauce: Boil the stock in a small saucepan until reduced by half, about 10 minutes. Stir in the saffron and salt. Remove from the heat, stir in the arrowroot slurry, return to the heat, and boil until thickened and clear, about 30 seconds. Cover and keep warm.

To serve: Heap the potatoes on a plate, making a deep well in the center with the back of a spoon. Fill with the sauce and sprinkle with the chives.

Nutritional Profile per Serving: Calories—92; calories from fat—27; fat (gm)—3 or 5% daily value; saturated fat (gm)—1; sodium (mg)—187; cholesterol (mg)—1; carbohydrates (gm)—13; dietary fiber (gm)—1

✖ STEAK AND PEPPERS ON FETTUCCINE

Jim and Christine Caruso wrote us to say, "When we decided to start eating healthier, we thought we would be leaving some great tastes behind us. But Jim has been able to use his creativity to enhance low-fat meals to our total satisfaction and delight."

Shortly after they moved from New York City to New Orleans, they cooked for Jim's brother and his family for the first time. Jim reports, "I received their highest compliments. The rosemary and thyme provided high notes that were very pleasing. The Hungarian paprika provided a bite that was pronounced but not overpowering."I hope this easy dish with its flavorful arrowroot-thickened sauce pleases you and your loved ones as well.

Time Estimate:
  Hands-on, 25 minutes
Serves 4

1/2 teaspoon light olive oil with a dash of toasted sesame oil
12 ounces (340 g) flank steak, cut in very thin slices
   across the grain
1/8 teaspoon freshly ground sea salt
1/4 teaspoon freshly ground pepper
8 ounces uncooked fettuccine noodles

Sauce
1/2 teaspoon light olive oil with a dash of toasted sesame oil
1 medium onion, peeled and sliced lengthwise
2 cloves garlic, bashed, peeled, and chopped
2 tablespoons low-sodium tomato paste
1 tablespoon hot Hungarian paprika
1 teaspoon dried thyme
1/2 teaspoon dried rosemary

1 medium red bell pepper, cut into 1 1/2-inch (4-cm) strips
1 medium green bell pepper, cut into 1 1/2-inch (4-cm) strips
8 mushrooms, sliced thick
1 cup low-sodium beef stock (page 231)
1/2 teaspoon freshly ground sea salt
1 teaspoon Worcestershire sauce
1 tablespoon arrowroot mixed with 2 tablespoons low-
   sodium beef stock (slurry)

Heat the oil in a large nonstick frying pan; when it's smoking hot, cook and stir the meat until just browned. Don't let it get tough and dried out. Sprinkle with the salt and pepper, remove from the pan, and keep warm. Don't wash the pan.

Cook the fettuccine noodles according to package directions.

The sauce: Pour the oil into the same frying pan, add the onion and garlic, and fry until they start to wilt and color. Push them to one side of the pan and add the tomato paste. Cook and stir the paste, allowing it to caramelize and darken. When it has turned a dark red color, add the paprika, thyme, rosemary, red and green peppers, and mushrooms. Stir until well coated with the tomato paste and seasonings and cook for 2 minutes. Add the stock, salt, and Worcestershire sauce, scraping the pan to deglaze it. Bring to a boil and cook for just 2 minutes. You want the peppers to stay crisp and colorful. Stir the cooked meat into the sauce and heat through. Remove from the heat, stir in the arrowroot slurry, return to the heat, and bring to a boil to thicken and turn clear, about 30 seconds. Divide the cooked fettuccine among individual plates and top with the sauced steak and peppers.

Nutritional Profile per Serving: Calories—390; calories from fat—90; fat (gm)—10 or 15% daily value; saturated fat (gm)—3; sodium (gm)—421; cholesterol (mg)—97; carbohydrates (gm)—47; dietary fiber (gm)—5

❖ FRESH STRAWBERRY PIE

The crunchy texture of the crust is outstanding and the arrowroot provides a shimmering gloss to a fruit glaze that is much more translucent than cornstarch. Wow! Just like a French patisserie! My thanks to Lizzie Burt for this tremendously appealing dessert.

Red strawberries with a shiny gloss of berry fruit sauce (color, texture, aroma)

Garnish with fresh strawberries with hulls on (color)

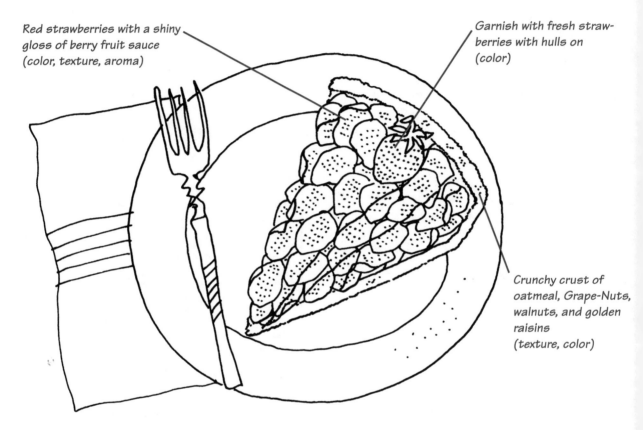

Crunchy crust of oatmeal, Grape-Nuts, walnuts, and golden raisins (texture, color)

Time Estimate:
  Hands-on, 30 minutes
Serves 10

The Crust
6 tablespoons chopped walnuts
3/4 cup instant oatmeal cereal
3/4 cup Grape-Nuts cereal
3/4 cup golden raisins

The Filling
1 (12-ounce) (340-g) carton frozen fruit juice concentrate, such as strawberry, apple, or cran-raspberry, thawed
3 tablespoons arrowroot or cornstarch
4 cups fresh strawberries, rinsed, hulled, and cut in half

In keeping with my notion of seeking out talented culinary professionals from all walks of life, we went the extra mile with **Elizabeth Rosalie Burt**!

Lizzie has now completed seven Hawaii Ironman Triathlons, was her Age Group Champion in 1987, and has run in three Boston Marathons. She works in preventive medicine, where she has been a tremendous catalyst in her community.

In 1992 Lizzie launched the "Taste of Health" in Ann Arbor, Michigan, attracting ten restaurants who served healthy food to about 200 attendees. In 1993, the size doubled, and in 1994 almost 1,000 people attended.

With registered dietitian Nelda Mercer, Lizzie has written a book called *High Fit— Low Fat*, which she uses when teaching classes at the University of Michigan Med Sport Preventive Cardiology Program. Lizzie has noticed that "People who have developed illness related to lifestyle habits often have a fear of failure in the kitchen; a lack of confidence that they can replace shortcuts like deep frying and high-fat take-out foods."Lizzie's answer is to demystify cooking by showing people simple techniques and loads of shortcuts through actual demonstrations in her classes.

These are the kind of creative ripples that help to change the world. Why not find out if someone in your community is teaching the same thing? Call your local hospital and ask for a registered dietitian. Who knows: perhaps you could play a valuable part in the process.

The crust: Preheat the oven to 400°F (205°C). Blend the walnuts, oatmeal, and Grape-Nuts in a food processor fitted with a steel blade. With the machine running, add the raisins through the feed tube, and continue to purée until the mixture has the consistency of crunchy coarse meal.

Spray a 10-inch (25-cm) pie dish with vegetable oil cooking spray. Press the puréed crust mixture evenly into the dish, extending it well up the side. Bake in the middle of the oven for 7 minutes, or until firm to the touch and lightly golden in color. Remove from the oven and place on a rack to cool.

The filling: Make a slurry by mixing 3 tablespoons of the fruit juice concentrate with the arrowroot or cornstarch. Pour the remaining fruit juice into a saucepan and bring to a boil. Remove from the heat, stir in the arrowroot slurry, return to the heat, and stir until thickened and clear. If using cornstarch, simmer the mixture for an additional 30 seconds to remove the starchy flavor. Remove from the heat and let cool.

When the crust and sauce are cool, fold the berries into the sauce and pile the mixture into the crust. This is best assembled no more than 2 hours before serving to avoid dilution of the glaze.

Nutritional Profile per Serving			
	Classic	Springboard	Daily Value
Calories	491	232	
Calories from fat	216	36	
Fat (gm)	24	4	6%
Saturated fat (gm)	11	0.38	2%
Sodium (mg)	96	112	5%
Cholesterol (mg)	47	0	0%
Carbohydrates (gm)	70	51	17%
Dietary fiber (gm)	4	4	16%
Classic compared: Sky-high Strawberry Pie			

3

WHITE SAUCES

*White coating sauces with strained yogurt
as a base for everything from meat to pasta.*

With the exception of the Americanized Italian
creamy pasta dishes (Alfredo and Carbonara),
one of the most radical changes in the culinary
field has been the disappearance of the Sauce Béchamel
(white), Sauce Velouté (milk and stocks), Blanquette and
Friccasée (white creamy stews) that have cloaked or
masked natural food flavors for generations.

Clearly there is now a preference for great individual
tastes and their synergy with one or two other balanced
ingredients. The blanketing sauce of flour and milk with or
without cheese simply overwhelms or at least lessens the
complexity of flavors achieved by wise selection.

In this technique, you discover a white coating sauce that doesn't mask the flavors beneath and is virtually fat free.

BASIC WHITE SAUCE

Yields 2½ cups

3 cups light-colored flavorful liquid
3 tablespoons cornstarch mixed with 6 tablespoons liquid (slurry)
1 cup strained yogurt (page 234), at room temperature
Salt, pepper, and garnish to taste

Pour the liquid into a medium saucepan, bring to a boil, and boil until reduced by half, about 10 minutes. Remove from the heat, stir in the cornstarch slurry, return to the heat, and boil until thickened and clear, stirring constantly, about 30 seconds. Remove from the heat and let cool. Place the yogurt in a small bowl, add the sauce, and stir gently until all the lumps are gone. Return to the saucepan, season, garnish, and reheat gently over low heat.

Tips and Hints

- The liquid must match the main ingredients, usually chicken stock, vegetable stock, or white wine.
- The basic rule is 1 tablespoon cornstarch to thicken each 1 cup of liquid.
- Before adding the cornstarch, mix it with double the amount of liquid to form a slurry.
- Always boil for 30 seconds to clear the starchy taste.
- The strained yogurt should be strained for at least 12 hours when using it for white sauce, to make it as lump-free as possible.
- Never boil the white sauce during reheating or the yogurt will break into pieces.

"Who was that masked main dish anyhow?"

White sauce, "the masked stranger," has almost left the scene.

Turkey Pastrami Paprikash

I created this recipe for Shirley Szalko based on the ingredients in her Food Preference List and her Czechoslovakian heritage. Shirley thought that my idea of substituting the white sauce with strained yogurt instead of sour cream was "wonderful."

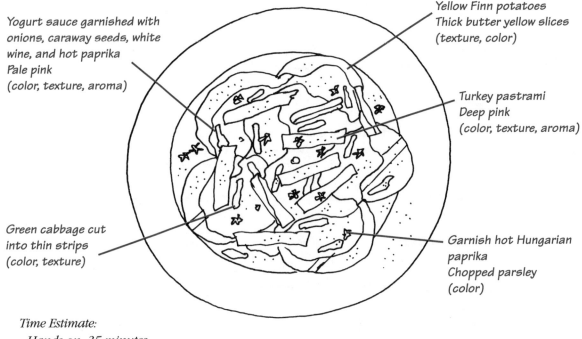

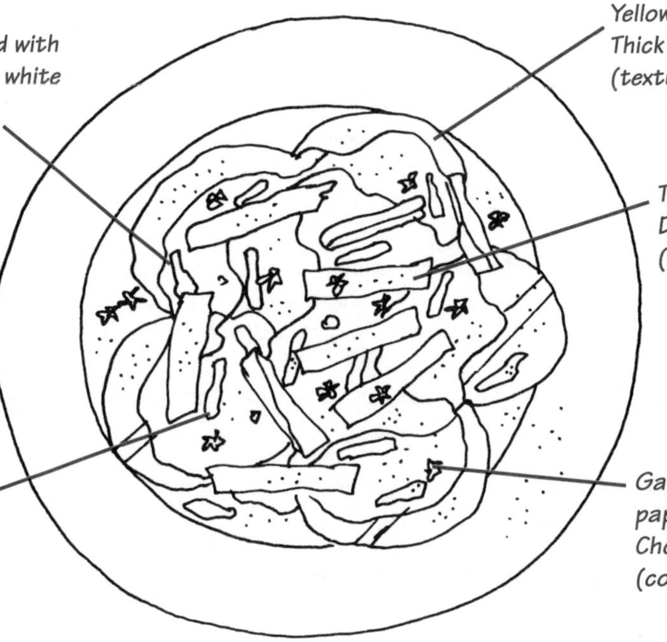
Yogurt sauce garnished with onions, caraway seeds, white wine, and hot paprika
Pale pink
(color, texture, aroma)
Yellow Finn potatoes
Thick butter yellow slices
(texture, color)
Turkey pastrami
Deep pink
(color, texture, aroma)
Green cabbage cut into thin strips
(color, texture)
Garnish hot Hungarian paprika
Chopped parsley
(color)

Time Estimate:
Hands-on, 35 minutes
Serves 4

White Onion Sauce

1 teaspoon light olive oil with a dash of toasted sesame oil
1 pound (450 g) yellow onions, peeled and sliced lengthwise
4 cloves garlic, bashed, peeled, and chopped
1 teaspoon hot Hungarian paprika (see sidebar)
3 cups low-sodium chicken stock (page 231)
3 tablespoons cornstarch mixed with 6 tablespoons dealcoholized white wine (slurry)
1 cup strained yogurt (page 234)
1 teaspoon hot Hungarian paprika

The Paprikash

1½ pounds (675 g) Yukon Gold or Yellow Finn potatoes, peeled and sliced 1/2 inch (1.5 cm) thick (you will want a total of 12 slices)
1/8 teaspoon freshly ground white pepper
Half a 2-pound (900-g) cabbage, cut into 1/4-inch (0.75-cm) strips
1/2 teaspoon caraway seeds
1/8 teaspoon freshly ground sea salt
1 teaspoon hot Hungarian paprika
8 ounces turkey pastrami, cut into 1/4-inch (0.75-cm) thick slices, then cut into batons about 2 inches (5 cm) long
2 tablespoons fresh chopped parsley

HUNGARIAN HOT VS. SPANISH SWEET PAPRIKA

This recipe calls for hot Hungarian paprika specifically. There is also a Spanish version, but it's mostly sweet and not as complex. The Hungarian paprika gets its depth of flavor from the inclusion of the ground seed pod in the powder. The hot version can be found in specialty food stores, sometimes packaged in a small linen sack. Incidentally, hot paprika is not native to Hungary, but it is considered its national spice.

⋈ EXTRA MEAL

Double the recipe for the white onion sauce. When you get through reducing it, transfer half the sauce to a bowl and let it cool in the refrigerator. Divide the cooled sauce into 2 resealable plastic bags. Flatten the bags, expelling the air. Label and date them. When you're ready to use the thawed sauce, thicken it with the cornstarch and add the yogurt. You can also use the frozen sauce in the side dish that follows.

The white onion sauce: Pour the oil into a high-sided 11-inch (28-cm) skillet on medium heat and fry the onions for 2 minutes. Reduce the heat to low, add the garlic and paprika, cover, and simmer for 10 minutes.

While the onion is simmering, pour the chicken stock into a medium-sized saucepan on high heat and boil until reduced to 2 cups, about 10 minutes. Remove from the heat, stir in the cornstarch slurry, return to the heat, and boil for 30 seconds, until clear and thick, stirring constantly. Remove from the heat and throw in a couple of ice cubes to drop the temperature rapidly.

Spoon the yogurt into a small bowl and stir gently until all the lumps are gone. Slowly whisk the cooled chicken stock into the yogurt, then pour it into the skillet over the onions. Stir in the paprika.

The paprikash: Pour at least 3 inches (8 cm) of water into a steamer pot and bring to a boil. Place the potatoes in a steamer basket or tray, sprinkle with the pepper, fit the basket into the pot, cover, and steam until just tender, about 15 minutes.

Transfer the cabbage pieces to a steamer tray, separate well, and sprinkle with the caraway seeds, salt, and half the paprika. If you are using a bamboo steamer, you can place the steamer tray right on top of the potatoes, cover, and steam for 5 minutes. Lay the turkey pastrami on top of the cabbage, cover, and steam for 5 minutes.

Combine the onion sauce with the steamed cabbage and pastrami, and heat through, *slowly* over *low* heat (do not boil it!).

To serve: Place three slices of steamed potatoes onto each plate and spoon the paprikash over the top, with a scattering of paprika and parsley.

Nutritional Profile per Serving			
	Classic	**Springboard**	**Daily Value**
Calories	960	395	
Calories from fat	558	54	
Fat (gm)	62	6	9%
Saturated fat (gm)	25	2	10%
Sodium (mg)	2,825	814	34%
Cholesterol (mg)	288	33	11%
Carbohydrates (gm)	59	62	21%
Dietary fiber (gm)	7	6	24%
Classic compared: Blanquette of Lamb à l'Ancienne			

✖ CREAMY PEAS

A basic white sauce can dress up almost any side dish, from vegetables to pasta. Just vary the seasoning and garnish to match your ingredient. For instance: With sweet potatoes I'd simply heighten the flavor with a dab of maple syrup. Apples would be lovely with a garnish of fresh chopped sage. And it's all mixed together in less than 10 minutes when you make the white sauce in a double batch and freeze it, following the instructions on the preceding page. This particular pea dish is a great accompaniment to lamb.

Time Estimate:
  Hands-on, 15 minutes
Serves 4

1/2 recipe White Onion Sauce (page 34), without the cornstarch slurry or yogurt, thawed (or just whip up the White Sauce on page 33 without the cornstarch slurry or strained yogurt steps)
3 cups petit peas
1 tablespoon plus 2 teaspoon cornstarch mixed with 3 tablespoons water (slurry)
1/2 cup strained yogurt (page 234)
1 tablespoon chopped fresh mint
1/4 teaspoon freshly ground sea salt

Heat the thawed white onion sauce in a medium saucepan. Add the peas and cook just long enough to heat through, about 2 minutes. They should still retain their bright green color. Remove from the heat, stir in the cornstarch slurry, return to the heat, and boil about 30 seconds.

Place the yogurt in a small bowl. Pour some of the peas and sauce into the yogurt, mix well, then whisk the yogurt mixture into the hot vegetables. Stir in the mint and salt and it's ready to serve.

Nutritional Profile per Serving: Calories—157; calories from fat—9; fat (gm)—1 or 2% daily value; saturated fat (gm)—0.3; sodium (mg)—286; cholesterol (mg)—1; carbohydrates (gm)—27; dietary fiber (gm)—6

✖ CREAMY PESTO WITH HOT PASTA

Page Huletz is a flight attendant. Since changing her eating habits and resisting fat, she's lost 20 pounds and stayed that way for 2 years. She sent us a pesto recipe which I suggested she make cheesier by adding strained yogurt—a good start to achieve your own weight-loss goals?

Time Estimate:
  Hands-on, 20 minutes
Serves 4

8 ounces (225 g) uncooked linguine noodles
2 Roma tomatoes, diced

Pesto
1½ cups fresh basil leaves (packed tightly), rinsed and dried
1/4 cup walnuts
Juice of 1 lemon
2 cloves garlic, bashed and peeled
1/3 cup strained yogurt (page 234)
1/4 cup freshly grated Parmesan cheese
1/2 teaspoon freshly ground black pepper
1/2 teaspoon freshly ground sea salt

Cook the pasta according to package directions for *al dente,* just until tender. Drain and set aside.

While the pasta is cooking, put all the pesto ingredients in a food processor and process for 30 seconds. Scrape the sides and process 30 more seconds.

To serve: Transfer the hot pasta to a warm serving bowl and toss with the pesto until well coated. Scatter the ruby red pieces of Roma tomatoes on top and bring to the table for your lucky guests.

Nutritional Profile per Serving: Calories—348; calories from fat—72; fat (gm)—8 or 12% daily value; saturated fat (gm)—2; sodium (mg)—426; cholesterol (mg)—6; carbohydrates (gm)—55; dietary fiber (gm)—3

PESTO ON PASTA PRONTO!

The pesto must be ready to add to the pasta the moment that it has been drained. Please don't reheat pesto, for it will curdle.

❌ CREAMY GARAM MASALA CHICKEN

Gerri Gilliland's idea for a sauce that infuses cardamom into the yogurt while it is being strained gives the spice a maturation time that is necessary for its subtly sweet and pungent essence. The chicken would be lovely with steamed basmati rice, fresh mango, and chapatis.

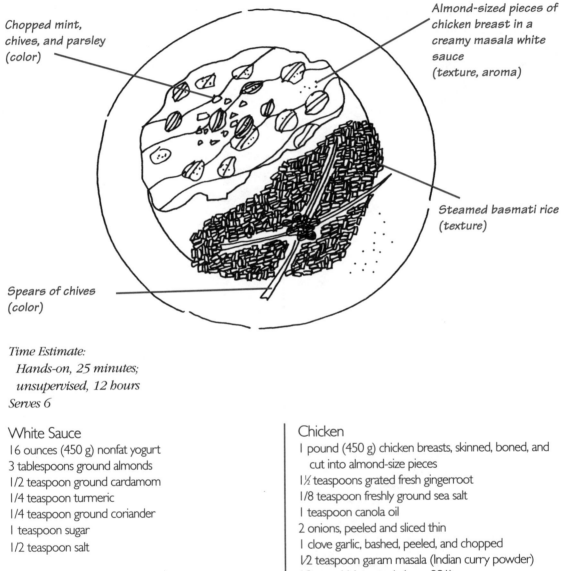

Chopped mint, chives, and parsley (color)

Almond-sized pieces of chicken breast in a creamy masala white sauce (texture, aroma)

Steamed basmati rice (texture)

Spears of chives (color)

Time Estimate:
  Hands-on, 25 minutes;
  unsupervised, 12 hours
Serves 6

White Sauce
16 ounces (450 g) nonfat yogurt
3 tablespoons ground almonds
1/2 teaspoon ground cardamom
1/4 teaspoon turmeric
1/4 teaspoon ground coriander
1 teaspoon sugar
1/2 teaspoon salt

Chicken
1 pound (450 g) chicken breasts, skinned, boned, and
  cut into almond-size pieces
1½ teaspoons grated fresh gingerroot
1/8 teaspoon freshly ground sea salt
1 teaspoon canola oil
2 onions, peeled and sliced thin
1 clove garlic, bashed, peeled, and chopped
1/2 teaspoon garam masala (Indian curry powder)
1/2 cup chicken stock (page 231)
Juice of 1 lime
1 tablespoon cornstarch

I do wish that you could hear **Gerri Gilliland** tell you her story in her own soft Irish brogue—you'd get a real feeling for this truly delightful and creative person.

In an earlier era, we both poured cream over everything that seemed edible. "When I hit 35," Gerri explained, "things changed and I found myself a few pounds heavier. I also found that a lot of my friends and customers" (Gerri has three restaurants, Gilliland's, Jake and Annie's, and Lulu in Santa Monica, California) "were starting to look at their diets and slowly change their eating habits.

"So I pioneered a new page on our menu called 'High Fiber, Low Fat and Vegetarian,' comprising salads, entrees, desserts, and coffee drinks. It's so popular I cannot tell you. We can't keep the Moroccan Vegetarian Couscous in the house, it sells so fast."

So do please visit Gerri at one of her restaurants and get her to talk. She has a delightful way of describing delicious things. Her recent cookbook, *Grills & Greens*, was nominated for a James Beard Award.

The white sauce: The day before, combine all the ingredients, place in a yogurt strainer, and refrigerate for 12 hours. Discard the whey.

The chicken: The day of serving, put the chicken in a small bowl, sprinkle with the ginger and salt, and refrigerate for 1 hour.

Heat the oil in a nonstick skillet and fry the onions until they are soft and just translucent. Do not allow them to color. Add the garlic, garam masala, and the marinated chicken breasts, and simmer gently for 5 minutes. Using a slotted spoon, remove the chicken from the pan, leaving the juices.

In a small bowl, combine the chicken stock, lime juice, and cornstarch, stir into the pan juices, and simmer gently, stirring constantly, for 3 minutes. Remove from the heat and gradually whisk a couple of tablespoons of the warm sauce into the strained yogurt. When that is well incorporated, stir the yogurt into the pan juices. Return the chicken to the pan and just heat through, but do not boil or the yogurt will curdle.

Nutritional Profile per Serving			
	Classic	**Springboard**	**Daily Value**
Calories	356	191	
Calories from fat	207	54	
Fat (gm)	23	6	9%
Saturated fat (gm)	13	1	5%
Sodium (mg)	665	370	15%
Cholesterol (mg)	112	43	14%
Carbohydrates (gm)	11	12	4%
Dietary fiber (gm)	1	1	4%
Classic compared: Creamed Chicken			

4
BROWN ONION SAUCES

Slowly caramelized onions are the base for a rich, dark sauce for any kind of hearty dish.

What I want to do here is to take a look into the future through a classic preparation to discover the genius of making the brown sauce. I borrow some techniques in order to introduce a swiftly made, dark, glossy, and aromatic brown sauce that, with only small ingredient variations, can become a universal condiment sauce, a sauce that complements the flavor of the main ingredient rather than extending it.

The good old onion forms the base for so many dishes that it works well as a complementary sauce flavor. When onions are heated carefully with a small amount of oil, their sugar content slowly caramelizes (especially with the naturally sweet varieties, like Vidalia, Walla Walla, and Maui) and turns them an appetizing deep rich brown color.

BASIC BROWN ONION SAUCE
Yields 2 cups

1/4 teaspoon light olive oil with a dash of toasted sesame oil
2 large sweet onions, peeled and diced fine
1 teaspoon dill seed
1 teaspoon caraway seed
1 cup deeply colored flavorful liquid
1 cup de-alcoholized red wine
1 tablespoon arrowroot mixed with 2 tablespoons de-alcoholized red wine (slurry)

Heat the oil in a large skillet on medium heat and fry the onions, dill, and caraway for 5 minutes. Add the stock and wine, scraping up all the pan residues into the liquid, and simmer for 5 minutes. Remove from the heat, stir in the arrowroot slurry, return to the heat, and stir until thickened and clear, about 30 seconds.

Tips and Hints
- Find the sweetest variety of onions in season and buy them as fresh as possible (ask someone in the produce section for a recommendation).
- You will need a fairly high heat to brown the onions; medium will do but be patient, as it will take 15 to 20 minutes to develop color without scorching.
- Beef stock, tomato purée, red wine, ham hock stock, a deeply colored vegetable stock, or any combination will provide depth of color to the sauce.

Inadvertently, Graham wore his blue suit while serving a brown sauce.

❉ BANGERS AND MASH

Marilyn Schermerhorn loves sausage and my brown onion sauce. I paired her up with a lower-fat sausage and, because Marilyn also likes Chinese food, I adapted a dish I had in Hong Kong called Silver Cloud Pierced with a Thousand Golden Arrows . . . which turned out to be sausages (bangers) and mashed potatoes!

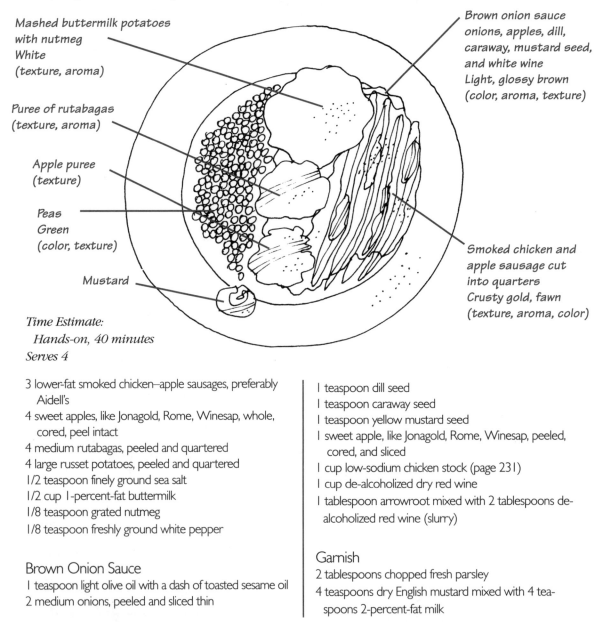

Mashed buttermilk potatoes with nutmeg
White
(texture, aroma)

Puree of rutabagas
(texture, aroma)

Apple puree
(texture)

Peas
Green
(color, texture)

Mustard

Brown onion sauce
onions, apples, dill, caraway, mustard seed, and white wine
Light, glossy brown
(color, aroma, texture)

Smoked chicken and apple sausage cut into quarters
Crusty gold, fawn
(texture, aroma, color)

Time Estimate:
  Hands-on, 40 minutes
Serves 4

3 lower-fat smoked chicken–apple sausages, preferably Aidell's
4 sweet apples, like Jonagold, Rome, Winesap, whole, cored, peel intact
4 medium rutabagas, peeled and quartered
4 large russet potatoes, peeled and quartered
1/2 teaspoon finely ground sea salt
1/2 cup 1-percent-fat buttermilk
1/8 teaspoon grated nutmeg
1/8 teaspoon freshly ground white pepper

Brown Onion Sauce
1 teaspoon light olive oil with a dash of toasted sesame oil
2 medium onions, peeled and sliced thin

1 teaspoon dill seed
1 teaspoon caraway seed
1 teaspoon yellow mustard seed
1 sweet apple, like Jonagold, Rome, Winesap, peeled, cored, and sliced
1 cup low-sodium chicken stock (page 231)
1 cup de-alcoholized dry red wine
1 tablespoon arrowroot mixed with 2 tablespoons de-alcoholized red wine (slurry)

Garnish
2 tablespoons chopped fresh parsley
4 teaspoons dry English mustard mixed with 4 teaspoons 2-percent-fat milk

At 66 years of age, *Marilyn Schermerhorn* tells me she doesn't have any health problems, but does need to lose 70 pounds. However, Marilyn says she's not going to go on "a diet" again. Instead she's convinced that she needs to change the way she cooks and eats permanently.

MINTY PEAS

2 cups frozen or fresh peas
1/4 cup water
1 tablespoon brown sugar
1 tablespoon mint leaves

In a medium saucepan, bring the water, mint, and sugar to a boil and simmer the peas until they are tender, about 5 to 10 minutes for fresh, 3 minutes for frozen.

✠ EXTRA MEAL

Double the recipe for the Brown Onion Sauce. Before you thicken or add the baked apple to it, dip out half the sauce. Cool in the refrigerator in an open flat container. Divide the sauce into 3 resealable plastic bags. Flatten them, expelling all the air, date, and label. Freeze for up to 6 months. The sauce is a great base for gravies, soups, and stews, and wonderful in the recipe that follows.

Ask the meat manager at your local grocery store where you can find lower-fat sausages. You can also call or write to Aidell's Sausage Company, 1575 Minnesota Street, San Francisco, CA 94107, (415) 285-6660.

Preheat the oven to 350°F (180°C). Place the sausages and apples together on a shallow baking pan and bake for 30 minutes. Remove the peel from the apples and mash three, reserving one for the sauce below.

In a medium saucepan, boil the rutabagas in water to cover for 30 minutes. Drain, return to the same pot, and mash until smooth.

In another medium saucepan, bring the potatoes to a boil in water, add 1/4 teaspoon of the salt, and cook for 20 minutes. Drain, return to the same pot over very low heat, cover with a kitchen towel, and let steam-dry for 15 minutes. Mash the boiled potatoes with the buttermilk, nutmeg, white pepper, and the remaining 1/4 teaspoon salt until smooth.

The brown onion sauce: While the bangers and mash are cooking, heat the oil in a high-sided skillet on medium high heat, add the onions, dill, caraway, and mustard seed and cook, uncovered, 5 minutes without stirring. Add the sliced apple, stir once, cover, and cook for 5 minutes. Pour in the stock and wine, stirring and scraping all the pan residues up into the liquid until the bottom of the pan is perfectly clean, and simmer 5 minutes. Remove from the heat, stir in the arrowroot slurry, return to the heat, and bring to a boil to thicken, about 30 seconds. Mash the reserved baked apple, stir into the sauce, and set aside.

To serve: Place one scoop each of the mashed potatoes, apple, and rutabaga down the center of each serving plate. Slice each sausage into quarters lengthwise. Ladle some sauce on one side of the mash and top the sauce with three quarters of sausage. Spoon some minty peas on the other side of the mash. Garnish with the parsley and a tablespoon of the mustard mixture next to the sausage.

Nutritional Profile per Serving			
	Classic	**Springboard**	**Daily Value**
Calories	748	696	
Calories from fat	522	90	
Fat (gm)	58	10	15%
Saturated fat (gm)	21	3	15%
Sodium (mg)	2606	820	34%
Cholesterol (mg)	124	60	20%
Carbohydrates (gm)	43	118	39%
Dietary fiber (gm)	6	15	60%
Classic compared: Pork Sausages and Mashed Potatoes			

✳ Potatoes Baked with Apples and Onion Sauce

Time Estimate:
 Hands-on, 15 minutes;
 unsupervised, 60 minutes
Serves 4

1 cup Brown Onion Sauce, thawed (page 41)
4 small russet potatoes, peeled and sliced thin
1 sweet apple, peeled and sliced thin
2 ounces (50 g) Canadian bacon, chopped fine
1¼ teaspoon light olive oil with a dash of toasted
   sesame oil

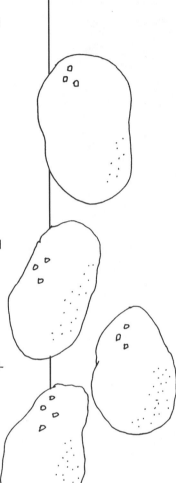

Preheat the oven to 350°F (180°C). Steam the potato slices for 5 minutes, remove from the heat, and cool under running water.

Layer half the potatoes in an oiled 9 x 9-inch (23 x 23-cm) baking dish. Scatter the apple and Canadian bacon over the potatoes. Pour the brown onion sauce evenly on top. Arrange the rest of the potato slices in an overlapping pattern on the sauce and press down. Brush with the oil. Bake uncovered for 1 hour.

Nutritional Profile per Serving: Calories—212; calories from fat—27; fat (gm)—3 or 0.05% daily value; saturated fat (gm)—1; sodium (mg)—195; cholesterol (mg)—7; carbohydrates (gm)—42; dietary fiber (gm)—5

✖ CREAMY FRENCH ONION SOUP

In her Food Preference List, Lisa Powell told me that she liked brown onion sauces and soups. Violà! *Just for her, and all you other onion soup lovers out there . . .*

Time Estimate:
 Hands-on, 40 minutes;
 unsupervised, 30 minutes
Serves 4

1 teaspoon light olive oil with a dash of toasted sesame oil
2 pounds (1 kg) yellow onions, peeled and sliced
1 cup de-alcoholized white wine
1 quart (944 ml) low-sodium chicken stock (page 231)
1/4 teaspoon freshly ground white pepper
1 tablespoon Dijon mustard
1 cup nonfat milk

Garnish
4 slices French bread, cut into cubes and baked until dry
1/4 cup freshly grated Parmesan cheese

Heat the oil in a heavy-bottomed stock pot, add the onions, and toss to release the oils, about 2 minutes. Reduce the heat to low and cook, uncovered, for 40 minutes. Watch them carefully and stir often to keep from browning. They will reduce in volume and become very soft. Add the wine and allow it to cook off. When it has evaporated, stir in the chicken stock, pepper, and mustard and let it cook, uncovered, for 30 minutes.

Strain the onions and purée in a blender or processor. Stir the onion purée back into the soup with the milk and heat through. Ladle into serving bowls and garnish with the croutons and Parmesan cheese.

Nutritional Profile per Serving: Calories—236; calories from fat—45; fat (gm)—5 or 8% daily value; saturated fat (gm)—2; sodium (mg)—403; cholesterol (mg)—6; carbohydrates (gm)—37; dietary fiber (gm)—4

VENISON AU CHOU CROQUANT
(VENISON WITH CRUNCHY CABBAGE)

Even if you don't have access to venison, don't miss this recipe: the brown sauce is so rich in flavor it's almost impossible to believe that it isn't loaded with fat. A great substitute for the venison would be a pork tenderloin. But the standout is Michel Bouit's crunchy, minty green cabbage, studded with chopped hazelnuts.

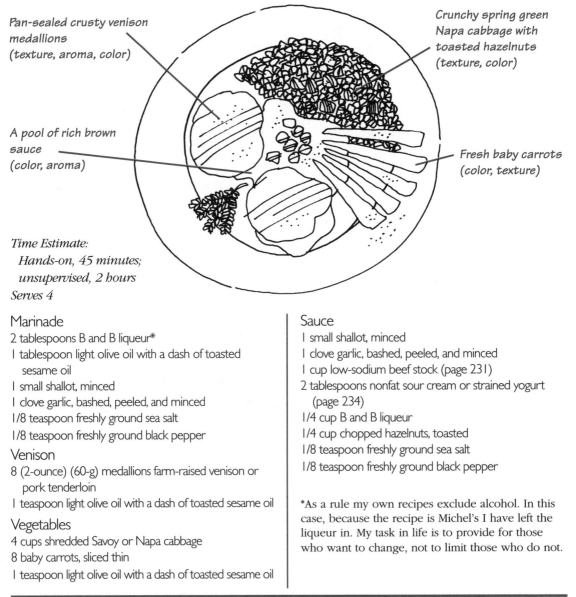

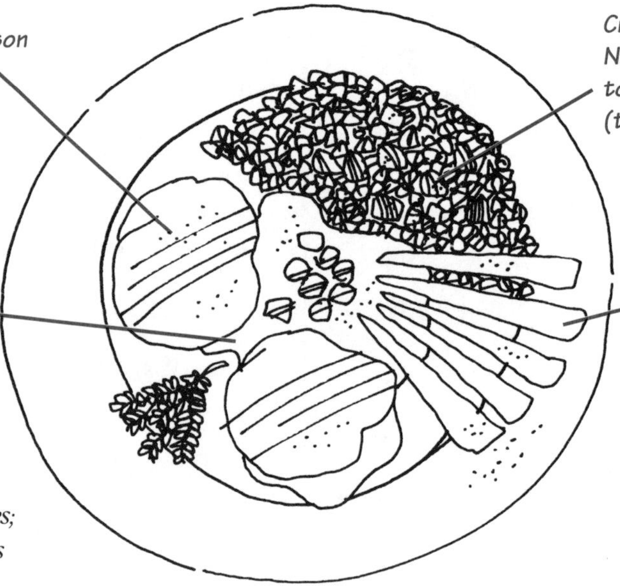
Pan-sealed crusty venison medallions (texture, aroma, color)
Crunchy spring green Napa cabbage with toasted hazelnuts (texture, color)
A pool of rich brown sauce (color, aroma)
Fresh baby carrots (color, texture)

Time Estimate:
Hands-on, 45 minutes; unsupervised, 2 hours
Serves 4

Marinade

2 tablespoons B and B liqueur*
1 tablespoon light olive oil with a dash of toasted sesame oil
1 small shallot, minced
1 clove garlic, bashed, peeled, and minced
1/8 teaspoon freshly ground sea salt
1/8 teaspoon freshly ground black pepper

Venison

8 (2-ounce) (60-g) medallions farm-raised venison or pork tenderloin
1 teaspoon light olive oil with a dash of toasted sesame oil

Vegetables

4 cups shredded Savoy or Napa cabbage
8 baby carrots, sliced thin
1 teaspoon light olive oil with a dash of toasted sesame oil

Sauce

1 small shallot, minced
1 clove garlic, bashed, peeled, and minced
1 cup low-sodium beef stock (page 231)
2 tablespoons nonfat sour cream or strained yogurt (page 234)
1/4 cup B and B liqueur
1/4 cup chopped hazelnuts, toasted
1/8 teaspoon freshly ground sea salt
1/8 teaspoon freshly ground black pepper

*As a rule my own recipes exclude alcohol. In this case, because the recipe is Michel's I have left the liqueur in. My task in life is to provide for those who want to change, not to limit those who do not.

Listen to one sentence from **Michel Bouit**, or even a few syllables, and you are plunged into France. His accent rolls around his mouth; words chase memories of food gone past and recipes to come.

Michel is a chef's chef, devoted to the kitchen and its classical practice. As executive director of the American Culinary Guild Cup, "Bocuse d'Or Competition," and professional culinary consultant, he is a man who cherishes standards of excellence.

Given this lofty perch, what does Michel have to say about my current interest in lower-fat levels? "People today are very knowledgeable about good food and nutrition. They are very aware of the connection between what they eat and how they feel." Perhaps it was his very French accent that made me stop to think about the link between eating and feeling. Michel wasn't talking about swooning with pleasure, but a whole body reaction.

Currently Michel has his own company, which specializes in the coordination of culinary events, both nationally and internationally. He adds, "As chefs we are the leaders in the food industry. We have the responsibility to monitor the pulse of our customers and design our menus accordingly."

Bon appétit is possible after all!

TO FLAMBÉ WITH FLOURISH

Flaming enhances a sauce, giving it a lusty rich flavor. Be careful never to pour liquor directly from the bottle into the pan; rather, measure out the required amount and set the liquor bottle well away from the stove. You might want to have a large pan lid ready, to douse the flames quickly if they seem out of control. Don't flambé over a high heat or the alcohol will burn off before you can ignite it. All you need is slightly warm alcohol for a flambé. Remove the warm pan from the heat, pour in the liqueur, and return to the heat, on medium. Stand back from the burner and with a long kitchen or fireplace match ignite the liqueur. Stand back until the flame disappears.

KNOW YOUR ANTELOPE

Michel uses blackbuck antelope. He says, "The blackbuck is extremely fine grained with a mild flavor. It is originally native to India and surrounding countries. Evolving near the equator, the blackbuck develops almost no body fat and retains the highest percentage of moisture of any harvested wild game meat."

The marinade: In a medium bowl combine all the marinade ingredients, place the meat in the marinade, and refrigerate for about 2 hours.

The vegetables: Blanch the cabbage and carrots in a large pot of boiling water for 1 minute. Drain, refresh the vegetables in cold water, and set aside to drain thoroughly. Just before serving, heat a large skillet, add the oil, and fry the vegetables until just heated through.

The venison: Pour the oil into a heavy-based skillet on medium heat. Lift the meat from the marinade and dry well with paper towels. Place the meat in the pan and sear the medallions for about 3 minutes per side. Remove from the pan.

The sauce: In the same heavy-based skillet on medium heat, fry the shallot and garlic for 2 minutes. Return the medallions to the pan, add the liqueur, and flambé. When the flames have subsided, remove the meat and keep warm in the oven. To the same skillet, add the stock, increase the heat to high, and boil until it is reduced to about 3/4 cup, about 5 minutes. In a small bowl, mix 1 tablespoon of the reduced stock into the sour cream or strained yogurt, then stir the mixture into the hot sauce. Keep warm but do not boil.

To serve: Pool the sauce onto warm plates and place 2 medallions in each pool. Spoon the cabbage and carrots onto the plate and sprinkle with toasted hazelnuts, salt, and pepper.

Nutritional Profile per Serving			
	Classic	Springboard	Daily Value
Calories	579	351	
Calories from fat	189	126	
Fat (gm)	21	14	22%
Saturated fat (gm)	10	2	10%
Sodium (mg)	285	405	17%
Cholesterol (mg)	224	94	32%
Carbohydrates (gm)	34	17	6%
Dietary fiber (gm)	3	5	20%
Classic compared: Ruby Venison Ragout			

5 ROASTED MEATS AND GRAVIES

Straining the fat out of cooking juices and supplementing them with other low-fat flavorful liquids, like wine or citrus juice, make lower-fat gravies in seconds.

Traditionally, roast meat gravy is made with highly saturated fat from pan drippings. The problem is compounded when it's thickened with a mixture of flour and butter—a gravy that is easily 40 percent fat.

Eliminating almost all of this fat is quite easy. First, there's an essential piece of equipment called the fat strainer cup. This indispensable tool has a spout that comes out of the bottom instead of the top. You simply pour your pan drippings or stock into the cup and let it sit for a few minutes, during which time you can actually see the fat rise to the top. Now it's a simple matter of pouring out the fat-free liquid that has accumulated on the bottom, stopping when the fat comes to the spout.

Nonfat thickening is easily accomplished by using arrowroot or cornstarch. So if you keep the serving portion of meat to about 4 ounces (the size of a pack of playing cards), your roast meat and gravy dinner with vegetables can run 25 to 30 percent of calories from fat, which is the ceiling recommended by the American Heart Association for healthy individuals. Dig in!

Tips and Hints

- Gravy is best made with a liquid that matches the main ingredients and is reduced in volume. Don't forget unsweetened fruit juices—after all, what is wine but an original base of squeezed grapes?
- A fat strainer cup is an essential piece of equipment.
- *Please* be sure that the gravy and serving plates are hot. An arrowroot-thickened gravy will become slippery if allowed to cool.

In the fat strainer cup, you can actually see the fat float to the top.

Roast Pork with Apple Gravy

Al Bannauch noted on his Food Preference List that he liked roast meats and gravies, so I sent him this recipe. His wife, Mary, served it at a dinner party for 10 people she describes as "real roast lovers." Did anyone know they were eating a lower-fat version? Nobody guessed, reports Mary, and none of the apple gravy was left over. Please make sure you complement your roast with colorful side vegetables. My suggestions are below.

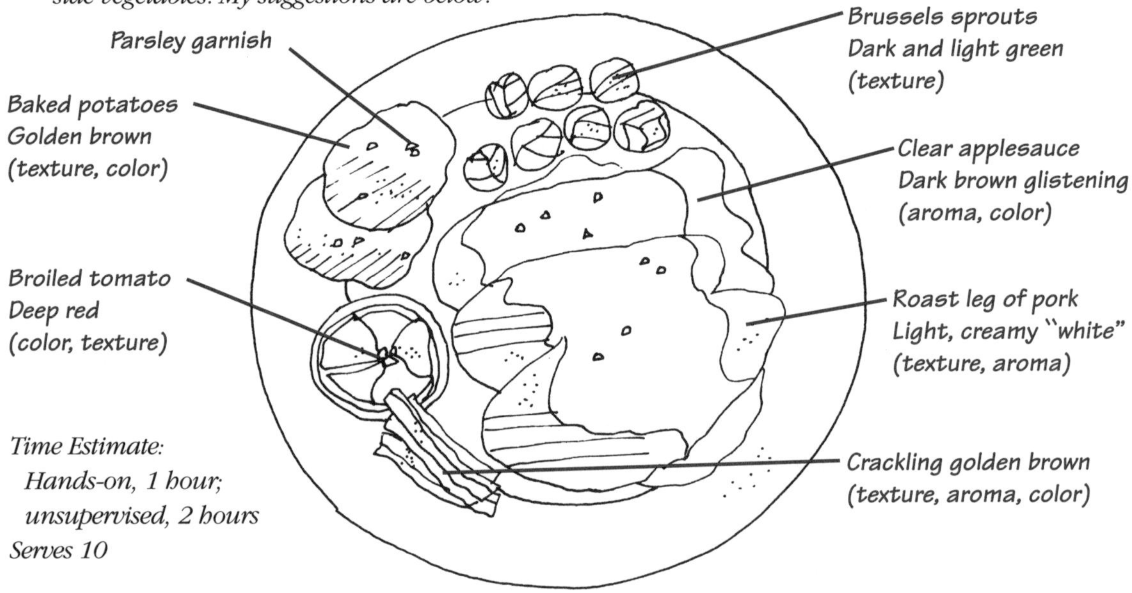
Parsley garnish
Baked potatoes
Golden brown
(texture, color)
Broiled tomato
Deep red
(color, texture)
Brussels sprouts
Dark and light green
(texture)
Clear applesauce
Dark brown glistening
(aroma, color)
Roast leg of pork
Light, creamy "white"
(texture, aroma)
Crackling golden brown
(texture, aroma, color)

Time Estimate:
Hands-on, 1 hour;
unsupervised, 2 hours
Serves 10

1 (6-pound) (2.7-kg) leg mid-roast, rind on and shank off (see directions on page 51)

Seasoning Rub

3 cloves garlic, bashed, peeled, and chopped
10 sage leaves, roughly chopped
1/8 teaspoon freshly ground sea salt
1/8 teaspoon freshly ground black pepper

Outer Crust Seasoning

1/8 teaspoon freshly ground sea salt
1 teaspoon caraway seed

Apple Gravy

2 cups unsweetened apple juice (not from concentrate)
2 tablespoons arrowroot mixed with 1/4 cup unsweetened apple juice (slurry)
1/4 cup chopped fresh parsley

The seasoning rub: Preheat the oven to 350°F (180°C). Purée the garlic, sage, salt, and pepper in a food processor or with a mortar and pestle until it's a paste. Spread the paste on the cut surface of the roast and up into the bone cavity—this will let the flavors penetrate the meat while it roasts. Place the prepared roast on a rack and close the open end with metal skewers. Lace it up with butcher's twine and tie securely.

The outer crust seasoning: Rub the salt and caraway seeds into the incisions in the rind. Place the roast on its rack in a roasting pan, pour in 2 cups of water, and bake for 2½ hours, or until the internal temperature measures 175°F (80°C). Throughout the baking process, check to make sure there is water in the bottom of the pan. Remove from the oven, transfer the roast to a cutting board, and let it rest for 20 minutes. Reserve the juices in the pan.

Make delicious crisp cracklings: Cut off the rind, scrape off and discard the white layer of fat from the inside, and place the rind on a baking sheet. Slide under the broiler until it gets really crisp, about 5 minutes. Remove from the

Scoring the Rind

Ask your butcher to remove the bone. To score the rind, make an incision with a sharp serrated knife just through the surface of the rind and around the circumference of the roast. Continue making the incision moving down the roast, leaving a 1/4-inch (1.5-cm) space between cuts.

Vegetable Side Dishes

Roast Potatoes, Brussels Sprouts, and Broiled Tomatoes
Serves 10
10 medium Yellow Finn or Yukon Gold potatoes
1½ pounds (675 g) Brussels sprouts
1½ cups unsweetened apple juice
3¾ teaspoons arrowroot mixed with 2½ tablespoons
   water (slurry)
5 large tomatoes, washed and halved
1/2 teaspoon freshly ground sea salt
1/2 teaspoon freshly ground black pepper
2 tablespoons chopped fresh basil

Scrub the potatoes, cut in half, and place on a broiler pan, flat side up. Bake with the roast for the last 30 minutes of the cooking process. To finish, brush with a little of the pan liquid and brown under the broiler for about 8 minutes.

For the Brussels sprouts, cut off the bottom 1/8 inch (0.5 cm) and make a deep X incision in the base. Remove any tough or discolored outside leaves. Place the Brussels sprouts and apple juice in a large skillet, bring to a boil, cover, reduce the heat to medium, and cook for 10 minutes. Remove from the heat, stir in the arrowroot slurry, return to the heat, and boil until thickened and clear, about 30 seconds. Place the tomato halves on a broiler tray, sprinkle with the salt, pepper, and basil, and broil until just brown, about 2 minutes.

✂ Extra Meal

Leftover roast pork will make another delicious meal in the recipe following, Roast Pork Stir-Fry (page 52).

Mary and Al Bannauch are both retired now from their jobs at Sears, and Mary says because they're not as active, they watch what they eat. They invited eight friends over to sample this dish, and although Mary had to substitute a pork loin, she reports that it all went "very well" and "I'm going to make this again. The gravy was the hit of the evening—no one noticed that it was low fat. And the house had the nicest aromas from the fresh herbs. Everyone who walked in the door commented on it."

oven, cut off all the surface fat and discard. Cut the cracklings into 4 x 2-inch (10 x 5-cm) pieces.

The gravy: Put the roasting pan with the reserved pan juices directly on a stovetop burner, add the apple juice, bring to a boil, then pour through a sieve into a fat strainer. Let sit for a few minutes until the fat has floated to the surface. Pour the fat-free juice from the strainer into a small saucepan. Bring the liquid to a boil, remove from the heat, stir in the arrowroot slurry, return to the heat, and bring to a boil to thicken and clear, about 30 seconds.

To serve: Serve three slices of the pork, about 1/4 inch (0.75 cm) thick each, and one piece of the crisp cracklings on individual serving plates. Please note that one piece of crackling this size could add between 10 and 15 grams of fat to the meal total. Ladle with the gravy and garnish with a sprinkle of the parsley. The pork would be wonderful served with Roasted Potatoes, Brussels Sprouts, and Broiled Tomatoes.

Nutritional Profile per Serving			
	Classic	Springboard	Daily Value
Calories	1179	871	
Calories from fat	594	279	
Fat (gm)	66	31	48%
Saturated fat (gm)	21	10	50%
Sodium (mg)	416	341	14%
Cholesterol (mg)	294	226	75%
Carbohydrates (gm)	37	65	22%
Dietary fiber (gm)	7	10	40%
Classic compared: Roast Leg of Pork with Spiced Peaches			

✄ ROAST PORK STIR-FRY

Time Estimate:
  Hands-on, 35 minutes
Serves 4

2 teaspoons light olive oil with a dash of toasted sesame
  oil
2 carrots, sliced thin on the diagonal
1 large stalk celery, cut in 1/4-inch (0.75 cm) diagonal
  slices
4 ounces (125 g) jicama, cut in matchsticks
4 ounces (125 g) snow peas, topped and tailed
2 cloves garlic, bashed, peeled, and chopped fine
12 thin quarter-size slices of fresh gingerroot, chopped
  fine
1 bunch green onions, sliced on the diagonal, white and
  green parts separate
8 ounces (225 g) leftover roast pork, cut in small strips
1/2 cup unsweetened apple juice
2 tablespoons low-sodium soy sauce
11/2 teaspoons arrowroot mixed with 1 tablespoon
  apple juice (slurry)
4 cups cooked long-grain white rice

Heat half the olive oil in a large skillet and fry the carrots, celery, jicama, and snow peas for 2 minutes. Transfer the cooked vegetables to a bowl and set aside.

Heat the remaining teaspoon of oil in the same skillet and fry the garlic, ginger, and white part of the green onion for 2 minutes. Transfer the seasonings to a small bowl and set aside. Place the pork in the same hot pan and stir-fry about 3 minutes. Return the cooked vegetables and seasonings to the pork and stir-fry until heated through, about 2 minutes. Pour in the apple juice and soy sauce and bring to a boil. Remove the pan from the heat, stir in the arrowroot slurry, return to the heat, and boil until thickened and clear, about 30 seconds.

Serve the pork and vegetables with the rice, garnished with the chopped green parts of the green onions.

Nutritional Profile per Serving: Calories—432; calories from fat—90; fat (gm)—10 or 15% daily value; saturated fat (gm)—3; sodium (mg)—173; cholesterol (mg)—47; carbohydrates (gm)—61; dietary fiber (gm)—4

BROCCOLI, WITH THE STALKS, PLEASE!

The lovely lady I created this recipe for, Angela, says that while she's fond of broccoli, she never before realized how good the *stalks* could be. Try them today.

Wash 2 pounds (900 g) of broccoli well. Cut off 2 inches (5 cm) of the bottom stalk and peel the rest of the stalk up to the florets. Cut off the peeled stalks 1 inch (2.5 cm) below where the florets begin to branch out. Cut the stalks into 1/4 inch (0.75 cm) diagonal slices. Break apart the florets, leaving some stem on each. When the chicken is cooked and out of the oven, put 1 inch (2.5 cm) of water in a steamer pot, place the broccoli stalks and florets on a steamer tray, cover the pot, and steam until just tender, about 2 1/2 minutes.

�֍ Roast Chicken with Cranberry Gravy

I really liked this lovely red and tangy cranberry gravy for roast chicken. I sent the recipe to Angela Stratton, who cooked this for her husband without telling him that it was low fat. Angela reports that the following comments must therefore be "sincere." He said it was "bursting with flavor," "tastes like a $50 dinner at Joseph's Restaurant," and was "really good to look at." Angela says, "We shall definitely be having it again." Why don't you try it, too? I think the perfect side vegetable is broccoli.

Time Estimate:
  Hands-on, 30 minutes;
  unsupervised, 90 minutes
Serves 4

1 (3½-pound (1.5-kg) whole chicken
1 whole clove garlic, smashed
1/4 teaspoon freshly ground sea salt
1/4 teaspoon freshly ground black pepper
1 (2-inch) (5 cm) sprig fresh rosemary
15 sage leaves
6 sprigs thyme
2 pounds (900 g) sweet potatoes, peeled and cut into 1-inch (2.5-cm) slices

Cranberry Gravy
Neck, heart, and gizzard from the chicken
1/2 onion, peeled and sliced
4 whole cloves
1 clove garlic, bashed, peeled, and sliced
10 peppercorns
1 (2-inch) (5-cm) sprig fresh rosemary
1 cup low-sodium chicken stock (page 231)
1/4 teaspoon freshly ground sea salt

1½ cups cranapple juice, divided
2 tablespoons dried cranberries
1½ tablespoons arrowroot mixed with 3 tablespoons cranapple juice (slurry)

The chicken: Preheat the oven to 350°F (180°C). Wash the chicken inside and out and drain. Rub the inside with the garlic and sprinkle with salt and pepper. Stuff the herbs into the cavity and tie the legs together. Place on a rack in a roasting pan large enough to hold the chicken and the sweet potatoes. Bake until the internal temperature reaches 165°F (75°C), about 1½ hours. After 1 hour, put the sweet potatoes in the pan and let them bake for the remaining 30 minutes. Remove from the oven and transfer the chicken and sweet potatoes to a carving board, reserving the cooking juices in the pan.

The cranberry gravy: In a saucepan, combine the chicken parts, onion, cloves, garlic, peppercorns, rosemary, chicken stock, salt, and 1 cup of the cranapple juice. Cover, bring to a boil, lower the heat, and simmer for 1 hour.

After the chicken has been removed from the oven, finish the gravy by pouring a little of the strained gravy liquid into the roasting pan to deglaze it. Then pour the pan residue into a fat strainer. Pour the defatted juices into a medium-sized saucepan with the rest of the strained gravy liquid, add the remaining 1/2 cup of cranapple juice and the dried cranberries, and bring to a boil. Remove from the heat, stir in the arrowroot slurry, return to the heat, and bring to a boil to thicken and clear, about 30 seconds.

To serve: Carve the chicken into thin slices and nestle them beside the sweet potatoes, ladled with the gravy. Steamed broccoli florets and stalks would complete the picture.

Nutritional Profile per Serving: Calories—539; calories from fat—81; fat (gm)—9 or 14% daily value; saturated fat (gm)—3; sodium (mg)—437; cholesterol (mg)—115; carbohydrates (gm)—67; dietary fiber (gm)—8

✖ ROAST SMOKED PORK LOIN

Tom Douglas' rich shallot and carrot gravy is a bold accompaniment to any meat roast. The Maillard Reaction (page 180) caramelizes the carrots and shallots, adding a depth of flavor that warms the heart and soul.

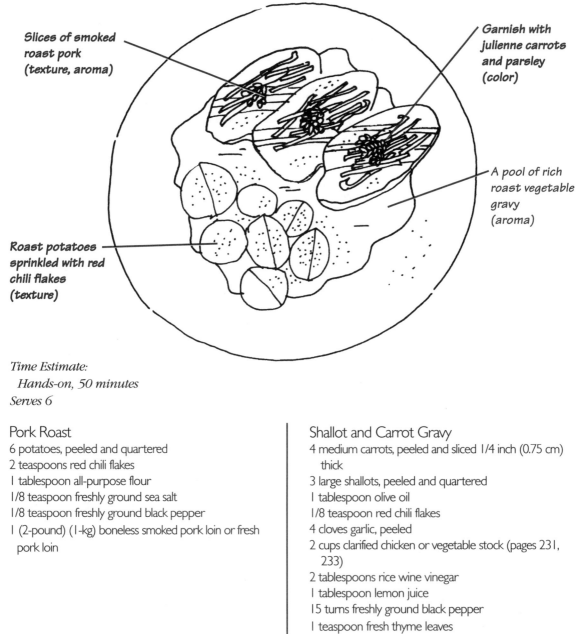

Slices of smoked roast pork (texture, aroma)

Garnish with julienne carrots and parsley (color)

A pool of rich roast vegetable gravy (aroma)

Roast potatoes sprinkled with red chili flakes (texture)

Time Estimate:
  Hands-on, 50 minutes
Serves 6

Pork Roast

6 potatoes, peeled and quartered
2 teaspoons red chili flakes
1 tablespoon all-purpose flour
1/8 teaspoon freshly ground sea salt
1/8 teaspoon freshly ground black pepper
1 (2-pound) (1-kg) boneless smoked pork loin or fresh pork loin

Shallot and Carrot Gravy

4 medium carrots, peeled and sliced 1/4 inch (0.75 cm) thick
3 large shallots, peeled and quartered
1 tablespoon olive oil
1/8 teaspoon red chili flakes
4 cloves garlic, peeled
2 cups clarified chicken or vegetable stock (pages 231, 233)
2 tablespoons rice wine vinegar
1 tablespoon lemon juice
15 turns freshly ground black pepper
1 teaspoon fresh thyme leaves

Tom Douglas tells me that he's strongly influenced by a paradox that almost reaches dual identity. "On the whole, I'm sick of 'lite,'" he says. "And yet, as a people, we are too fat." He reconciles this by dreaming of smaller center-of-the-plate meat portions and more creative vegetable presentations.

Tom has won his culinary spurs among Seattle's various eaters at his Dahlia Lounge by creating exactly this kind of high drama, so startlingly comfortable that you are not even aware of his lighter touch. He does a potato gnocchi with a roasted tomato sauce and a Kaso cod with seaweed salad that both sell very well and look wonderful.

Tom hopes that restaurants will remain "places of community, courtship and discussion," which is exactly what happens at the Dahlia. The fact is that Tom likes to eat anfd he's real, and that's fun, and that's good for the digestion.

A RENAISSANCE GRAVY

This roast gravy can accent any roast meat: pork, beef, chicken, or turkey. If you're using the gravy for roast pork or beef, make sure that the carrots and shallots are very well browned and caramelized before adding them to the stock. This will make the rich-looking gravy that you traditionally expect to come with pork or beef.

The roast: Preheat the oven to 375°F (175°C). Parboil the potatoes for 10 minutes, drain, and pat dry. Combine the red chili flakes with the flour, salt, and pepper and lightly sprinkle over the pork and the potatoes. Place the pork and potatoes in a roasting pan and bake for 45 minutes.

The shallot and carrot gravy: While the roast is cooking, place the carrots and shallots in a separate roasting pan in a single layer and drizzle with the olive oil. Let stand for 15 minutes. Sprinkle with the chili flakes and garlic and put in the oven. Cook until slightly caramelized and tender, about 15 to 20 minutes. Remove the vegetables from the oven and transfer to a medium saucepan. Add the stock, vinegar, lemon juice, and pepper to the pan and simmer for 5 minutes. Place in the food processor with the thyme and purée until very smooth. If the gravy is too thin, reduce by boiling over high heat until you achieve the desired thickness. If too thick, add a little more water, or stock if you have it.

Remove the smoked pork and potatoes from the pan and pour off any pan drippings. Add the gravy to the pan, and place on top of the stove. Over gentle heat, stir the gravy until any crusty bits adhering to the pan have incorporated into the sauce.

To serve: Slice the pork and distribute it with the potatoes and vegetables on plates. Drizzle with the gravy, serving the rest of the gravy on the table.

Nutritional Profile per Serving			
	Classic	**Springboard**	**Daily Value**
Calories	661	432	
Calories from fat	270	90	
Fat (gm)	30	10	15%
Saturated fat (gm)	11	3	15%
Sodium (mg)	683	233	10%
Cholesterol (mg)	197	119	40%
Carbohydrates (gm)	24	37	12%
Dietary fiber (gm)	2	4	16%
Classic compared: Roast Pork and Gravy			

6

STRAINED YOGURT

Plain nonfat yogurt strained overnight becomes a dense, creamy fresh "cheese" for savory spreads, sauces, and toppings.

If you have an interest in food and modern trends in the restaurant business you cannot avoid the word "signature" to describe a particular flavor or style based upon one or more ingredients. I'm prepared to admit that my signature includes strained yogurt.

The simple process of leaving plain nonfat yogurt to stand for 4 hours or overnight drains out the liquid whey and reduces the volume by 50 percent, leaving you with a considerably thickened and creamier yogurt, what many call a fresh cheese. This can be done in advance so you have it on hand for any need. (See Basic Strained Yogurt, page 234.)

I love strained yogurt plain and use it in place of butter on my toast. But I have also found it a great boost to my most creative cookery: to whiten light-colored reduced chicken, fish, and vegetable stocks; as a base for salad dressings; and for both dessert and savory toppings. Without a particle of fat, it contributes the fine flavor of a dairy product, an essential dense whiteness, a smooth mouthfeel, and a pleasant acidic "bright note."

Tips and Hints

- Select a plain yogurt that uses *acidophilus bulgaricus* culture, listed on the carton label. Be sure that there are no thickeners, as these prevent the whey from escaping. Dannon is an example of a good brand.
- Choose the degree of fat that pertains to your health needs. I use nonfat yogurt in all my recipes. The higher the fat content, the more mouthroundful the strained yogurt will have.
- You can strain the yogurt in a specifically designed strainer or in a mesh sieve lined with a coffee filter or cheesecloth. It will partially strain in 2 hours at room temperature and 8 hours in the refrigerator. Allow 12 hours in the refrigerator for a dense, lump-free cheese.
- You can't strain too much, so start with the largest carton of yogurt you can find and keep it refrigerated for handy use. The volume reduces by half after straining. It keeps a week refrigerated.
- To prevent the low-fat yogurt from breaking (curdling) when used as a sauce thickener, first thicken the liquid with cornstarch. Place the yogurt in a small bowl and pour the thickened sauce into it very slowly, stirring gently. Return to the heat and warm through without boiling.

"OK, faster now!! You can do it! Make it burn!"

How not to "strain yogurt."

✖ BREAST OF CHICKEN IN SWEET PEPPER SAUCE

Vibrant with red, green, and yellow bell peppers, fragrant with fresh cilantro, this creamy sauced chicken dinner has it all—it's even ready in less than one hour! It's also a classic example of using strained yogurt to make a creamy white sauce that you'll be able to duplicate in many other of your own dishes. It was springboarded from a recipe sent to me by Jean Ferbert, who said she liked to use a sweet pepper salsa on baked potatoes, salads, and chicken. The dinner is complete with baked sweet potatoes and steamed broccoli on the side.

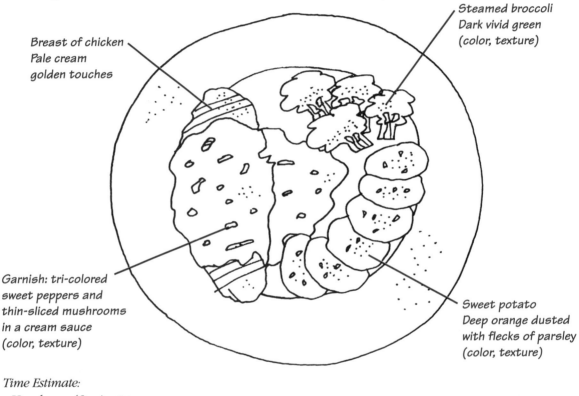

Breast of chicken
Pale cream
golden touches

Steamed broccoli
Dark vivid green
(color, texture)

Garnish: tri-colored
sweet peppers and
thin-sliced mushrooms
in a cream sauce
(color, texture)

Sweet potato
Deep orange dusted
with flecks of parsley
(color, texture)

Time Estimate:
  Hands-on, 40 minutes
Serves 4

1/4 teaspoon light olive oil with a dash of toasted sesame oil

4 (6-ounce) (170-g) chicken breast halves, skin on

1 bunch green onions, trimmed and chopped fine

3 cloves garlic, bashed, peeled, and chopped

1 each red, yellow, and green bell pepper, cored, seeded, and diced fine

1/4 teaspoon freshly ground black pepper

1/8 teaspoon freshly ground sea salt

1 cup de-alcoholized white wine

4 ounces (125 g) mushrooms, thinly sliced

2 tablespoons chopped fresh cilantro

1 tablespoon cornstarch mixed with 2 tablespoons of de-alcoholized white wine (slurry)

1/4 cup strained yogurt (page 234)

4 baked sweet potatoes, seasoned with cardamom

1 pound (450 g) broccoli florets, steamed

Heat the oil in a medium skillet on medium heat and fry the chicken for 2 minutes on each side. Remove from the pan, strip off and discard the skin, and set aside.

In the same skillet, fry the onions, garlic, and diced bell peppers for 1 minute. Return the chicken breasts to the pan, sprinkle with the pepper and salt, cover, and cook for 5 minutes. Transfer the chicken and vegetables to a warm plate.

Deglaze the skillet with the wine. Stir in the mushrooms and cilantro and boil for 1 minute. Remove from the heat, stir in the cornstarch slurry, return to the heat, and bring to a boil for 30 seconds to thicken and clear. Remove from the heat and lightly but thoroughly stir in the strained yogurt. Return to very low heat, add the reserved chicken and vegetables, and heat through. Divide the sauced chicken and vegetables on plates with sweet potato and broccoli on the side.

Jean Ferbert says she tries to cook "very, very, very low fat" for herself and her husband. While she has never had any health concerns, her husband had a cholesterol problem. But now they've learned a whole new way of low-fat eating and really enjoy it. Jean says, "It gives me a feeling that I'm taking care of my body and my husband,  and it feels good protecting us."

To cut back on fat even more in this recipe, Jean told me that she just took the skin off the chicken and steamed it. She reports that the chicken is quite moist with this cooking method. She also suggests flavoring the steaming water with garlic, dill, or lemon, so that flavor just steams up through the meat.

Nutritional Profile per Serving			
	Classic	**Springboard**	**Daily Value**
Calories	527	383	
Calories from fat	135	45	
Fat (gm)	26	5	8%
Saturated fat (gm)	15	1	5%
Sodium (mg)	562	203	8%
Cholesterol (mg)	149	87	29%
Carbohydrates (gm)	40	43	14%
Dietary fiber (gm)	7	7	28%
Classic compared: Chicken Breast in Wine and Cream Sauce			

✖ STRAINED YOGURT WITH MARMALADE OR FRUIT SPREAD

Perhaps the biggest benefit to me from strained yogurt has been its use as a savory spread on all my breads, replacing butter and cheese. I use it plain, as in the recipe below, but you might want to flavor it with garlic, onion, your favorite fresh herbs, or other seasonings. Of course, strained yogurt also works well sweetened and used as a top-ping for desserts in place of whipped cream (I did mention that this stuff is versatile, didn't I?).

Time Estimate:
  Hands-on, 5 minutes
Serves 4

8 teaspoons of strained yogurt (page 234)
8 teaspoons marmalade or fruit spread
4 English muffins or 4 slices of bread, toasted

Spread 1 teaspoon of the strained yogurt on each toasted muffin half with 1 teaspoon of the marmalade or fruit spread.

Nutritional Profile per Serving: Calories—221; calories from fat—36; fat (gm)—4 or 6% daily value; saturated fat (gm)—1; sodium (mg)—154; cholesterol (mg)—240; carbohy-drates (gm)—41; dietary fiber (gm)—3

✖ OVEN-FRIED CHICKEN

Because she enjoys "fresh bright tastes" in her cooking, Bonnie Gorden grows all sorts of vegetables and herbs in her own backyard. In fact, Bonnie reported that the herbs she used in this recipe were either fresh or dried from her own garden. She thought the strained yogurt, mustard, and bread crumb coating for the chicken gave it "good taste and texture." She recommends cutting the chicken breasts into thin strips before breading if you like it crispier. Herb Mashed Potatoes and Broiled Tomatoes complete the dish.

Time Estimate:
  Hands-on, 20 minutes;
  unsupervised, 15 minutes
Serves 4

Herb Mashed Potatoes
4 large russet potatoes, peeled and cut into quarters
1/2 cup nonfat buttermilk
1/4 teaspoon freshly ground white pepper
1/8 teaspoon freshly ground sea salt
1/4 cup finely chopped fresh basil
1/8 cup finely chopped fresh Italian parsley

Chicken
4 (6-ounce) (170-g) boneless, skinless chicken breast
  halves
1/4 cup strained yogurt (page 234)
2 tablespoons Dijon mustard
1 cup Italian bread crumbs

Broiled Tomatoes
4 large tomatoes
4 teaspoons freshly grated Parmesan cheese
1/4 teaspoon freshly ground black pepper

The herb mashed potatoes: In a large pot, boil the potatoes for 30 minutes, drain, and return to the same pot over low heat. Put a kitchen towel over the top and let them dry out for 15 minutes. In a medium-sized bowl, mash together the boiled potatoes, buttermilk, pepper, and salt. Stir in the basil and parsley leaves and mix well. Set aside and keep warm.

The chicken: Preheat the oven to 350°F (180°C). Pound the chicken breasts to flatten until about 1/4 inch (0.75 cm) thick. In a large bowl, combine the yogurt and mustard. Spread the bread crumbs out on a large plate. Roll the chicken breasts in the yogurt mixture, then in the bread crumbs to cover well. Place on a flat greased baking pan and bake for 15 minutes. Remove from the oven and cover to keep warm while cooking the tomatoes.

The tomatoes: Cut the tomatoes in half, place on a baking sheet, and sprinkle with the Parmesan cheese and black pepper. Pop under the broiler for 5 minutes until the cheese and the tomatoes are lightly browned.

To serve: Slice each chicken breast across the grain into 5 pieces and fan out on individual dinner plates. Place some mashed potatoes and two tomato halves on the side.

Nutritional Profile per Serving: Calories—508; calories from fat—72; fat (gm)—8 or 12% daily value; saturated fat (gm)—3; sodium (mg)—493; cholesterol (mg)—98; carbohydrates (gm)—61; dietary fiber (gm)—6

❖ GRILLED SALMON WITH GARLIC CUCUMBER RELISH AND MARINATED PEPPERS

Reviewers call Mary Sue Milliken's food "fiesta-bright, stylishly funky, pleasantly raucous and vividly authentic." I think this dish exhibits the best of those qualities. The pickling cucumbers, pressed before adding to the strained yogurt, are a revelation. Regular cucumbers in a yogurt sauce often weep and make it watery and bitter. But the pressed pickling cucumbers stand up to the yogurt and don't dilute it, thus the sauce remains truly creamy.

Charbroiled juicy
fresh salmon
(texture, color,
aroma)

A rainbow of roasted
red, green, and yellow
bell peppers
(color, texture)

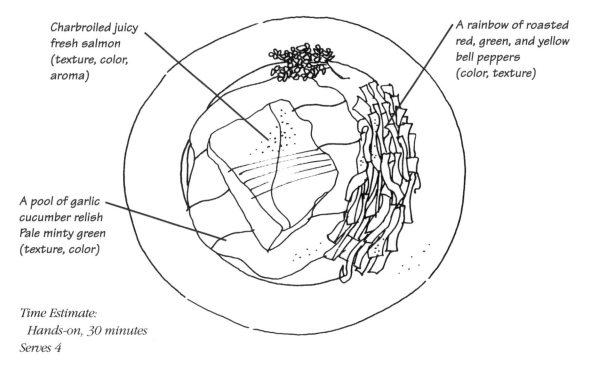

A pool of garlic
cucumber relish
Pale minty green
(texture, color)

Time Estimate:
  Hands-on, 30 minutes
Serves 4

Garlic Cucumber Relish
4 small pickling cucumbers, peeled and seeded
2 cloves garlic, bashed, peeled, and chopped very fine
1/8 teaspoon freshly ground sea salt
1/8 teaspoon freshly ground black pepper
3/4 cup strained nonfat yogurt (page 234)

Bell Peppers
1 each red, green, and yellow bell pepper, roasted,
  peeled, and seeded (see sidebar)
1 tablespoon extra virgin olive oil
1 tablespoon chopped fresh oregano
1 teaspoon red wine vinegar
Salt and freshly ground black pepper

Salmon
4 (4-ounce) (125-g) skinless, boneless salmon fillets
1/8 teaspoon freshly ground sea salt
1/8 teaspoon freshly ground black pepper

Mary Sue Milliken and her partner Susan Feniger's restaurants, Border Grill and CITY, in Los Angeles are well known as a haven for vegetarians, not that Mary Sue has banned beef, either at home or at the restaurant. "Susan and I have what we call the moderate approach. Excessive amounts of anything would be unhealthy and moderate amounts of most anything can't be bad for you."

While measuring moderation might be hard for the casual home cook, Mary Sue and Susan have obviously wrestled this issue to the ground and succeeded with an effective compromise. Their hugely successful vegetarian platter combines not only the freshest produce but also cooking methods that enhance that freshness. They also feature grilled fish and poultry set on a pool of fresh salsa or fruit compote. Another popular section of their menu is entrees based primarily on grains with much smaller portions of meat or poultry.

Mary Sue strongly believes that "we shall be returning to a diet that our ancestors ate naturally: abundant in grains and vegetables, using meats as garnish or flavoring."

IT'S EASY TO ROAST YOUR OWN VEGETABLES

Just seed and slice the peppers and place them flat on a baking sheet, cut side down. Broil until their skin blackens, put in a paper bag, and let steam for 15 minutes. Rub off the skin and dig in—your peppers will have an irresistible smoky sweet taste.

The relish: Grate the cucumbers, using the coarse side of your grater, set in a sieve, and cover with plastic wrap. Set a weight on the cucumbers, such as the lid of a pot or a can, and leave for 30 minutes to extract as much water as possible. Make a fine paste of the garlic by placing it on a hard surface and working it with a knife until a paste is formed. Place the drained cucumbers, garlic, salt, pepper, and strained yogurt in a bowl and mix well. Refrigerate until serving time.

The bell peppers: Cut the roasted peppers into thin strips and transfer to a bowl. Add the olive oil, oregano, vinegar, salt, and pepper. Toss gently and set aside at room temperature until serving time.

The salmon: Preheat the oven to broil or grill for at least 5 minutes. Line the broiler pan with foil. Season the salmon with the salt and pepper and broil close to the flame for 2 to 3 minutes per side or until desired doneness is achieved. Do not overcook.

To serve: Present the cooked fillets atop a pool of cucumber relish with a mound of marinated peppers alongside. Couscous would also be a wonderful accompaniment to this dish.

Nutritional Profile per Serving			
	Classic	Springboard	Daily Value
Calories	894	270	
Calories from fat	702	90	
Fat (gm)	78	10	15%
Saturated fat (gm)	13	2	10%
Sodium (mg)	1078	536	22%
Cholesterol (mg)	149	69	23%
Carbohydrates (gm)	16	17	6%
Dietary fiber (gm)	2	2	8%
Classic compared: Salmon with Lemon Cucumber Sauce			

7

SMOOTH VEGETABLE SAUCES

Pureed cooked vegetables seasoned with herbs and spices are a flavorful and textural base for sauces, vegetables, and casseroles.

P robably you will believe me if I say that I sometimes get *really* excited by some of our research.
This time I'm over the moon!

I'd been looking for a basic springboard technique that
would use naturally smooth-textured vegetables to
replace the mouthfeel and density provided by fats and
cereal starches, to use as delectable and satisfying sauces
on pasta, chicken breasts, whole grains, et al. I'd used
puréed and seasoned green peas, butter beans, garbanzo
beans, and winter squash successfully in past experiments.
But in recent days I stumbled over two sweet ones:

parsnips and sweet potatoes. I'm sure you can think of many cooked vegetables and fruits that are densely textured but without grainy or fibrous strands for your own springboard experiments: sweet potatoes, yams, parsnips, carrots, winter squash, mangoes, pears, apricots, nectarines, plums . . . the list goes on and on.

BASIC SMOOTH VEGETABLE SAUCE

1/4 teaspoon light olive oil with a dash of toasted sesame oil
1 pound (450 g) vegetable or fruit, peeled and sliced thin
1 (14-ounce) (400-g) can evaporated nonfat milk

Heat the oil in a large nonstick skillet and fry the sliced vegetable or fruit just to caramelize the starch sugars, about 5 minutes. This will deepen the eventual flavor and make the final sauce more complex. Now steam the browned produce until it is absolutely soft, varying with the produce. When pinched between your fingers it should slip as if oiled.

Drop the steamed pieces into a food processor or wide-bodied blender. Add the evaporated milk and whiz for 3 minutes into a smooth, creamy purée. Season to taste with spices, herbs, or freshly grated Parmesan cheese, but be careful not to overwhelm the produce.

Tips and Hints

- For a pouring sauce, add a little more evaporated milk, stock, or wine.
- I like a little fresh lime juice with sweet fruits and vegetables—but be careful not to overwhelm the taste.

Graham stumbles over two sweet vegetables.

✄ MACARONI AND CHEESE

Diane Moss has two children who love (that means eat without bribery or threat) macaroni and cheese, the type that comes complete "in-the-box." Her need was for an alternative that would be consumed with equal gusto but with much less fat. After a bit of back and forth between us, we seem to have won the day, but then you might know that you never can tell . . . with children.

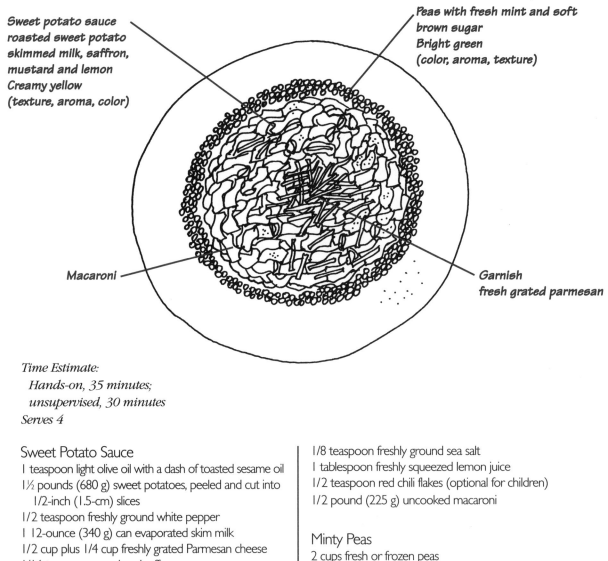

Sweet potato sauce
roasted sweet potato
skimmed milk, saffron,
mustard and lemon
Creamy yellow
(texture, aroma, color)

Peas with fresh mint and soft brown sugar
Bright green
(color, aroma, texture)

Macaroni

Garnish
fresh grated parmesan

Time Estimate:
  Hands-on, 35 minutes;
  unsupervised, 30 minutes
Serves 4

Sweet Potato Sauce
1 teaspoon light olive oil with a dash of toasted sesame oil
1½ pounds (680 g) sweet potatoes, peeled and cut into 1/2-inch (1.5-cm) slices
1/2 teaspoon freshly ground white pepper
1 12-ounce (340 g) can evaporated skim milk
1/2 cup plus 1/4 cup freshly grated Parmesan cheese
1/16 teaspoon powdered saffron
1/2 teaspoon dry mustard

1/8 teaspoon freshly ground sea salt
1 tablespoon freshly squeezed lemon juice
1/2 teaspoon red chili flakes (optional for children)
1/2 pound (225 g) uncooked macaroni

Minty Peas
2 cups fresh or frozen peas
1 teaspoon chopped fresh mint
2 teaspoons brown sugar

Diane Moss has had a problem losing weight. After a diet, any lost weight just seemed to spring back—with extra poundage!

Today she's trying to emphasize a low-fat, portion-controlled lifestyle. This helps Diane with her weight problem (she's lost 50 pounds over the last year) and contributes toward her goal of establishing healthy eating habits for her husband and two young children.

Diane tried three or four variations of this recipe. The adults liked the recipe, but the children thought it was too sweet and too hot. So out went the chili flakes and the brown sugar on the peas. Diane baked the sweet potatoes, added more cheese, and served the peas plain and . . . *voilà!* The kids liked that the best. Diane also tried puréed parsnips in the sauce—the kids did a thumbs down. Pureed butter beans was the next experiment, which the kids liked as far as taste, but they didn't like the texture (not as fluffy as grainy sweet potatoes). So . . . the final decision was sweet potatoes without chili and plain minty peas.

✂ **EXTRA MEAL**
Double the sweet potato sauce recipe and freeze half. Store in a large resealable plastic bag. Flatten the bag, expel all the air, label, and date. Use it within 6 months. I enjoyed it in the au gratin vegetable dish that follows.

The sweet potato sauce: Pour the oil into a large skillet over medium-high heat, toss in the sweet potatoes and 1/4 teaspoon of the white pepper, and fry until lightly brown and caramelized, about 10 minutes. Pour at least 2 inches (5 cm) of water in your steamer pot and bring to a boil. Transfer the sweet potatoes to a steamer tray, place atop the boiling water, cover, and steam for 30 minutes. Remove the tray and set it aside to cool. When the potatoes have cooled, transfer them to a large food processor. Add the evaporated milk and 1/2 cup of the Parmesan cheese and whiz together for 3 minutes. Stir in the saffron, dry mustard, salt, lemon juice, chili flakes, and the remaining white pepper and pulse in the food processor until the texture is light and creamy.

Cook the macaroni according to package directions and drain well.

In a large pot, combine the cooked macaroni and the sauce and keep warm on very low heat, being careful it doesn't stick or burn.

The minty peas: In a medium saucepan, bring water to a boil and simmer the peas, mint, and sugar until the peas are tender—about 5 to 10 minutes for fresh, 3 minutes for frozen.

To serve: Spoon the macaroni and cheese onto serving plates and surround with the peas on the outer edge. Sprinkle with the remaining 1/4 cup of Parmesan cheese.

Nutritional Profile per Serving			
	Classic	Springboard	Daily Value
Calories	531	586	
Calories from fat	180	72	
Fat (gm)	20	8	12%
Saturated fat (gm)	12	4	20%
Sodium (mg)	1421	598	25%
Cholesterol (mg)	61	18	6%
Carbohydrates (gm)	61	100	33%
Dietary fiber (gm)	2	8	32%
Classic compared: Packaged Macaroni and Cheese Dinner			

✖ Broccoli and Cauliflower au Gratin

A gorgeous blend of gold and green, this traditional family favorite method of serving vegetables just got a lot healthier—less fat, certainly, but also a super increase in beta carotene and vitamin A from the sweet potato sauce in the preceding recipe. Use it as a vegetarian entree or a dressy side dish.

Time Estimate:
  Hands-on, 15 minutes;
  unsupervised, 30 minutes
Serves 4

1 small head cauliflower, stems trimmed, cut into florets
1 large bunch broccoli, stems trimmed, cut into florets
1 recipe frozen Sweet Potato Sauce (page 66), thawed
1/8 teaspoon paprika
2 tablespoons chopped fresh parsley

Preheat the oven to 375°F (190°C). Blanch the cauliflower and broccoli in boiling water and drain well. Place in alternating rows in a 9 x 9-inch (23 x 23-cm) baking dish. Pour the sweet potato sauce over the top, dust with paprika, and bake uncovered for 30 minutes. Remove from the oven, sprinkle with parsley, and bring to the table.

Nutritional Profile per Serving: Calories—332; calories from fat—63; fat (gm)—7 or 11% daily value; saturated fat (gm)—4; sodium (mg)—539; cholesterol (mg)—17; carbohydrates (gm)—50; dietary fiber (gm)—6

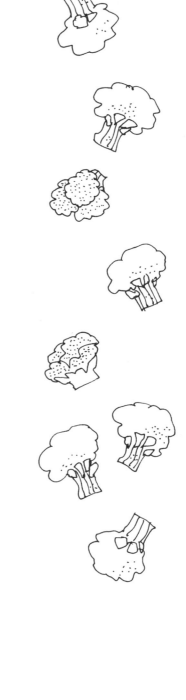

Corn Chowder

All smooth vegetable sauces have the potential to become great soups! Leftover sauce is a great beginning for tomorrow's soup. Identify one of the basic herbs that went into the making of the original sauce (for instance: cilantro in this recipe) and add a little more along with a cup or two of stock.

Pureed corn is the main ingredient for this quick and easy chowder. I created it based on a recipe from Tracy Johnston. Tracy started trying to convert all their favorite comfort foods to very low-fat versions when her husband was put on a low-fat diet for medical reasons. In this recipe, Tracy suggested using a chicken stock base rather than evaporated milk to control dairy intake. I leave the choice to you.

Time Estimate:
Hands-on, 40 minutes
Serves 4

1 pound (450 g) plus 1 cup frozen corn kernels, thawed
1 (12-ounce) (340 g) can evaporated skim milk or low-sodium chicken stock (page 231)
1 teaspoon light olive oil with a dash of toasted sesame oil
2 green onions, sliced very thin
2 ounces (60 g) Canadian bacon, sliced very thin and cut in slivers
1/2 a zucchini squash, cut into matchsticks
2 large Roma tomatoes, seeded and diced

Purée 1 pound (450 g) of the corn in a processor, adding only as much of the evaporated milk or stock as you need to keep it moving. Whiz for about 3 minutes to get it really smooth.

Heat the oil in a medium saucepan and fry the onions and Canadian bacon for 1 minute. Add the zucchini, stir well, and remove from the heat. Pour the corn purée through a strainer into the saucepan with the vegetables and bacon. Press hard with a wooden siever or spatula to get all the liquid. Add the rest of the evaporated milk or stock and the remaining 1 cup of corn. Return to the heat on medium low, stirring often. When it's hot, stir in the diced tomatoes and serve.

Nutritional Profile per Serving: Calories—254; calories from fat—27; fat (gm)—3 or 10% daily value; saturated fat (gm)—1; sodium (mg)—308; cholesterol (mg)—10; carbohydrates (gm)—48; dietary fiber (gm)—7

Rosemary Chicken with Butternut Sauce

You might think that chef Martin Frost has created a huge culture clash here: North American butternut squash meets Mexican cilantro on the couscous-covered road to Morocco—but, s'il vous plaît, mesdames et monsieurs, *have a go at it. It really works!*

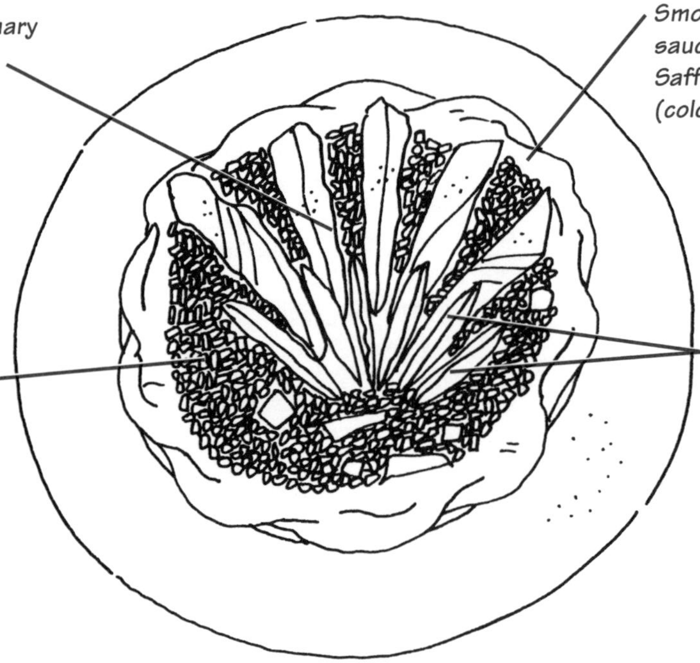

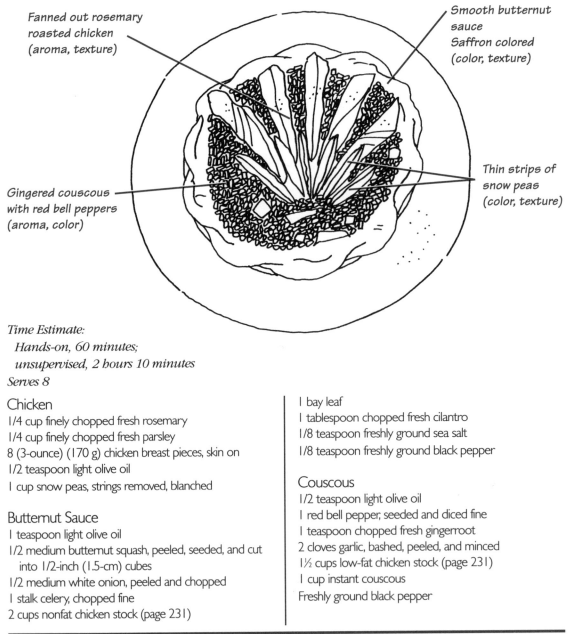

Fanned out rosemary roasted chicken (aroma, texture)
Smooth butternut sauce Saffron colored (color, texture)
Gingered couscous with red bell peppers (aroma, color)
Thin strips of snow peas (color, texture)

Time Estimate:
Hands-on, 60 minutes;
unsupervised, 2 hours 10 minutes
Serves 8

Chicken

1/4 cup finely chopped fresh rosemary
1/4 cup finely chopped fresh parsley
8 (3-ounce) (170 g) chicken breast pieces, skin on
1/2 teaspoon light olive oil
1 cup snow peas, strings removed, blanched

Butternut Sauce

1 teaspoon light olive oil
1/2 medium butternut squash, peeled, seeded, and cut into 1/2-inch (1.5-cm) cubes
1/2 medium white onion, peeled and chopped
1 stalk celery, chopped fine
2 cups nonfat chicken stock (page 231)
1 bay leaf
1 tablespoon chopped fresh cilantro
1/8 teaspoon freshly ground sea salt
1/8 teaspoon freshly ground black pepper

Couscous

1/2 teaspoon light olive oil
1 red bell pepper, seeded and diced fine
1 teaspoon chopped fresh gingerroot
2 cloves garlic, bashed, peeled, and minced
1½ cups low-fat chicken stock (page 231)
1 cup instant couscous
Freshly ground black pepper

I wanted you to meet chef **Martin Frost** of the Four Seasons Clift Hotel in San Francisco because of his award-winning past, his present standards of excellence, and the fact that we both came over from the British Isles.

When I dined at his restaurant, he suggested I eat a chicken breast served on a molded island of perfectly seasoned couscous set on a flavorful sea of broth. It was this dish that inspired me to create the Chilean Sea Bass on page 74.

Four Seasons Hotels have been offering what they call an "alternative cuisine" for many years. On average about half of their luncheon trade is alternative and 10 to 15 percent at dinner.

Martin told me, "In the last five years, healthy cuisine is no longer a trend but a way of life." He went on to explain that "As the quality, taste, and presentation are constantly improved, more chefs are embracing a healthier style that is here to stay. With this food style you can still be creative, and innovative, and not endanger your healthy body."

I love it! And so will you when you stop for a break at Martin Frost's restaurant.

The chicken: Combine the rosemary with the parsley and stuff under the skin of each chicken breast. Place the chicken breasts on a plate, cover, and refrigerate for at least 2 hours to allow the herbs to perfume the chicken flesh.

The butternut sauce: Heat the olive oil in a medium skillet on medium heat and fry the squash, onion, and celery for 4 to 5 minutes, but do not allow to color. Add the chicken stock and bay leaf and simmer, uncovered, for 25 minutes. Add the cilantro and cook for another 5 minutes. Remove and discard the bay leaf and purée the sauce in a blender. Season with salt and pepper.

The couscous: Heat the olive oil in a medium skillet over medium heat and fry the bell pepper, ginger, and garlic for 3 minutes. In a separate pot, or in the microwave, bring the chicken stock to a boil. Add the couscous and hot chicken stock to the bell pepper mixture, stir with a fork, and cover for 5 minutes. Remove from the heat, stir with a fork, and season with freshly ground black pepper. Set aside, covered, to keep warm.

Finish the chicken: Preheat the oven to 350°F (180°C). Heat a large ovenproof skillet over medium heat, add the oil, and fry the chicken breasts, skin side down, until the chicken skin is golden brown. Remove any excess oil with a paper towel and turn the breasts over. Place the chicken, in the skillet, in the oven for 5 to 8 minutes until cooked but still juicy.

To serve: Spoon the couscous into a ring on the center of the plate. Remove the skin from the chicken breasts, slice, and fan on top of the couscous. Spoon the sauce around the couscous and garnish with thin strips of snow peas.

Nutritional Profile per Serving			
	Classic	**Springboard**	**Daily Value**
Calories	1116	233	
Calories from fat	612	36	
Fat (gm)	68	4	6%
Saturated fat (gm)	35	1	5%
Sodium (mg)	1885	142	6%
Cholesterol (mg)	280	43	14%
Carbohydrates (gm)	62	25	8%
Dietary fiber (gm)	7	3	12%
Classic compared: Blanquette of Chicken			

8

VINAIGRETTE BROTHS AND SAUCES

Easy oil and vinegar base vinaigrettes are enlivened with broths, juices, herbs, and spices to become tasty sauces.

On a recent book tour for *Creative Choices*, I had the great good fortune to have lunch with chef Martin Frost of the Four Seasons Clift in San Francisco. He knew of my interest in light-hearted matters and ordered my lunch for me from among his repertoire. All Four Seasons hotels have been trend setters in what they call alternative cuisine.

The dish was incredibly simple and beautifully done: a chicken breast nestled on top of a perfectly cooked mound of couscous. Around the outside was a moat of dark brown brothlike vinaigrette in the place of the traditional beurre blanc or worse! (For the recipe, see page 74.) It was wonderful and an inspiration to me to experiment with these delicious thin sauces.

Most sauces, of course, hang together because a starch provides the binding. With vinaigrettes, there is no starch and the basic vinegar and oil must somehow combine (emulsify). Like all simple-looking things, there is much to be understood. Let me share my findings to date.

Tips and Hints

Graham experiments with delicious thin sauces.

- If you add prepared mustard and beat or blend it with the vinegar and oil, you get the emulsion, but you also fracture the quality of really good virgin olive oils. When using less flavorsome, less expensive canola or olive oils, this doesn't matter.
- Fresh herbs, a clove or two of garlic, a stiff purée of cooked vegetables (see page 65 for smooth vegetable sauces) or sieved tomato sauce (see page 206 for our marinara) also supply a shorter-lived emulsion.
- Juices from poaching fish, braising meats, or cooking vegetables can be combined with cooked vegetables and herbs in a blender, then drizzled with oil and vinegar and whizzed together just before serving.
- To keep within acceptable limits of oil and fat in vinaigrettes, use a maximum of 1 tablespoon of oil for each 1/4 cup of sauce (30 percent of calories from fat). But less is better, and 1 teaspoon per 1/4 cup will still give you the flavor and texture needed.

✤ Smoked Chilean Sea Bass with Thai Vinaigrette

In her Food Preference List, Katie Wagner indicated that she enjoyed Asian food, especially from Thailand. Add to this her love of fish, and I came up with this extremely unusual combination of flavors. If you have a taste for the exotic you'll love this smoky seafood supper or luncheon dish.

Katie says her family loved this dish, even her two young sons! She has no Asian food market where she lives, but she says looking for the lemon grass is worth the search. Her husband didn't know what he would think about couscous, but he thought the fish stock and other ingredients flavored it quite well.

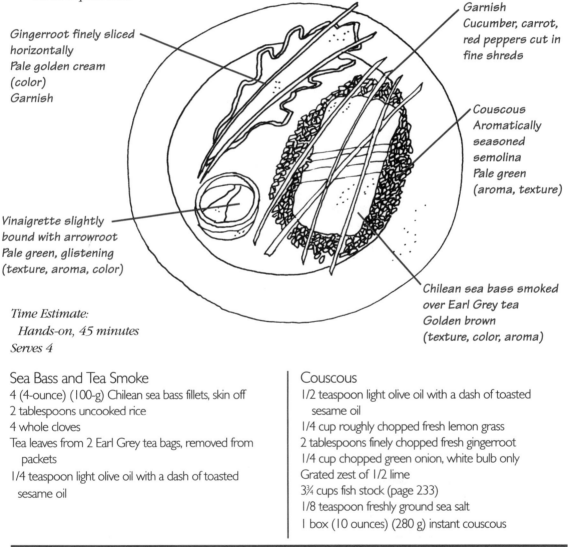

Gingerroot finely sliced horizontally
Pale golden cream (color)
Garnish

Garnish
Cucumber, carrot, red peppers cut in fine shreds

Couscous
Aromatically seasoned semolina
Pale green (aroma, texture)

Vinaigrette slightly bound with arrowroot
Pale green, glistening (texture, aroma, color)

Chilean sea bass smoked over Earl Grey tea
Golden brown (texture, color, aroma)

Time Estimate:
  Hands-on, 45 minutes
  Serves 4

Sea Bass and Tea Smoke

4 (4-ounce) (100-g) Chilean sea bass fillets, skin off
2 tablespoons uncooked rice
4 whole cloves
Tea leaves from 2 Earl Grey tea bags, removed from packets
1/4 teaspoon light olive oil with a dash of toasted sesame oil

Couscous

1/2 teaspoon light olive oil with a dash of toasted sesame oil
1/4 cup roughly chopped fresh lemon grass
2 tablespoons finely chopped fresh gingerroot
1/4 cup chopped green onion, white bulb only
Grated zest of 1/2 lime
3¾ cups fish stock (page 233)
1/8 teaspoon freshly ground sea salt
1 box (10 ounces) (280 g) instant couscous

Vinaigrette

I cup reserved seasoned fish stock (see directions below)
I tablespoon thinly sliced fresh gingerroot
1/4 cup thinly sliced fresh lemon grass
3 tablespoons freshly squeezed lime juice
I tablespoon low-sodium soy sauce
2 tablespoons light olive oil
1/4 teaspoon toasted sesame oil
2 tablespoons fresh cilantro leaves
12 fresh mint leaves

2 teaspoons arrowroot mixed with 4 teaspoons
   reserved vinaigrette (slurry) (see directions below)

Raw Vegetable Garnish

I (5- to 6-inch) (13- to 15-cm) piece of fresh gingerroot,
   sliced into 4 flat pieces lengthwise
2 green onions, sliced lengthwise into whisper-thin pieces
I red bell pepper, cut into long toothpick-size strips
1/2 English cucumber, cut into long thin strips
I carrot, cut into long thin strips
Mint leaves, sliced thin

Katie Wagner has been practicing low-fat cooking for 5 years. As an aerobics instructor, she felt that her students should learn how to exercise *and* eat a minimum of fat.

No longer an aerobics teacher, Katie now cooks low-fat for her husband (both his father and grandfather died early of heart disease) and two sons. Although both Katie and her husband are from South Dakota and grew up on a steady diet of red meat and potatoes, they don't eat that at all now. Instead, they do a lot of experimenting. Even her two boys are encouraged to choose a night of the week to buy the food and prepare the meal of their choice.

The sea bass and tea smoke: Rinse and pat dry the fish fillets with a paper towel. Cut 3 sheets of heavy-duty aluminum foil into 15-inch (38-cm) squares. Roll the edges under to form a circle that fits in the bottom of a Dutch oven. The pot should not be made of a light alloy or alloy bonded to other metals. Cast iron, cast aluminum, or Steelon pans work fine. You should have a foil "saucer" approximately 5 inches (13 cm) in diameter. When the edge is rolled to about 1 inch (2.5 cm) high, stop and flatten the foil. Depress the center to hold the smoke ingredients.

In the depression of the aluminum foil saucer, sprinkle the rice on the bottom, the cloves, and then the contents of the tea bags. Place the foil dish in the bottom of the Dutch oven, cover the pan tightly, and cook over high heat until the ingredients in the foil start smoking, about 5 minutes.

Brush a long-legged steamer basket with the olive oil. Place the sea bass on the steamer platform. Put into the Dutch oven over the smoke ingredients, cover, and continue smoking over high heat until cooked through, about 8 minutes. Remove from the heat and let cool.

(continued)

The couscous: Pour the oil into a medium saucepan and fry the lemon grass, ginger, green onion, and lime zest for 2 minutes. Add the stock and bring to a boil. Turn the heat down and simmer for 10 minutes to allow for infusion and reduction. Strain into a large measuring cup—you want to have 3 cups of liquid. Reserve 1 cup for the vinaigrette. Pour the remaining 2 cups back into the saucepan and bring back to a boil. Stir in the salt and couscous, cover, remove from the heat, and let stand for 5 minutes.

The vinaigrette: In a medium saucepan, combine the reserved stock, ginger, and lemon grass and boil until reduced to 1/2 cup, about 10 minutes. Strain into a blender jar. Add the lime juice, soy sauce, olive oil, sesame oil, cilantro, and mint leaves and whiz for 2 minutes to emulsify or hold together. Reserve 1½ tablespoons. Pour the rest into a small saucepan and bring to a boil. Remove from the heat, stir in the arrowroot slurry, return to the heat, and bring to a boil to thicken and clear, about 30 seconds.

To serve: Make a mound of couscous on each plate and place a smoked fillet on top. Arrange the raw vegetable garnish (reserving the mint) around the plate. Ladle the vinaigrette atop the sea bass and garnish it with slivers of mint.

⚡ EXTRA MEAL

The vinaigrette in this recipe is great to have standing by as a light sauce for salmon, shrimp, and other seafood; for an example, see the orange roughy recipe that follows. Double the vinaigrette portion of the recipe. Pour the extra into ice cube trays and freeze. When it's frozen solid, pop the cubes out of the trays and store them in resealable freezer bags. Expel as much air as possible, label, and date. They will last for 6 months.

Nutritional Profile per Serving			
	Classic	**Springboard**	**Daily Value**
Calories	867	499	
Calories from fat	486	99	
Fat (gm)	54	11	17%
Saturated fat (gm)	8	2	10%
Sodium (mg)	1008	395	16%
Cholesterol (mg)	120	60	20%
Carbohydrates (gm)	54	63	21%
Dietary fiber (gm)	8	4	16%
Classic compared: Seafood Salad with Blue Lake Beans and Sweet Corn in Saffron Vinaigrette			

✖ ORANGE ROUGHY POACHED IN VINAIGRETTE

I can't wait for you to try this dish: The wonderful fresh flavors of mint and lime are brightened with fresh ginger, spicy chili paste, and balsamic vinegar. Then the pineapple smooths it all out and pulls it together. Use the vinaigrette ice cubes from the preceding recipe, or just whip it up fresh in minutes.

Time Estimate:
 Hands-on, 25 minutes
Serves 4

1/2 teaspoon light olive oil with a dash of toasted
  sesame oil
1 yellow onion, peeled and chopped
2 cubes (1/4 cup) frozen Vinaigrette (page 75)
1/4 cup low-sodium chicken stock (page 231)
1 cup chopped pineapple
8 thin quarter-size slices fresh gingerroot, diced fine
1/4 teaspoon roasted chili paste
1 tablespoon balsamic vinegar
4 (4-ounce) (125-g) orange roughy fillets
4 cups cooked long-grain white rice
2 tablespoons shredded fresh mint
1/2 teaspoon red chili flakes

Heat the oil in a small skillet on medium heat and fry the onion for 3 minutes. Remove from the heat and set aside.

In another large skillet, heat the vinaigrette cubes until melted, then stir in the cooked onion, chicken stock, pineapple, ginger, chili paste, and balsamic vinegar. Place the fish fillets on top, cover, and simmer gently for 8 minutes.

Serve the fish and vegetables immediately with rice, sprinkled with the fresh mint and chilli flakes.

YOU WON'T CHILL OUT ON CHILI PASTE

This is an extremely hot and spicy seasoning that must be used judiciously. It's readily available in the Asian section of your supermarket—along with many other different seasonings and spices that you'll love to discover and use often.

Nutritional Profile per Serving: Calories—359; calories from fat—27; fat (gm)—3 or 5% daily value; saturated fat (gm)—1; sodium (mg)—117; cholesterol (mg)—62; carbohydrates (gm)—53; dietary fiber (gm)—2

What happens when you don't use chili paste judiciously?

✠ Chinese Chicken Salad

Erik Rogers describes himself as a single graduate student who's "not a great cook" but who does like "having a few key recipes that I can use when I entertain friends." He sent me his Chinese chicken salad recipe to see if I could lower the fat. He prepared my modified recipe in its spicy vinaigrette for friends who had already tasted his original recipe and . . . they loved it! Erik did say that the one thing they requested was a garnish of chopped cashews, which he had traditionally served.

Time Estimate:
  Hands-on, 25 minutes;
  unsupervised, 45 minutes
Serves 4

Chicken
2 (6-ounce) (170 g) boneless, skinless chicken breast halves
1 tablespoon low-sodium soy sauce
1 clove garlic, bashed, peeled, and chopped
1 teaspoon sugar
1 teaspoon de-alcoholized white wine
1 teaspoon hoisin sauce
1/2 teaspoon light olive oil with a dash of toasted sesame oil
1 tablespoon sesame seeds

Noodles
2 ounces (75 g) uncooked bean thread noodles (cellophane noodles)
1/4 teaspoon toasted sesame oil

Vinaigrette
1/4 cup low-sodium chicken stock (page231)
2 tablespoons rice wine vinegar
1 tablespoon low-sodium soy sauce
1/2 teaspoon red chili flakes
1 large clove garlic, bashed, peeled, and chopped
1 green onion, minced
2 teaspoons toasted sesame oil

Salad
1/2 head Chinese cabbage or iceberg lettuce, shredded
1/2 head romaine, shredded
1/2 head red leaf lettuce, shredded
4 green onions, sliced on the diagonal
1 bunch cilantro, leaves only, washed and dried
12 tomato wedges
Chopped cashews (optional)

The chicken: Cut the chicken into strips across the grain and place in a medium bowl. In a small bowl, combine the soy sauce, garlic, sugar, wine, and hoisin sauce and stir until the sugar dissolves. Pour over the chicken strips and marinate in the refrigerator for 30 minutes to 2 hours.

The noodles: Cook the noodles in boiling water for 1 minute. Drain, rinse under cold water, and drain well. Toss with the sesame oil and spread out very thin on a cookie sheet. Bake for 45 minutes at 400°F (205°C) until golden brown and very crisp.

The vinaigrette and salad: In a small bowl, whisk the vinaigrette ingredients together. In a large serving bowl, toss the shredded greens, onions, cilantro, and vinaigrette. Break the toasted noodles into small pieces and scatter them on top.

To finish the chicken: Pour the oil into a large skillet on medium heat. Drain the chicken, pat it dry, and transfer to the skillet with the sesame seeds. Cook, stirring and tossing, for 3 minutes. Add the chicken to the noodles and greens and toss until completely mixed. Divide among plates and garnish with the tomato wedges and a sprinkle of chopped cashews (optional).

Nutritional Profile per Serving: Calories—229; calories from fat—63; fat (gm)—7 or 11% daily value; saturated fat (gm)—1; sodium (mg)—369; cholesterol (mg)—47; carbohydrates (gm)—18; dietary fiber (gm)—3 (cashews not included)

Grilled Halibut in Apple Cider Vinaigrette

Joy Delf's concept of reduced apple cider is the secret in this vinaigrette sauce: it provides a firm and fulfilling flavor that is light, airy, and bold, all at the same time.

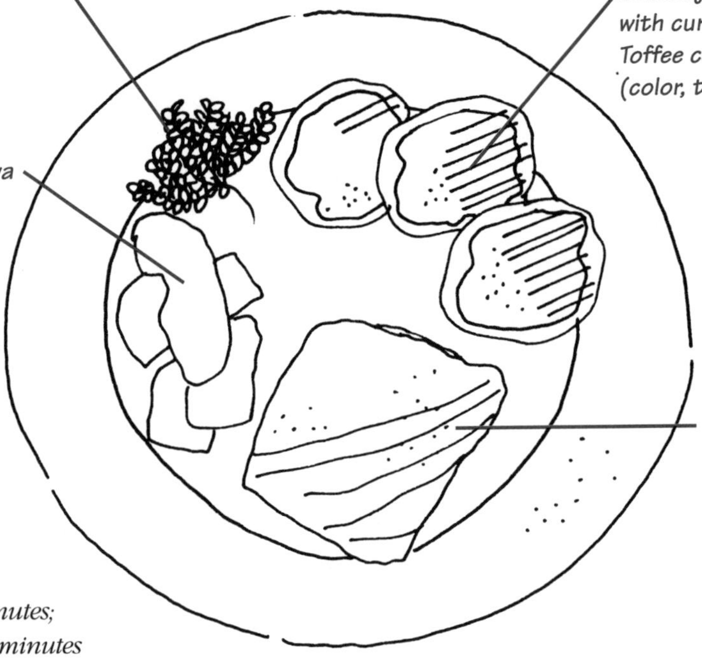

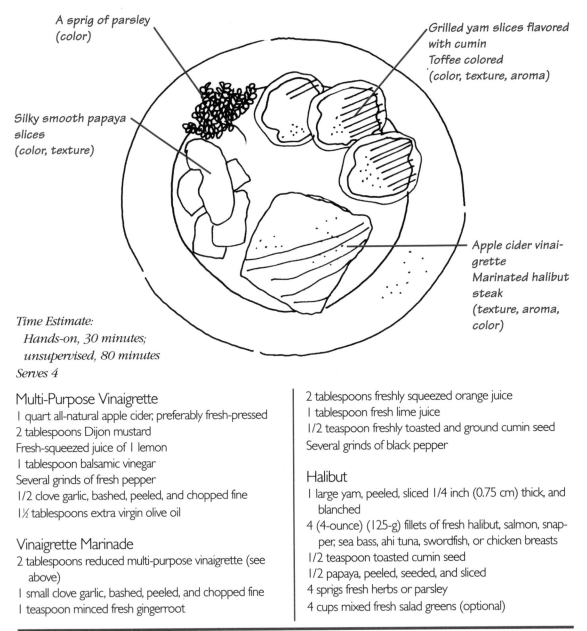

A sprig of parsley
(color)
Grilled yam slices flavored
with cumin
Toffee colored
(color, texture, aroma)
Silky smooth papaya
slices
(color, texture)
Apple cider vinai-
grette
Marinated halibut
steak
(texture, aroma,
color)

Time Estimate:
Hands-on, 30 minutes;
unsupervised, 80 minutes
Serves 4

Multi-Purpose Vinaigrette

1 quart all-natural apple cider, preferably fresh-pressed
2 tablespoons Dijon mustard
Fresh-squeezed juice of 1 lemon
1 tablespoon balsamic vinegar
Several grinds of fresh pepper
1/2 clove garlic, bashed, peeled, and chopped fine
1½ tablespoons extra virgin olive oil

Vinaigrette Marinade

2 tablespoons reduced multi-purpose vinaigrette (see above)
1 small clove garlic, bashed, peeled, and chopped fine
1 teaspoon minced fresh gingerroot
2 tablespoons freshly squeezed orange juice
1 tablespoon fresh lime juice
1/2 teaspoon freshly toasted and ground cumin seed
Several grinds of black pepper

Halibut

1 large yam, peeled, sliced 1/4 inch (0.75 cm) thick, and blanched
4 (4-ounce) (125-g) fillets of fresh halibut, salmon, snapper, sea bass, ahi tuna, swordfish, or chicken breasts
1/2 teaspoon toasted cumin seed
1/2 papaya, peeled, seeded, and sliced
4 sprigs fresh herbs or parsley
4 cups mixed fresh salad greens (optional)

For many years now, **Joy Delf** and I have been collaborating in the field of risk reduction and flavor enhancement among the gourmet establishment.

Joy began reducing fat in the early '80s. Her husband had gained about 15 pounds during her "gourmet" cooking phase, which was "loaded with butter and rich sauces."

Joy sized up the problem with her metabolism milestone theory. "We could not eat the way we used to prior to age 30, our first milestone of metabolism. We have since noticed another notch around the age 40 mark. We know what to expect in the decades to come!"

Joy began with learning how substitutions work, and she tells me her early attempts were not that great. It took about a year, but gradually she and her husband began to appreciate the pleasures of eating again. When Joy started teaching her "Low Calorie Conscious Gourmet" classes, they were always packed.

I am delighted that she could share a recipe with us. She is a consummate professional, the best in her field I've ever met.

The multi-purpose vinaigrette: In a medium saucepan, bring the cider to a boil. Reduce the heat and simmer, uncovered, until the volume reduces to 1/2 cup, about 45 minutes. Remove from the heat and let cool. Transfer 2 tablespoons of the reduced cider to a bowl and whisk with the mustard, lemon juice, vinegar, pepper, and garlic. Then whisk in the olive oil, a little at a time. Refrigerate until needed. Cover and refrigerate the remaining reduced cider to make future batches of the vinaigrette. Remove from the refrigerator about 15 minutes before using.

The vinaigrette marinade: Combine all marinade ingredients in a wide nonmetal pan.

The halibut: Preheat the broiler or grill. Dredge both sides of the yam slices in the marinade, remove them to a baking sheet, and sprinkle with the cumin. Dredge the fish fillets in the marinade and let stand for 15 minutes at room temperature. Remove the fish, pat mostly dry, and arrange on another baking sheet. Put both the fish and the yams in the oven and broil or grill at the same time until the fish is opaque but still moist. Joy Delf grills fish for 10 minutes per inch (2.5 cm) of flesh thickness. Grill the yam slices until they are nicely browned and cooked through.

To serve: Arrange the fish and yam slices on a plate with thin slices of fresh papaya and sprigs of fresh herbs. Joy serves this with mixed fresh salad greens lightly tossed with a little of the multi-purpose vinaigrette.

Nutritional Profile per Serving			
	Classic	Springboard	Daily Value
Calories	623	312	
Calories from fat	396	36	
Fat (gm)	44	4	6%
Saturated fat (gm)	8	0.69	3%
Sodium (mg)	784	205	9%
Cholesterol (mg)	119	60	20%
Carbohydrates (gm)	16	47	16%
Dietary fiber (gm)	2	3	12%
Classic compared: Marinated Broiled Swordfish with Vinaigrette			

9

BAO SYANG

Shallow-frying fragrant onion, garlic, herbs, and spices in cooking oil perfumes the entire dish with irresistible smells and flavor.

*B*ao Syang in Chinese means "exploded into fragrance." It is quite literally a sudden release of the volatile oils contained in such flavorings as onion, garlic, gingerroot, shallots, green onions, leeks, citrus zest, chili (and all other peppers), and Szechwan peppercorns ("flower pepper," not hot but aromatic). You can't release these oils at boiling or simmering temperatures—only when oil is used at medium high heat, not hot enough to scorch. The point is to flavor your cooking oil and perfume your dish with irresistible-flavor oils.

I learned about this term from Barbara Tropp's *The*

Modern Art of Chinese Cooking. If your love of good food extends to Asian cooking, this book is a must.

Tips and Hints

- Start out with the three famous flavors: 6 green onions, 6 thin quarter-sized disks of fresh gingerroot, and 2 cloves of finely chopped garlic. If you like a zip of heat in your food, try 1 small chili pepper, diced.
- I slice, crush, shred, and pound the aromatics listed above until they are mere wisps. Then, using just enough oil to explode their oil sacs, I shallow-fry them for a minute or two, then remove them to a side plate to be returned later on.
- With the pan now throbbing with fragrance, I continue to cook. When a liquid is added, I return the wispy flavorings and let them practically dissolve into the sauce.

Bao-Syang is Chinese for "Exploded into Fragrance."

✖ FRIED RICE

Joe Presley is just finishing high school, but the Food Preference List he sent me reads like that of a well-seasoned gourmet. I ended up creating a fried rice for him. The result is delicious, and a perfect example of bao syang *in action. I do recommend that you make the rice the day before for the best texture in the final dish.*

Garnish: Wisps of green onion

Parboiled white rice and wheat berries fried with Canadian bacon, spring onions, sun dried tomatoes, and peas Fawn, whites, greens pinks, and deep red (texture, aroma, color)

Egg omelet
Golden brown and yellow
(color, texture, aroma)

Time Estimate:
  Hands-on, 30 minutes
Serves 4

Seasoned Rice

1/2 cup (118 ml) uncooked wheat berries
2⅔ cups (628 ml) low-sodium chicken stock (page 231)
1⅓ cups (314 ml) uncooked long-grain converted white rice
1 tablespoon light olive oil with a dash of toasted sesame oil

Omelet

7 quarter-size slices peeled fresh gingerroot, chopped very fine
3 cloves garlic, bashed, peeled, and chopped very fine
6 green onions, chopped very fine
1/2 teaspoon light olive oil with a dash of toasted sesame oil
1 ounce (25 gm) Canadian bacon, rind removed, cut into 1/4-inch (.75-cm) dice

1 cup liquid egg substitute
1/16 teaspoon freshly ground sea salt
1/8 teaspoon freshly ground white pepper
Dash of cayenne pepper (optional)
1 teaspoon low-sodium soy sauce

Vegetables

1/2 teaspoon light olive oil with a dash of toasted sesame oil
3 ounces (75 gm) Canadian bacon, rind removed, cut into 1/4-inch (.75-cm) dice
10 sun-dried tomatoes, soaked for 10 minutes in boiling water and drained, cut into strips
1¼ cups frozen peas
4 green onions, diced

Garnish

1 green onion

At 17 years old, **Joe Presley** has no immediate health problems. He was just home watching television one summer when he caught the Graham Kerr television program habit and became convinced enough to try creative cooking (his mom says that he's got a pair of suspenders that help him do a great Graham imitation—accent and all).

Joe says, "I'd read a little bit about bao syang in the Minimax Cookbook but I hadn't ever really used it until I tried this fried rice. I would use it again—it really pepped up the omelet."

The day before, prepare the wheat berries and rice as follows: Soak the wheat berries in 2 cups of water for 8 hours or overnight. Strain, transfer the wheat berries to a medium saucepan, add 3 cups of water, cover, and bring to a boil. Reduce the heat and simmer for 2 hours. Drain and rinse well.

The seasoned rice: Pour the stock into a medium saucepan, bring to a boil, add the rice, stir once, reduce the heat to a simmer, cover, and cook for 15 minutes. When cool, spread out on a plate and let sit to dry out overnight in the refrigerator.

The omelet: Mix the gingerroot, garlic, and onions and divide into 3 equal parts. This *bao syang* mixture will be used throughout the recipe where specified for an explosion of fragrance and flavor. Pour 1/2 teaspoon oil into a medium nonstick skillet over medium-high heat, add the first third of the *bao syang* mixture, and fry for 30 seconds. Add the Canadian bacon and fry for 30 more seconds. Pour in the egg substitute, salt, pepper (and cayenne pepper for people who like it spicy), and reduce the heat to medium, stirring the mixture up from the bottom in small circular motions. When the omelet is set, but still soft on top, slide a spatula underneath to loosen it. Slide onto a plate and sprinkle with soy sauce. Cut into strips about 1/2 inch (1.5 cm) wide, then cut in half again. Set aside.

The vegetables: Pour 1/2 teaspoon oil into a large skillet over medium-high heat, add the second part of the *bao syang* mixture, and fry for 30 seconds. Add the Canadian bacon and fry for 30 more seconds. Add the tomatoes, peas, and green onions, stirring quickly to heat through. Remove from the skillet and set aside.

Pour the 1 tablespoon oil into the same skillet over medium-high heat, add the remaining third of the *bao syang* mixture, and fry for 30 seconds. Add the cooked rice and wheat berries and toss well to distribute the oil throughout the dish. Return the vegetables to the pan and cook while stirring well, about 4 minutes.

To serve: Spoon the rice mixture onto individual serving plates and garnish with the sliced omelet (brown side up) and long thin wisps of green onion between the slices of omelet.

✂ EXTRA MEAL

The fried rice and vegetables from this recipe are the perfect stuffing for Chinese dolma in the following recipe. Double the rice and vegetables, taking out half and cooling in the refrigerator. Divide this half into two resealable plastic bags. Pat them flat and expel all the air. Label and date the packages and freeze for up to 6 months.

Nutritional Profile per Serving			
	Classic	**Springboard**	**Daily Value**
Calories	779	462	
Calories from fat	333	72	
Fat (gm)	37	8	12%
Saturated fat (gm)	8	5	25%
Sodium (mg)	2066	730	30%
Cholesterol (mg)	238	13	4%
Carbohydrates (gm)	84	65	22%
Dietary fiber (gm)	4	6	24%
Classic compared: Ham and Egg Fried Rice			

CHINESE DOLMA

Inspired by the Greek classic stuffed grape leaves, with Chinese fried rice in the middle, and garnished with Mexican salsa—let's call it triple fusion. The fried rice can be made ahead and frozen when you make the recipe that precedes.

Time Estimate:
Hands-on, 25 minutes;
unsupervised, 5 minutes
Serves 4; yields 12 dolmas

2 bunches collard greens, washed
1/2 recipe Seasoned Rice and Vegetables (page 84)
1/2 cup commercial tomato salsa

Select 24 of the best-looking whole collard leaves and carefully cut off their stems. Place in a steamer tray and steam for 4 minutes. Transfer the cooked leaves to a plate.

To assemble: Lay out a cooked collard leaf, vein side up. Place 1/4 cup of the fried rice in the center. Drop 1 teaspoon of salsa on top of the rice. Fold the stem end of the leaf over the rice. Fold in the two sides and roll the bundle, firmly enclosing the rice. Repeat with the remaining leaves. Steam for 5 minutes to heat through.

Nutritional Profile per Serving: Calories—274; calories from fat—36; fat (gm)—4 or 6% daily value; saturated fat (gm)—1; sodium (mg)—716; cholesterol (mg)—7; carbohydrates (gm)—48; dietary fiber (gm)—7

Selecting the best-looking collard leaves

✖ WOW BAO CHICKEN SOUP

"Wow bao . . . WOW!!" is how Bob Kerschner began his reaction letter to this recipe. He continued, "Recipes, like road maps, should provide specific directions which allow you to always move from point A to Z. A good recipe also provides you with many opportunities to move off the main road, where, with a bit of imagination and some sense of adventure, any number of exciting results may be obtained."

Bob thought that my substitutions to his original recipe established a "flavor rivalry pleasing to the taste buds." He suggested it might be an interesting change if thin strips of lean pork and cabbage were substituted for the chicken and vegetables in my recipe . . . but that's another road to travel. How about joining us?

Time Estimate:
  Hands-on, 45 minutes
Serves 4

Chicken
4 ounces (100 g) skinless, boneless chicken breast, trimmed of all visible fat
Zest of 1/2 lime (1 teaspoon), grated
Zest of 1/2 lemon (1 teaspoon), grated
1 teaspoon fresh gingerroot, minced
2 teaspoons cornstarch

Broth
1/4 teaspoon light olive oil
1/4 teaspoon sesame oil
1 clove garlic, bashed, peeled, and chopped
8 quarter-size thin slices fresh gingerroot
4 green onions, roughly chopped
4 cups low-sodium chicken stock (page 231)

2 tablespoons lemon juice
1/4 teaspoon cayenne pepper
4 teaspoons rice wine vinegar

Vegetables
1 large carrot, sliced 1/8 inch thick (0.5 cm) on the diagonal
2 ounces (50 g) snow peas, strings removed and cut in half diagonally
4 large mushrooms, sliced into 4 slices
2 green onions, sliced 1/4 inch thick (0.75 cm) on the diagonal

1⅓ cups cooked rice
2 teaspoons grated lemon zest

The chicken: Cut the chicken breast in half lengthwise, then across into thin strips. In a small bowl, toss the strips with the lemon and lime zests, ginger, and cornstarch, making sure each piece is well coated. Put in the refrigerator and let marinate for at least 1/2 hour.

While the chicken marinates prepare the broth: Pour the oils into a medium saucepan over medium heat, toss in the garlic, ginger, and onions, and cook for 4 minutes. Add the stock, lemon juice, cayenne pepper, and vinegar, and bring to a boil. Reduce the heat and simmer for 5 minutes. Strain the stock into another medium saucepan.

Return the stock to a boil. Remove the chicken from its marinade and pat dry with paper towels. Drop the meat and carrots into the boiling stock and boil for 1 minute. Add the rest of the vegetables, stir, and just heat through. Remove from the heat.

To serve: Scoop the rice into a large bowl. Ladle the soup around the rice and sprinkle with the lemon zest.

Nutritional Profile per Serving: Calories—162; calories from fat—27; fat (gm)—3 or 5% daily value; saturated fat (gm)—1; sodium (mg)—91; cholesterol (mg)—16; carbohydrates (gm)—23; dietary fiber (gm)—2

✖ CLAMS WITH BLACK BEAN SAUCE

The bao syang *burst of fragrance here comes from Jon Rowley's zesty sauce of black beans, ginger, garlic, and red chili clinging to each clam, imparting zing to your taste buds with each bite. This is serving your guests the unexpected, and that's exciting.*

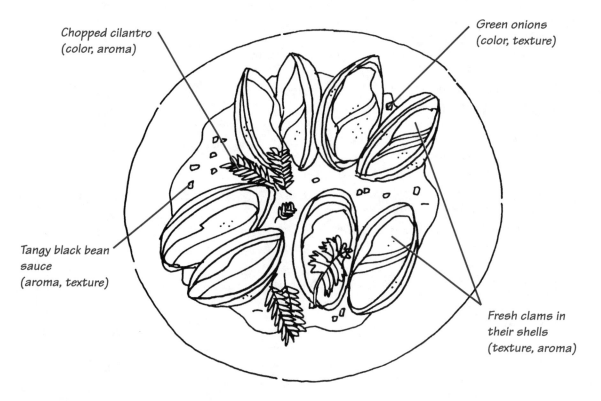

Chopped cilantro
(color, aroma)

Green onions
(color, texture)

Tangy black bean
sauce
(aroma, texture)

Fresh clams in
their shells
(texture, aroma)

Time Estimate:
  Hands-on, 45 minutes
Serves 6

2 tablespoons fermented black beans*
1 teaspoon canola oil
2 tablespoons slivered or chopped fresh gingerroot
1 tablespoon minced garlic
1 dried red chile, seeds removed and sliced
4 pounds (2 kg) live clams, well scrubbed
1 cup low-salt vegetable stock (page 233)
2 tablespoons sherry or de-alcoholized white wine

1 teaspoon toasted sesame oil
2 tablespoons cornstarch mixed with 1/4 cup
  de-alcoholized white wine (slurry)
2 tablespoons chopped green onions
1 tablespoon chopped fresh cilantro

*Available in Asian food stores and many supermarkets.

Jon Rowley's been turning some personal corners recently. You may already know him from guest appearances on my public broadcasting television series. He is my (and dozens of other food professionals') resident expert on fresh seafood.

Those of us who know and love his enthusiasm have been aware of his commitment to the soil, and to fruit and vegetables that have integrity. Jon is now turning his persuasive mind to fresh produce of all kinds. "More and more people," he suggests, "now understand how food choices affect personal health, the health of our society, and the health of the planet."

Jon is convinced that the end of the twentieth century is an important phase in human evolution. He gets almost prophetic: "The arithmetic of an expanding population eating off the top of the food chain doesn't compute." "Off the top" means eating the animals that eat the grains that we can eat far more efficiently. In other words, Jon is calling for a diet that is largely vegetarian by the year 2000, and he has one word for its importance: "essential."

Jon's own diet has become largely grains and vegetables, with a small amount of fish and shellfish. "The fascinating thing is that instead of feeling deprived, I find the food, while lighter in the body, is full of flavor and completely satisfying."

Please ponder his phrase "lighter in the body." look for that body feedback when you eat a meal.

A LOVINGLY CLINGY SAUCE

This clam sauce really needs to hug the clams inside their shells. As the amount of juice that comes from clams varies widely, you may need a little more or less cornstarch in order to get the sauce to lovingly cling to its clam.

Soak the fermented black beans in 1 cup of water for 20 minutes. Rinse the beans and mince them. Heat the canola oil in a large stockpot or steamer, add the black beans, ginger, garlic, and chile, and stir over low heat until fragrant, about 2 minutes. Add the clams, vegetable stock, sherry, and sesame oil. Cover the pot and simmer until the clams open, about 5 minutes. Turn off the heat. Transfer the clams to soup bowls and keep warm. Add the cornstarch slurry to the pan juices and gently bring to a boil, stirring constantly. When the sauce has thickened, about 1 minute, add the green onions and cilantro.

To serve: Spoon the sauce over the clams. You might want to soak up this delicious tangy broth with crusty bread rolls or chapatis.

Nutritional Profile per Serving			
	Classic	**Springboard**	**Daily Value**
Calories	834	178	
Calories from fat	270	27	
Fat (gm)	30	3	5%
Saturated fat (gm)	15	.36	2%
Sodium (mg)	689	217	9%
Cholesterol (mg)	277	24	8%
Carbohydrates (gm)	37	23	8%
Dietary fiber (gm)	2	1	4%
Classic compared: Clams Mariniere			

10 EGG SUBSTITUTES

With the yolk removed, the cholesterol and fat-free egg white becomes the "egg" for all kinds of egg dishes and baking.

In 1973–74, when I was videotaping my first nutrition-oriented television program, called *Take Kerr*, liquid egg substitute was also making its debut. It took me thirteen years to get over my first unsuccessful experiments. Somehow I saw egg substitute as an unnatural test tube creation, rather than what it is: 99 percent egg white mixed with beta carotene for color and a touch of natural coagulant—probably derived from seaweed (it's a secret).

If you haven't tried one of the many brands now available you will find that it's a great low-fat cooking ingredient, not just for breakfast dishes but for your baking needs as well. You will have to forget what you know about traditional methods for cooking scrambled eggs and omelets using whole eggs. Liquid egg substitute just doesn't respond the same way. Try some of my techniques, listed below, and I think you'll have a new egg-habit going.

Tips and Hints

- For scrambled eggs: Push the egg into the middle of the pan with a flat-ended wooden spoon (or my spurtle), then keep moving it around the pan until it is heaped in the middle and is still very moist. Serve it quickly—it sets fast.
- For an omelet: Stir just once, then let it settle to cook gently. Spoon your filling down the center, at a 90 degree angle to the pan handle, then fold both sides over and turn out onto a plate.

❌ Fruit Soufflé Omelet

After working in a cardiologist's office for 11 years, Ronnee Bienstock really understands the importance of a heart-healthy diet. In this dish she took the Arnold Bennett omelet from Smart Cooking *and turned it into a dessert. She had problems with the wetness of fresh fruit in her recipe, so I substituted dried fruit and we added the orange yogurt sauce. Great stuff, Ronnee, it makes a splendid dessert!*

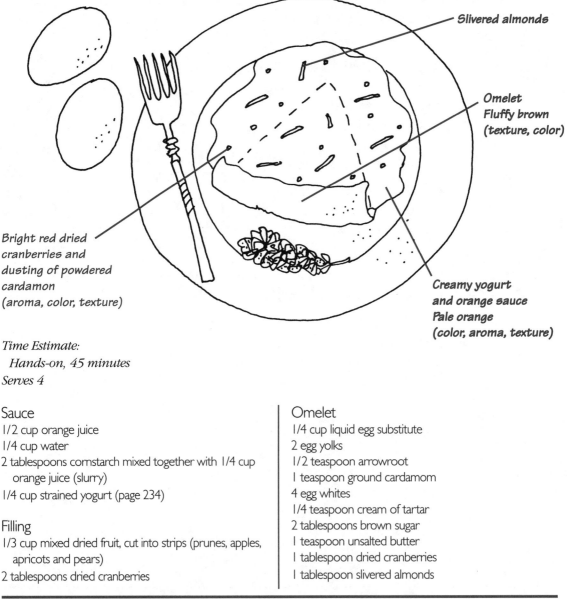

Slivered almonds

Omelet
Fluffy brown
(texture, color)

Creamy yogurt
and orange sauce
Pale orange
(color, aroma, texture)

Bright red dried
cranberries and
dusting of powdered
cardamon
(aroma, color, texture)

Time Estimate:
  Hands-on, 45 minutes
Serves 4

Sauce
1/2 cup orange juice
1/4 cup water
2 tablespoons cornstarch mixed together with 1/4 cup
  orange juice (slurry)
1/4 cup strained yogurt (page 234)

Filling
1/3 cup mixed dried fruit, cut into strips (prunes, apples,
  apricots and pears)
2 tablespoons dried cranberries

Omelet
1/4 cup liquid egg substitute
2 egg yolks
1/2 teaspoon arrowroot
1 teaspoon ground cardamom
4 egg whites
1/4 teaspoon cream of tartar
2 tablespoons brown sugar
1 teaspoon unsalted butter
1 tablespoon dried cranberries
1 tablespoon slivered almonds

Ronnee Bienstock says that her idea of living to "a ripe old age does not include being sick." At age 51, this grandmother likes to watch what she and her husband eat so they can continue their favorite activities, like hiking in the mountains.

Ronnee says she thinks this recipe would be great for brunch, with a nice salad and rolls. She had never thought of using dried fruit, and thought she liked the taste of it better than her idea of using fresh fruit.

The sauce: In a small saucepan bring the orange juice and water to a boil. Remove from the heat, stir in the cornstarch slurry, return to the heat, and bring to a boil for 1 minute to thicken and clear. Remove from the heat and let cool. Put the yogurt in a small bowl and gently whisk in the warm orange mixture.

The filling: Combine the mixed dried fruit and cranberries and set aside.

The omelet: In a small bowl, combine the egg substitute, egg yolks, arrowroot, and 1/2 teaspoon of the cardamon. In another bowl, beat the egg whites with the cream of tartar and brown sugar until they form soft peaks. Just before cooking, fold the egg yolk mixture into the egg whites until they are an even pale yellow color.

Preheat the broiler and set the rack 4 to 5 inches (10 to 13 cm) from the heating element. Set the skillet over medium heat and, when hot, add the butter, letting it sizzle until it looks light brown. Add the omelet mixture all at once and whisk it for about 10 seconds (count slowly). Now sprinkle the dried fruit filling over the top, pressing down with a fork to get it beneath the surface. Cook until the edges of the omelet come away from the pan, air holes start to appear on the top, and you can smell the brown sugar starting to caramelize, about 2 minutes. Immediately slide the pan under the preheated broiler and cook until a brown color appears on top and the omelet has risen, about 4 minutes. Remove from the oven, loosen the edges, and use a spatula to help you carefully shake it out of the pan onto a cutting board.

To serve: Cut into 4 wedges, place on individual serving plates, and spoon the sauce over the top. Garnish with the cranberries and almonds and a sprinkle of the remaining ground cardamom.

Nutritional Profile per Serving			
	Classic	**Springboard**	**Daily Value**
Calories	514	217	
Calories from fat	279	63	
Fat (gm)	31	7	11%
Saturated fat (gm)	17	3	15%
Sodium (mg)	166	119	5%
Cholesterol (mg)	381	115	38%
Carbohydrates (gm)	36	31	10%
Dietary fiber (gm)	1	2	8%
Classic compared: Strawberry Soufflé Omelet			

Mushroom and Spinach Omelet

I have called for chanterelle mushrooms in this recipe, knowing full well that they can only be found in the fall in certain places in our country. Please feel free to substitute other kinds of mushrooms. There are many varieties being grown domestically these days and available in supermarkets.

Time Estimate:
Hands-on, 20 minutes
Serves 4

8 cups spinach, washed and stemmed
1/4 teaspoon freshly ground black pepper
1/4 teaspoon freshly grated nutmeg
1 tablespoon unsalted butter
8 ounces chanterelle mushrooms, sliced
1 teaspoon chopped fresh dill weed
2 cups liquid egg substitute
2 tablespoons freshly grated Parmesan cheese

Put the spinach into a steamer tray, sprinkle with the pepper and the nutmeg, and place on top of a pot of boiling water. Cover and steam for 2 minutes. Remove from the heat and set aside.

Set a 10-inch (25-cm) skillet over medium heat. When hot, add the butter, letting it sizzle until it looks light brown. Toss in the mushrooms and dill and fry until tender, about 5 or 6 minutes. Pour the egg substitute over the mushrooms. Push the eggs toward the middle of the pan, allowing the undone egg to run down to the sides of the pan. Treat the egg substitute very gently and it will stay nice and creamy. Loosen the edges and with the help of a spatula carefully shake it out of the pan onto a cutting board.

To serve: Cut into 4 wedges. Press the excess water out of the spinach and fluff up. Place an omelet wedge on each plate and top with the spinach. Garnish with a sprinkle of the Parmesan cheese.

Nutritional Profile per Serving: Calories—161; calories from fat—36; fat (gm)—4 or 6% daily value; saturated fat (gm)—2; sodium (mg)—466; cholesterol (mg)—10; carbohydrates (gm)—15; dietary fiber (gm)—5

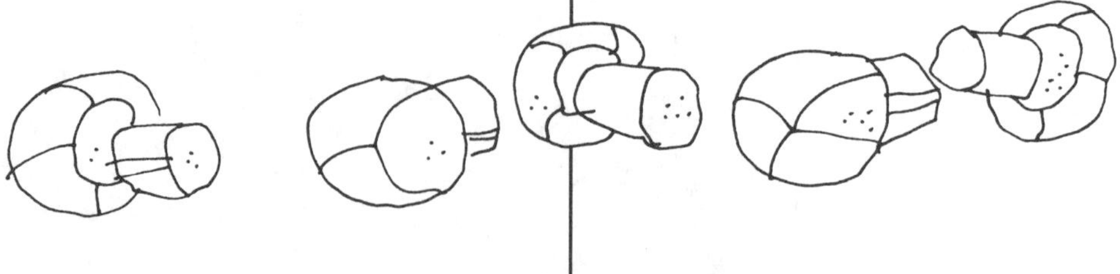

✖ CORNBREAD

*This really is a wonderful springboarders'
recipe. Imagine adding a few red chili flakes,
a pinch of cumin, a tablespoon of capers, a
few pine nuts? Come on—use it as a vehicle
for some of your favorite foods. It is based on
a "Delicious Cornbread Recipe" sent to me by
Hubert Goddard.*

Time Estimate:
Hands-on, 20 minutes;
unsupervised, 30 minutes
Serves 8

1 cup yellow corn meal
1 cup cake flour
1/2 teaspoon baking powder
2 teaspoons baking soda
1/4 teaspoon salt
1 tablespoon honey
1/2 cup liquid egg substitute
1½ cups low-fat buttermilk
2 tablespoons light olive oil

Preheat the oven to 350°F (180°C). Grease and
flour an 8-inch-square (20-cm) baking pan. Sift
the corn meal, flour, baking powder, soda, and
salt into a large mixing bowl. Pour the honey,
egg substitute, buttermilk, and oil into a small
bowl.

Stir the wet ingredients into the dry ingredients
gradually and gently, until mixed. Pour into the
prepared pan and bake for 30 minutes. Remove
from the oven, cut into squares, and serve hot
from the pan.

Nutritional Profile per Serving: Calories—176; calories from
fat—36; fat (gm)—4 or 6% daily value; saturated fat (gm)—
1; sodium (mg)—374; cholesterol (mg)—2; carbohydrates
(gm)—29; dietary fiber (gm)—2

✳ MING'S RICE-FILLED OMELET

Kweethai Chin Neill's creation is the easiest omelet you'll ever make: only folded over by one third, like a lovely linen napkin in a bread basket, which is lovingly folded back to reveal the excitement of the contents within. This omelet is so thin you could easily use it as a crêpe substitute.

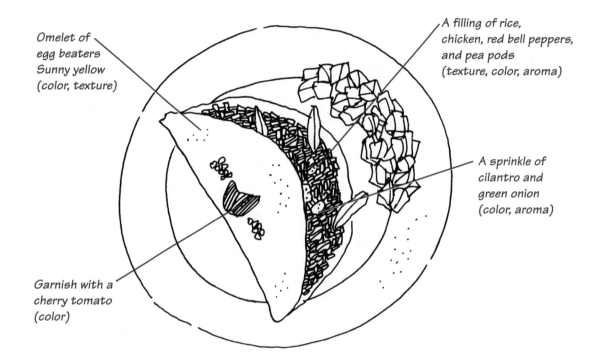

Omelet of egg beaters Sunny yellow (color, texture)

A filling of rice, chicken, red bell peppers, and pea pods (texture, color, aroma)

A sprinkle of cilantro and green onion (color, aroma)

Garnish with a cherry tomato (color)

Time Estimate:
  Hands-on, 30 minutes
Serves 2

Filling
1/2 teaspoon sesame oil
1/2 teaspoon olive oil
2 cloves garlic, bashed, peeled, and chopped fine
1 slice fresh gingerroot, chopped fine
2 tablespoons cubed cooked chicken meat (no skin)
1 cup fresh snow pea pods, strings removed
1/2 cup red bell peppers cut in 1/2-inch dice
1 cup cooked rice
2 teaspoons low-sodium soy sauce
Dash of cayenne pepper

Omelet
1 cup liquid egg substitute
1/8 teaspoon freshly ground sea salt
1/8 teaspoon freshly ground white pepper

Garnish
1 cup shredded lettuce
Fresh cilantro
Green onions
2 cherry tomatoes

The filling: Heat the two oils in a large skillet, add the garlic, ginger, and chicken, and stir-sizzle until fragrant. Add the snow peas and bell pepper and fry for 2 to 3 minutes, until the vegetables are just cooked. Add the rice, soy sauce, and cayenne pepper, remove from the heat, and keep warm while you make the omelet.

The omelet: Spray an 8-inch (20-cm) nonstick skillet with a small spritz of vegetable oil cooking spray. Heat the pan over medium heat. Pour the egg substitute into a small bowl and stir in the salt and pepper. Pour half the mixture into the pan to make a thin omelet. When just cooked, transfer to a warm dinner plate. Repeat with the rest of the egg substitute to make the second omelet.

To serve: Place the filling on 2/3 of the surface of the omelet. Flip the other 1/3 over. Place 1/2 cup of shredded lettuce on the side of the plate beside the omelet. Sprinkle with chopped green onions and cilantro leaves and top with a cherry tomato. Repeat with the second omelet. Serve immediately.

Nutritional Profile per Serving			
	Classic	**Springboard**	**Daily Value**
Calories	698	248	
Calories from fat	468	27	
Fat (gm)	52	3	5%
Saturated fat (gm)	27	.54	3%
Sodium (mg)	2702	642	27%
Cholesterol (mg)	568	7	2%
Carbohydrates (gm)	23	35	12%
Dietary fiber (gm)	2	4	16%
Classic compared: Farmer's Omelet			

II

WHOLE GRAINS

Packed with texture and nutrients, a huge variety of whole grains add ethnic creativity and satisfaction to meals.

As you'll recall, the idea behind the food pyramid is that we would do well to adjust what we eat so that we get more whole grains, from things like bread, cereal, rice, and pasta. Indeed, the pyramid's base of whole grains should be the first and broadest source of our daily calories, with the pyramid pinnacle, of fats, oils, and sweets, being the smallest.

Using the techniques in this chapter, you will discover how cooking whole grains can be easy, enjoyable, and even *swift*. I encourage you to experiment with the whole range of tastes and textures available to you: amaranth, pot barley, buckwheat (kasha, when toasted), corn (polenta, grits), millet, oats, pasta, quinoa, rice, rye, sorghum, wheat (from which is made bulgur wheat, couscous, semolina, triticale, wheat berries, rolled wheat, farina, wheat germ, seitan or "wheat meat"), wild rice, . . . phew!

All grains and grain products have three common elements: the outer shell, called BRAN; the inner life, called the GERM; and finally a compact supply of starch to feed the germ as it begins to grow, ENDOSPERM. When all three are intact, you have a whole grain. As whole grains are refined—for example, brown rice polished into white—they lose part of their ability to nourish.

Tips and Hints

- Wash all grains well and drain dry. Pan-fry them without oil at medium heat to toast them brown, being careful to avoid scorching. Cover with about double the quantity of liquid (for more flavor, use a stock), bring to a boil and simmer, covered, for the appropriate time.
- Depending upon their plant structure and the degree of refining, each kind of grain will vary in cooking time. Look on the package for exact specifics.
- Some grains, like wheat berries, need to be soaked overnight. Others, like bulgar and buckwheat, can be covered with boiling water and will cook in just 10 minutes. The "toughest" grains take up to 2 hours of simmering; but this can be shortened in a pressure cooker to 15 minutes.
- You can sprout wheat, pot barley, buckwheat, rice, rye, millet, flax, triticale, and amaranth seeds.

✖ WHOLE-GRAIN ISLAND ON A PARSNIP SEA

Tess Fields wrote to me with a dilemma: She loved parsnips, but could find very few recipes that featured them as a main ingredient. This led directly into a really radical whole-grain concept with an awesome creamy parsnip sauce that is a knockout: slightly sweet but oh what a velvet finish set against the textural "pop" of whole grains.

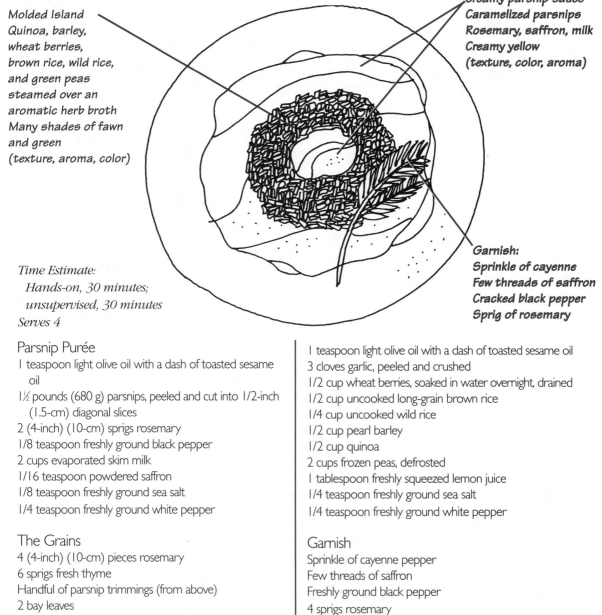

Molded Island
Quinoa, barley,
wheat berries,
brown rice, wild rice,
and green peas
steamed over an
aromatic herb broth
Many shades of fawn
and green
(texture, aroma, color)

Creamy parsnip sauce
Caramelized parsnips
Rosemary, saffron, milk
Creamy yellow
(texture, color, aroma)

Garnish:
Sprinkle of cayenne
Few threads of saffron
Cracked black pepper
Sprig of rosemary

Time Estimate:
  Hands-on, 30 minutes;
  unsupervised, 30 minutes
Serves 4

Parsnip Purée

1 teaspoon light olive oil with a dash of toasted sesame
  oil
1½ pounds (680 g) parsnips, peeled and cut into 1/2-inch
  (1.5-cm) diagonal slices
2 (4-inch) (10-cm) sprigs rosemary
1/8 teaspoon freshly ground black pepper
2 cups evaporated skim milk
1/16 teaspoon powdered saffron
1/8 teaspoon freshly ground sea salt
1/4 teaspoon freshly ground white pepper

The Grains

4 (4-inch) (10-cm) pieces rosemary
6 sprigs fresh thyme
Handful of parsnip trimmings (from above)
2 bay leaves

1 teaspoon light olive oil with a dash of toasted sesame oil
3 cloves garlic, peeled and crushed
1/2 cup wheat berries, soaked in water overnight, drained
1/2 cup uncooked long-grain brown rice
1/4 cup uncooked wild rice
1/2 cup pearl barley
1/2 cup quinoa
2 cups frozen peas, defrosted
1 tablespoon freshly squeezed lemon juice
1/4 teaspoon freshly ground sea salt
1/4 teaspoon freshly ground white pepper

Garnish

Sprinkle of cayenne pepper
Few threads of saffron
Freshly ground black pepper
4 sprigs rosemary

Two years ago **Tess Fields'** neighbor grew parsnips . . . and the rest is history. "He thought they were too weird and no wonder nobody ate them. But I cooked them and only three little pieces got to the table because I think they're delicious!"

Finn potatoes, poufed them out, and piped in curlicues of mashed yams."

Tess says she would like to get rid of the fat in her diet, but there's this boyfriend: "He's kind of tough. He'll eat low-fat, but he still likes to go to burger joints a lot. . . ."

Tess likes to cook low-fat and to make things beautiful. "Like one day I baked Yellow

Perhaps he would like a parsnip burger with cream?

The parsnip purée: Pour at least 3 inches (9 cm) of water into a steamer pot and bring it to a boil. Pour the oil into a large skillet over medium heat and fry the parsnip, rosemary, and black pepper until the parsnips become lightly brown and caramelized, about 10 minutes. Discard the rosemary, transfer the parsnips into a steamer tray, place it atop the pot of boiling water, cover, and steam for 30 minutes. Remove the tray of parsnips and set it aside to cool slightly. Refresh the steaming pot with water if needed for the grains.

The grains: While the parsnips are steaming, start the grains: Make a seasoning bag with the rosemary, thyme, parsnip trimmings, and bay leaf tied in a piece of cheesecloth. Pour the oil into a large stock pot on medium heat and fry the crushed garlic to release the oils, about 2 minutes. Pour in 6 cups of water, add the seasoning bag, and bring to a boil. Stir in the brown rice, wild rice, and barley and boil for 28 minutes. Stir in the quinoa and boil 2 minutes longer. Drain the grains, discarding the seasoning bag and liquid. Turn the grains out onto a steamer tray lined with cheesecloth, place atop a pot of boiling water, cover, and steam for 15 minutes.

Finish the parsnip purée: Transfer the cooled parsnips to a food processor, add 1½ cups of the evaporated milk, and whiz for 3 minutes. The texture should be very light, with a silky mouthfeel and the appearance of a whole-cream mousse. Stir in the saffron, salt, and white pepper. Reserve 4 tablespoons of the purée for garnish. Finish with the remaining 1/2 cup of evaporated milk for a more pourable purée.

Finish the grains: Turn the steamed grains out into a mixing bowl. Toss together immediately with the peas, lemon juice, salt, and white pepper.

To serve: Fill each serving bowl with equal amounts of the parsnip cream. Pack a small flan ring with the grains to mold and turn out on top of the parsnip cream. Garnish with a small dollop of the parsnip cream on top of each grain island and sprinkle with the cayenne pepper, saffron threads, black pepper, and a sprig of rosemary. If you can't find a flan ring, spoon the grains into a cup or small soup bowl to mold.

⚡ EXTRA MEAL

Double the grains in this recipe and you're on your way to making Beautiful Soup on the next page. But don't double the garlic—3 cloves is plenty for the double batch. Set aside half the grains mix after it's steamed. Cool in the refrigerator. Divide between 2 or 3 resealable plastic bags. Flatten, label, and date the bags.

Nutritional Profile per Serving			
	Classic	**Springboard**	**Daily Value**
Calories	555	706	
Calories from fat	216	54	
Fat (gm)	24	6	9%
Saturated fat (gm)	15	1	5%
Sodium (mg)	861	477	20%
Cholesterol (mg)	67	5	2%
Carbohydrates (gm)	76	140	47%
Dietary fiber (gm)	9	21	84%
Classic compared: Parsnip and Celery Cream with Rice Pilaf			

✖ Beautiful Soup

A double batch of the grains from the preceding recipe get you ready to dive into a really beautiful meal. I think it's the colors that are magnificent; warm brown broth, orange carrots, deep red kidney beans, all tied together by deep green and red Swiss chard. Nothing Minimalist about this soup—except the fat.

Time Estimate:
  Hands-on, 20 minutes;
  unsupervised, 20 minutes
Serves 4

1 teaspoon light olive oil with a dash of toasted sesame oil
1 medium onion, peeled ad diced
2 cloves garlic, bashed, peeled, and chopped
2 teaspoons Hungarian paprika
2 tablespoons low-sodium tomato paste
2 medium carrots, peeled and diced
2 (15-ounce) (425-g) cans low-sodium beef stock
1 bay leaf
2 sprigs fresh thyme
6 whole black peppercorns
2 whole cloves
3 sprigs fresh parsley
2 cups frozen extra Whole Grains (page 100), from your freezer
1 (15-ounce) (425-g) can low-sodium kidney beans, drained and rinsed
2 cups Swiss chard, cut into thin strips

Pour the oil into a large saucepan on medium heat and fry the onion, garlic, and paprika until the onion wilts. Push the vegetables to one side, add the tomato paste, and cook until the paste darkens. Add the carrots and stir to coat. Pour in the beef stock and bring to a boil. Wrap the herbs and whole spices in an herb ball or a square of cheesecloth and toss into the soup. Turn the heat down to medium and simmer for 10 minutes.

Stir in the whole grains, beans, and Swiss chard. Bring back to a boil and simmer 10 more minutes. Ladle the soup into bowls and serve crusty French bread on the side.

Nutritional Profile per Serving: Calories—314; calories from fat—36; fat (gm)—4 or 6% daily value; saturated fat (gm)—1; sodium (mg)—118; cholesterol (mg)—0; carbohydrates (gm)—56; dietary fiber (gm)—12

Mexican Baked Whitefish

Ron Stofer does a lot of camping in the spring and summer. He thinks this dish would be an impressive meal away from home. Ron goes on to say it would just be a matter of putting a portion or two in individual serving dishes and freezing. When camping, it would simply mean defrost, bake, and garnish. Good idea, Ron!

Time Estimate:
Hands-on, 40 minutes;
unsupervised, 20 minutes
Serves 4

Salsa
1/2 pound (225 g) tomatoes, chopped
1/4 cup chopped onion
1/2 cup chopped fresh cilantro
2 cloves garlic, bashed, peeled, and chopped

Mexican Pilaf
2 cups water
1 cup quinoa
1 teaspoon light olive oil with a dash of toasted sesame oil
1/2 cup chopped onion
1/2 medium red bell pepper, seeded and diced
1/2 medium yellow bell pepper, seeded and diced
1/4 cup chopped fresh cilantro
1/2 teaspoon red chili flakes
1/4 teaspoon freshly ground sea salt
4 fillets (1 pound) (450 g) orange roughy or other whitefish
1/4 pound (110 g) baby shrimp, cooked and peeled

The salsa: Pulse all the ingredients in a processor until coarsely chopped or finely chop with a knife. Set aside.

The pilaf: Bring the water to a boil in a saucepan. Add the quinoa and simmer for 10 minutes. Drain.

Preheat the oven to 350°F (180°C). Heat the oil in a medium-sized skillet over medium-high heat. Fry the onion for 2 minutes, then add the peppers and fry until they're slightly softened. Stir in the cooked quinoa, cilantro, red chili flakes, and salt; transfer to an 8 x 8-inch (20 x 20-cm) baking pan. Arrange the fish on top, dolloping each fillet with a quarter of the salsa. Bake for 20 minutes or until the quinoa is hot and the fish flakes easily when tested with a fork. Serve immediately, garnished with the baby shrimp.

Nutritional Profile per Serving: Calories—311; calories from fat—81; fat (gm)—9 or 14% daily value; saturated fat (gm)—2; sodium (mg)—253; cholesterol (mg)—118; carbohydrates (gm)—29; dietary fiber (gm)—4

✖ LIME, LAMB, AND BARLEY

Jerri Fifer Broyles first composed this recipe as a lime, lamb, and lentil creation, then substituted barley instead of the lentils. Barley or lentils? It really doesn't matter; they both work equally well.

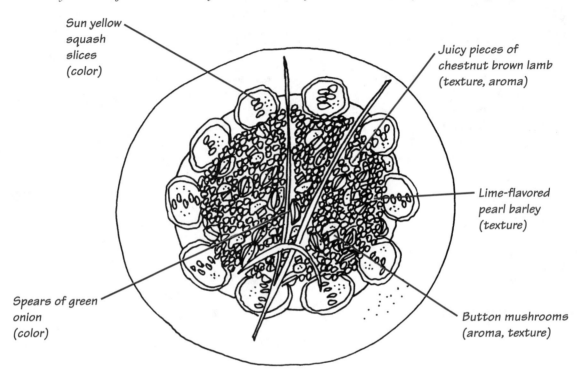

Sun yellow squash slices (color)

Juicy pieces of chestnut brown lamb (texture, aroma)

Lime-flavored pearl barley (texture)

Spears of green onion (color)

Button mushrooms (aroma, texture)

Time Estimate:
  Hands-on, 30 minutes;
  unsupervised, 30 minutes
Serves 4

1 cup pearl barley
6 cups water

Marinade

3 cloves garlic, bashed, peeled, and chopped
1 teaspoon chopped fresh rosemary leaves
1 teaspoon curry powder
3 drops lime oil or 1/2 teaspoon lemon extract
1/2 cup de-alcoholized red wine
1/8 teaspoon freshly ground black pepper

Casserole

8 ounces (250 g) very lean lamb, cut into thin strips
1 tablespoon light olive oil with a dash of toasted sesame oil
10 button mushrooms, quartered
1 cup crushed tomatoes
2 cups low-sodium chicken stock (page 231)
2 tablespoons chopped fresh thyme
2 tablespoons red currant jelly
2 tablespoons chopped fresh parsley
1 yellow squash, sliced into rounds and blanched
2 green onions, sliced lengthwise

Jerri Fifer Broyles owns and operates the Frog and Owl Café, 10 minutes outside of Highlands, North Carolina. The restaurant is literally miles from anywhere, but it's definitely on my map whenever Treena and I visit our daughter Tess and her family in that area of the world. "Why, that's only a three-hour drive," explained Jerri. "Lots of my customers come that far."

They come for what I've been told is the best country-style food and atmosphere in the United States. "A lot of my sauces are reductions, but the dishes aren't airy or wispy. They are right for my customers, who want comforting dishes that truly satisfy.

"Folks around here are mostly farmers," continued Jerri, "and raise a lot of pigs. While they appreciate well-cooked vegetables, they certainly would miss a good thick pork chop."

Recently Jerri has been testing the tide of opinion with greater focus on whole grains and less meat in very tasty combination dishes. "I'll just keep listening to my customers and serving them with the best I can."

Well, I thought, at least they've got good drive time for their digestion before hitting the sack.

Place the barley in a medium saucepan, add the water, bring to a rapid boil, and simmer for 40 minutes. Rinse in cold water, drain, and set aside.

The marinade: While the barley is cooking, whisk together the garlic, rosemary, curry powder, lime oil, red wine, and black pepper in a small bowl. Add the lamb, toss until well coated, and set aside in the refrigerator for at least 20 minutes.

The casserole: Remove the lamb from the marinade and pat dry. Pour the oil into a large skillet over medium heat, add the lamb, and brown it very well. Add the mushrooms, fry for 2 minutes, then remove the lamb and mushrooms to a plate and set aside. Add the tomatoes, chicken stock, thyme, and red currant jelly and boil on high heat to reduce by half, about 10 minutes. Return the lamb and mushrooms to the pan, along with the cooked barley and parsley, just until heated through, tossing carefully.

To serve: Ladle a portion of lamb and barley into the middle of each serving plate, and arrange the blanched yellow squash around as though they were petals on a sunflower. Lay a couple of green onion slices across the top and you're ready.

Nutritional Profile per Serving			
	Classic	**Springboard**	**Daily Value**
Calories	812	404	
Calories from fat	504	90	
Fat (gm)	56	10	17%
Saturated fat (gm)	29	3	15%
Sodium (mg)	1111	220	9%
Cholesterol (mg)	184	52	17%
Carbohydrates (gm)	7	56	4$
Dietary fiber (gm)		9	36%
Classic compared: Lamb, Barley, and Mushroom Casserole			

12 SEASONED RICE

Rice has heightened flavor by cooking each grain like a tiny sponge in broth, herbs, and spices.

One thing that hasn't changed for me is my commitment to rice. While individual recipes like the classic risotto can total 700 calories with as much as 26 grams of fat, this doesn't mean that hundreds of other methods are fattening.

Using good meat or vegetable stocks that have been concentrated in flavor by reduction (see pages 14–15) allows each rice grain to act like a tiny dry sponge that thirstily soaks up the grand flavors you've developed.

Tips and Hints

- Any type of rice can be a "seasoned sponge," but some have much better results than others. Those that do well are long-grain converted, basmati or Texmati, and arborio. The brown rices and short-grain "sticky" rice do not do as well.

"One thing that hasn't changed for me is my commitment to rice."

- All seasoned rice, including fried rice, must be precooked by boiling. In order to use less fat, I cook the rice in water or stock and avoid the early shallow frying of the raw grains so often seen in classic preparations. The stock increases the background flavor in every single grain as it cuts back on fat by 75 percent.

- Whenever possible, I color the rice a brilliant yellow with either turmeric (inexpensive) or powdered saffron (expensive). The choice depends upon how delicate and refined the flavor is in the final dish. If it's made with lobster tails or smoked salmon, then use saffron; for chicken bits or baby shrimp, turmeric will do.

✜ Afghan Lamb *Palow*

Carol Saia and her husband, Michael, love to have friends in for a totally different dining experience—an Afghan meal. She sent me several recipes to "fix." I used the seasoned rice technique of cooking the rice in stock and off we went. Our version dropped Carol's classic recipe from nearly 29 grams of fat to 16 grams and still held the great flavor of the original.

Lamb braised in a
spiced tomato stock
Highlight deep browns
(aroma, color, texture)

The rice "palow"
cooked in lamb stock
and saffron
Bright yellow
(color, aroma, texture)

Fine matchsticks of
carrot cooked in
brown sugar with
raisins and almonds
Bright glossy orange
(color, texture)

Time Estimate:
  Hands-on, 35 minutes
Serves 4

Seasoning
1/2 teaspoon cardamon seeds, shelled (about 12 seeds altogether)
1/2 teaspoon cumin seeds
16 whole cloves
1 (2-inch) (5cm) piece of cinnamon stick

Stock
11 ounces (300 g) roasted lamb bones
5 ounces (140 g) fat trimmings from the lamb shoulder (see above)
10 cups water
4 small bay leaves
Peelings from the 4 carrots (see below)
Peelings from the 2 onions (see below)
6 whole cloves

1 (1-inch) (2.5-cm) piece of cinnamon stick
1/2 teaspoon whole cumin seed
1/4 teaspoon freshly ground sea salt
1/4 teaspoon whole black peppercorns

Stew
1 pound (450 g) boneless lamb shoulder
1 teaspoon light olive oil with a dash of toasted sesame oil
2 onions, peeled and sliced lengthwise 1/4 inch (0.75 cm) thick
2 tablespoons low-sodium tomato paste
2 teaspoons seasoning (see above)
2 cups lamb stock (see above)
1/4 teaspoon salt
1 tablespoon arrowroot mixed with 2 tablespoons water (slurry)

Vegetable

1/2 teaspoon light olive oil with a dash of toasted sesame oil
4 carrots, peeled and cut into matchsticks
1 teaspoon brown sugar
1/4 cup dark raisins
2 tablespoons slivered almonds

Palow (Pilaf)

3 cups lamb stock (see above)
1/4 teaspoon freshly ground sea salt
1/2 inch (1.5 cm) ground saffron, heaped on the end of a pointed knife
1⅓ cups uncooked long-grain white rice, rinsed
1 tablespoon balsamic vinegar

THE FRESHEST AND LEANEST LAMB

Bone the lamb yourself to be sure it's perfectly fresh and remove all the visible fat possible. Purchase a 2-pound (900 g) lamb blade or shoulder steak. Using a sharp knife, remove the meat from the bone and trim off any visible fat. Cut the meat into 1/2-inch (1.5-cm) dice, which helps to spot some of the heavier concentrations of fat. You should end up with about 1 pound (450 g) of meat, 5 ounces (140 g) of fat, and 11 ounces (300 g) of bones. The fat and bones will be used for the stock.

✄ EXTRA MEAL

Double the entire recipe so you'll have leftovers to make the exotic sandwiches on the next page. You can also freeze the leftovers as a complete meal in itself. Mix everything well and freeze in resealable freezer bags in portions that make sense for your family. Flatten the bags, expelling as much air as possible, label, and date. Thaw before reheating.

The seasoning: Whiz the spices together in a small electric coffee grinder, or grind with a mortar and pestle. Spoon into a small bowl and set aside.

The stock: Place all the ingredients for the stock in a large pot with 8 cups of the water. Cook for 2 hours, adding the remaining 2 cups of water during the cooking to make up for evaporation. Strain the stock and discard the solids. Strain again into a fat strainer and discard the fat that rises to the top. Rinse the stockpot with a couple ounces of water to clean the sides.

Carol Saia and her husband, Michael, have lived in India, Afghanistan, Germany, and Holland, where they discovered the joy of making foods from different cultures. Afghan lamb *Palow* is not typical of the food Carol cooks on a daily basis. As a busy working mom who also home-schools her 6-year-old son, Carol told me that she wished there were a cookbook with low-fat, inexpensive recipes that she could freeze in multiple batches. Carol, this book's for you!

(continued)

Nutritional Profile per Serving			
	Classic	**Springboard**	**Daily Value**
Calories	899	662	
Calories from fat	423	144	
Fat (gm)	47	16	25%
Saturated fat (gm)	8	5	25%
Sodium (mg)	985	472	20%
Cholesterol (mg)	70	104	35%
Carbohydrates (gm)	10	85	28%
Dietary fiber (gm)	3	5	20%
Classic compared: Lamb and Rice with Carrots and Raisins			

The stew: Trim the lamb of all visible fat and cut it into 1⁄2-inch (1.5-cm) dice (see page 109). Heat the oil in a large high-sided skillet on medium heat and brown the lamb on one side, making sure the pieces are separate, for 5 minutes. Remove and set aside.

In the same skillet, cook the onion on medium heat for 2 minutes. Add the tomato paste and 1½ teaspoons of the seasoning and cook for 2 minutes. Stir in the browned lamb and the stock, cover, and simmer for 30 minutes. Just before serving, remove from the heat and stir in the remaining 1/2 teaspoon of the seasoning, 1/4 teaspoon salt, and the arrowroot slurry. Return to the heat, and bring to a boil to thicken and clear, about 30 seconds.

The vegetable: Pour the oil into a large skillet and fry the carrots and brown sugar on medium heat until the carrots are just tender. Add the raisins and almonds and stir together.

The pilaf: Bring the stock, salt, and saffron to a boil in a medium saucepan. Add the rice, stir lightly, reduce the heat, and simmer, covered, for 15 minutes.

To serve: Spoon a ring of rice on each dinner plate. Fill the center with carrots and the sauced lamb. Scatter a few more carrots around the edge and sprinkle with the balsamic vinegar.

✖ LAMB *PALOW* POP-UPS

Any manner of fillings can go into a pita bread, be frozen, and then be ready to pop into the oven for a quick and healthy lunch. I really liked this combination, made with leftover Afghan lamb palow *from the preceding recipe. Chutney is a flavorful and textural low-fat alternative to mayonnaise. I used mango here, but urge you to experiment with the different kinds available in the grocery store.*

Time Estimate:
 Hands-on, 20 minutes
Makes 16 pita halves

1 recipe of Afghan Lamb *Palow* (pages 108–110), stew
 and pilaf
1 package whole wheat pita bread
16 teaspoons mango chutney

Whiz the rice, vegetables, and lamb from the Afghan lamb *palow* in a processor to grind it into small pieces, but don't let it go to a paste.

Cut the pitas in half, spread each half with 1 teaspoon of the mango chutney, and fill with 1/4 to 1/2 cupof the *palow*. Place on a baking sheet and bake at 350°F (180°C) until heated through, about 5 minutes.

You can also make "freezer pitas" by cutting the pitas in half and filling with 1/4 to 1/2 cup of the *palow*. Press together until flat enough to fit into a toaster. Wrap each half individually, place in a resealable plastic bag and freeze.

When you are ready to eat them, remove from the freezer and let thaw. Slide in 1 teaspoon of the mango chutney and toast in your toaster. If you are in a real hurry, you can microwave them still frozen, then toast and add the chutney.

Nutritional Profile per Serving: Calories—256; calories from fat—36; fat (gm)—4 or 6% daily value; saturated fat (gm)—1; sodium (mg)—3; cholesterol (mg)—26; carbohydrates (gm)—39; dietary fiber (gm)—3

✖ WILD MUSHROOM RISOTTO

Risotto is one of my favorite types of seasoned rice dishes. Ida Penna wrote me indicating her love for this traditionally ultra-rich Italian classic. I'll wager that this creative version will make you a risotto lover too. If you've never tried dried mushrooms, I think you'll be pleasantly surprised by their delicate flavor but unusually meaty texture. With a crunchy green salad on the side and a crusty bread, you have the basis for a satisfying and hearty vegetarian entree.

Time Estimate:
  Hands-on, 40 minutes
Serves 4

5 cups low-sodium chicken stock (page 231)
1 ounce dried porcini mushrooms
12 sun-dried tomato halves
1 teaspoon light olive oil with a dash of toasted sesame oil
2 tablespoons finely chopped onion
1 clove garlic, bashed, peeled, and chopped fine
1 cup uncooked arborio rice
1/2 cup de-alcoholized white wine
1/4 teaspoon freshly ground black pepper
1/4 teaspoon freshly ground sea salt
1/2 cup freshly grated Parmesan cheese

Heat the chicken stock in a large saucepan. Remove from the heat, add the dried mushrooms, and let them sit for 20 minutes. Strain through a double thickness of paper towels or a coffee filter, saving the stock. Chop the mushrooms and set aside.

Submerge the dried tomatoes in boiling water and resuscitate for 2 minutes. Drain, press out and discard the water, cut the tomatoes into slivers, and set aside with the mushrooms.

Heat the oil in a heavy-bottomed saucepan and fry the onion and garlic for 3 minutes. Add the rice and toss until it's coated with oil. Pour in 1/2 cup of the stock and bring to a boil, stirring when mixture starts to stick. It should stay at a low boil. When the stock is absorbed, add the wine, stirring until it's absorbed. Continue adding half cupfuls of the stock until all the liquid is incorporated. Add the pepper, salt, and chopped vegetables with the last 1/2 cup of liquid. You don't have to stir the risotto constantly, but keep a close eye on it and stir whenever it starts to stick. You may not need all the stock. Stop cooking when the rice is soft but not mushy. It should take about 30 minutes.

To serve: Remove from the heat and stir in most of the cheese, saving just a little to sprinkle on each serving as a garnish.

Nutritional Profile per Serving: Calories—306; calories from fat—54; fat (gm)—6 or 9% daily value; saturated fat (gm)—3; sodium (mg)—544; cholesterol (mg)—10; carbohydrates (gm)—47; dietary fiber (gm)—2

✖ BEEF PILAF WITH CILANTRO AND ALLSPICE

Peter Kump's easy pilaf, fragrant with cilantro and allspice, is a flavor combination you will find interesting to sample.

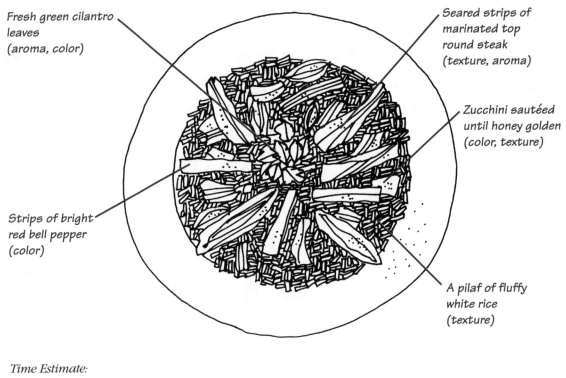

Fresh green cilantro
leaves
(aroma, color)

Seared strips of
marinated top
round steak
(texture, aroma)

Zucchini sautéed
until honey golden
(color, texture)

Strips of bright
red bell pepper
(color)

A pilaf of fluffy
white rice
(texture)

Time Estimate:
  Hands-on, 40 minutes;
  unsupervised, 50 minutes
Serves 6

Marinade
1 tablespoon red wine vinegar
2 teaspoons finely chopped fresh cilantro
1/2 teaspoon ground allspice
1 teaspoon extra virgin olive oil
1/4 teaspoon freshly ground black pepper
1/8 teaspoon freshly ground sea salt

Beef and Pilaf
1 (6-ounce) (200-g) top round steak, trimmed of all fat
3 medium zucchini, sliced lengthwise into 1/4-inch
    (0.75-cm) strips

1 teaspoon extra virgin olive oil
1/8 teaspoon freshly ground sea salt
2 medium onions, peeled and diced
2 cloves garlic, bashed, peeled, and chopped fine
1 red bell pepper, cored, seeded, and sliced into 1/4-inch
    (0.75-cm) strips
2 cups uncooked long-grain rice
1/2 cup de-alcoholized white wine
3½ cups low-sodium beef stock (page 231)
1/8 teaspoon freshly ground black pepper
Cilantro leaves for garnish

Peter Kump is a major influence in North American culinary matters. Quite apart from the steady influence exerted through his famous New York Cooking School, Peter is a great help to the James Beard Foundation, and, as such, is connected daily to the foremost chefs of our time.

In 1972, responding to growing customer interest, he began a new class called Lean Cuisine: Spa Cooking. "We have adjusted and changed our recipes," Peter explained, "to reflect the preference for lower fat, more vegetables and grains, and a general Mediterranean diet approach. Five years ago, we paid it little attention; but now we respect it."

When I pressed a crystal ball into Peter's hand and asked about the year 2000, he said, "I do think that we will see an increasing trend to control the fat in our diets but at the present time I find this limited to a depressingly small part of the population."

Well, Peter, I'll do my best to bring low-fat cooking to more and more people . . . with a little help from my friends.

Combine the marinade ingredients in a small bowl. Pour over the steak and let sit at room temperature for up to 30 minutes or refrigerate for up to 2 hours.

Remove the meat from the marinade and pat dry. Reserve the marinade. In a medium skillet with a tight-fitting lid, brown the meat over high heat for 2 minutes on each side. Remove the meat to a warm plate.

Brush the strips of zucchini with the olive oil and season with the salt. Using the same skillet, sauté the zucchini until golden for 3 minutes on each side. Remove and set aside. In the same skillet fry the onion, garlic, and red pepper for 1 minute. Add the rice, cooking and stirring until it begins to brown, about 5 minutes. Pour in the wine and deglaze the pan. Add the stock and the reserved marinade and bring to a boil. Reduce the heat, cover, and cook until the rice is tender and the liquid is absorbed, about 20 minutes.

Slice the steak in half lengthwise and then into thin slices on the diagonal. Then cut the zucchini strips into 1/4-inch (0.75-cm) pieces. When the rice is done, toss the beef, zucchini, and any accumulated juices with the rice and incorporate evenly. Season with the pepper. Garnish with the cilantro leaves, bring to the table, and spoon onto individual dishes.

An elegant presentation for this dish would be mounded on a beautiful serving plate, ringed with a brightly colored turban of crisp fresh julienned carrots, jicama, fennel, and red bell pepper tossed in a little of Joy Delf's Cider Vinaigrette (page 80).

Nutritional Profile per Serving			
	Classic	Springboard	Daily Value
Calories	297	358	
Calories from fat	117	36	
Fat (gm)	13	4	6%
Saturated fat (gm)	5	1	5%
Sodium (mg)	546	322	13%
Cholesterol (mg)	31	24	8%
Carbohydrates (gm)	35	62	21%
Dietary fiber (gm)	3	3	12%
Classic compared: Spanish Rice with Beef			

BEANS

Pureed into a buttery-smooth paste, canned beans are the convenient base for innumerable easy and nutrient-packed sauces, savory spreads, and soup thickeners.

This is what I call Brave New World food. Most people already know that beans are a nutritional superfood, even when they're precooked in the can and literally "ready to go." But cooked and puréed beans can be the butterlike base for innumerable sauces, even an extremely tasty and elegant bean terrine appetizer.

There are at least 16 varieties of beans available in supermarkets and food cooperatives across North America. In this book, I've used precooked canned beans and, whenever possible, those that are low sodium. This means that they are *very* fast food. The ideas for their use are quite varied and should give you lots of potential for springboarding.

Don't let those noisy upstarts raffinose and stachyose deter you from eating them. These unusual bean starches travel into the unprepared, underexercised North American intestine and can produce flatulence.

May I suggest that you start with small portions, literally only 1 tablespoon at a meal, using them as you would a condiment. Your unsuspecting digestive system will usually adapt as you build up the quantity. You can also try adding a tablespoon of rice wine vinegar to your favorite bean recipe when the cooking is complete. The vinegar changes the acid level of the dish and reduces your chances of having a gassy reaction. It also helps to pour off the water after soaking dried beans, then add fresh water, bring to a boil, pour off the second water, and then use fresh water to cook.

It's time to stop avoiding beans.

✖ BEAN TEREENA

It seemed an impossible task when the recipe came in from Lee Anderson: a sumptuous layered terrine (pâté) stuffed full of cheese and oil. We ran the numbers just for fun and a small slice as an appetizer was 496 calories and 82 percent fat! This was supreme challenge time. After hours upon hours of testing, a new recipe finally emerged—and it's an incredible feast for the senses. This is one of the all-time great dishes to emerge from my kitchen (that's why its name changed from Terrine to that of my wife, Treena). Thanks to Lee for the inspiration!

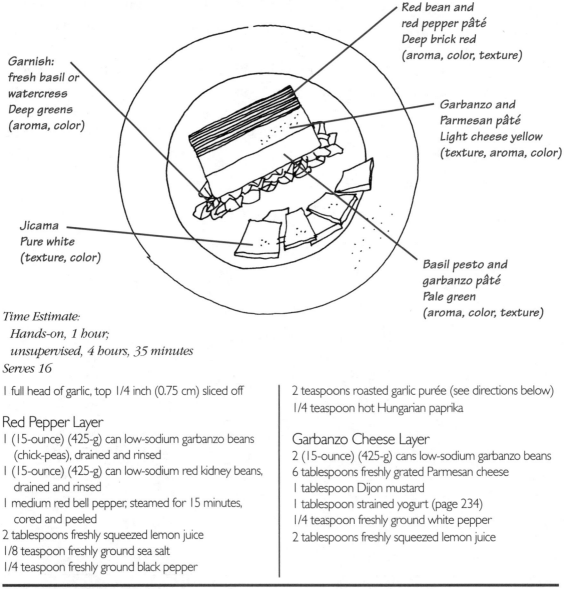

Red bean and
red pepper pâté
Deep brick red
(aroma, color, texture)

Garnish:
fresh basil or
watercress
Deep greens
(aroma, color)

Garbanzo and
Parmesan pâté
Light cheese yellow
(texture, aroma, color)

Jicama
Pure white
(texture, color)

Basil pesto and
garbanzo pâté
Pale green
(aroma, color, texture)

Time Estimate:
  Hands-on, 1 hour;
  unsupervised, 4 hours, 35 minutes
Serves 16

I full head of garlic, top 1/4 inch (0.75 cm) sliced off

Red Pepper Layer
I (15-ounce) (425-g) can low-sodium garbanzo beans
  (chick-peas), drained and rinsed
I (15-ounce) (425-g) can low-sodium red kidney beans,
  drained and rinsed
I medium red bell pepper, steamed for 15 minutes,
  cored and peeled
2 tablespoons freshly squeezed lemon juice
1/8 teaspoon freshly ground sea salt
1/4 teaspoon freshly ground black pepper

2 teaspoons roasted garlic purée (see directions below)
1/4 teaspoon hot Hungarian paprika

Garbanzo Cheese Layer
2 (15-ounce) (425-g) cans low-sodium garbanzo beans
6 tablespoons freshly grated Parmesan cheese
I tablespoon Dijon mustard
I tablespoon strained yogurt (page 234)
1/4 teaspoon freshly ground white pepper
2 tablespoons freshly squeezed lemon juice

Pesto Layer

1 (15-ounce) (425-g) can white beans, drained and rinsed
1 cup lightly packed fresh basil leaves, rinsed and drained
2 tablespoons freshly grated Parmesan cheese
1 teaspoon mashed roasted garlic purée (see directions below)

2 tablespoons freshly squeezed lemon juice
1/4 teaspoon freshly ground black pepper

Garnish

1 bunch watercress, rinsed and drained
1 (1-pound) (450-gm) jicama, peeled and cut into 48 wedges

Lee Anderson is a 49-year-old accountant and travel agent who is "struggling" with food, trying to learn how to convert his cooking to healthier dishes. He said he knew his original recipe was "ridiculously" high in fat and calories and admits that he's especially guilty of serving this kind of rich dish when he's entertaining. Lee thought my version was "good" and said he was going to make it for friends soon and get their reaction.

Preheat the oven to 375°F (190°C). Cut the root end off the head of the garlic, opening up the cloves. Wrap the garlic in foil and bake for 35 minutes. Immediately after it comes out of the oven, mash it to produce 1 level tablespoon of garlic purée. To do this, hold one end of the garlic head with a pot holder. Press the garlic out with the back of a knife. It will come out mashed. We found not much more than 1 tablespoon in a head of roasted garlic.

Note: Have a dipping bowl of water handy for your spatula when spreading the layers. This is very important for an even presentation.

Red pepper layer: Line an 8 x 4-inch (20 x 10-cm) loaf pan with a piece of plastic wrap that's big enough to fit over the whole terrine. Put all the ingredients for the red pepper layer in a processor and whiz for 3 minutes. (You may have to do this in batches.) Spread evenly in the bottom of the loaf pan.

Garbanzo cheese layer: Put all the ingredients for this layer in a processor and whiz for 4 minutes. Drop small amounts over the red pepper layer and spread gently and evenly; try to avoid getting any air pockets.

Pesto layer: Put all the ingredients for this layer into a processor and whiz until smooth, about 3 minutes. Spread evenly over the garbanzo cheese layer, cover with plastic wrap, and press down gently. Chill for 4 hours or overnight.

To serve: Uncover the top of the loaf pan. Lay a cutting board or plate over the top and invert. The bean loaf will fall right out. Remove plastic wrap. Slice into 16 pieces and serve on individual plates as a first course. Garnish with the watercress and jicama wedges.

⌘ EXTRA MEAL

Be sure to save leftover Beans Tereena or make a double batch for enchiladas tomorrow. (See the recipe that follows.)

Nutritional Profile per Serving

	Classic	Springboard	Daily Value
Calories	496	231	
Calories from fat	405	27	
Fat (gm)	45	3	5%
Saturated fat (gm)	20	1	5%
Sodium (mg)	732	163	7%
Cholesterol (mg)	86	2	0.6%
Carbohydrates (gm)	6	38	13%
Dietary fiber (gm)	1	8	32%

Classic compared: Provolone Terrine

✖ BEAN ENCHILADAS

Elegant Bean Tereena leftovers from the pre-ceeding recipe are transformed here into a familiar family favorite. I use a 4-inch (10-cm) size tortilla because they're the perfect size for children and fit easily into a loaf pan.

Time Estimate:
  Hands-on, 15 minutes;
  unsupervised, 15 minutes
Serves 4

1 (15-ounce) (425 gm) can low-sodium tomatoes
1 jalapeño pepper, seeded and chopped (leave the seed in if you like it hot)
1/4 teaspoon freshly ground sea salt
1 tablespoon fresh oregano (1 teaspoon dried)
1 cup Bean Tereena (page 116)
8 (4-inch) (10-cm) flour tortillas
2 tablespoons freshly grated Parmesan cheese

Preheat the oven to 350°F (180°C). Whiz the tomatoes, jalapeño, salt, and oregano in a blender or processor until the tomatoes are chopped but not smooth. Pour a little of the sauce into the bottom of a loaf pan.

Spoon 2 tablespoons of the Bean Tereena down the middle of each tortilla. Roll up and place on top of the sauce in the casserole. Cover the enchiladas with some more of the sauce, but don't drown them. Bake for 15 minutes. Pour the remaining sauce into a saucepan and just heat through.

To serve: Pour a pool of the sauce onto each serving plate, place 2 enchiladas on top, sprinkle with Parmesan cheese, and serve with a side salad of watercress or seasonal greens and your choice of low-fat dressing.

Nutritional Profile per Serving: Calories—346; calories from fat—54; fat (gm)—6 or 9% daily value; saturated fat (gm)—2; sodium (mg)—395; cholesterol (mg)—6; carbohydrates (gm)—58; dietary fiber (gm)—11

✜ Black Beans and Rice

I knew a dinner made from canned black beans would fit right in with Rich Horowitz's lifestyle. Rich, his wife, and two teenage sons are a family on the go who want to keep their meals low fat and high flavor. Rich found this recipe a bit too spicy. He recommends dropping the hot sauce and substituting a milder sauce with the brand name "Pickapeppa," which contains tomatoes, onions, sugar, vinegar, mangoes, raisins, tamarinds, salt, peppers, and spices—that's depth of flavor!

Time Estimate:
  Hands-on, 20 minutes;
  unsupervised, 35 minutes
Serves 4

1⅓ cups low-sodium chicken stock (page 231)
2/3 cup uncooked long-grain brown rice, rinsed
1 teaspoon light olive oil with a dash of toasted sesame oil
1 medium yellow onion, chopped
2 cloves garlic, bashed, peeled, and chopped
1 medium green bell pepper, seeded and chopped
1 medium red bell pepper, seeded and chopped
2 teaspoons dried oregano
1 (15-ounce) (425-g) can low-sodium black beans, drained and rinsed
3 tablespoons bottled hot sauce, such as Pickapeppa, or 1/2 teaspoon liquid hot red pepper sauce, such as Tabasco
1/4 teaspoon freshly ground sea salt

Fruit Salad
2 large oranges, peeled and sectioned
2 medium kiwifruit, peeled and sliced
1 large banana, peeled and sliced
2 limes
1/2 cup fresh chopped cilantro

4 (8-inch) (20-cm) flour tortillas

Pour the stock into a small saucepan, add the rice, bring to a boil, cover, reduce the heat, and simmer for 35 minutes.

Heat the oil in a large high-sided skillet on medium heat and fry the onion and garlic for 3 minutes. Add the bell peppers and oregano and cook for 3 more minutes. Stir in the cooked rice, beans, hot sauce, and salt; mix well and heat through.

Make a fruit salad in a small bowl by gently mixing the oranges, kiwifruit, and banana.

To serve: Divide the black beans among individual places, squeeze half a lime on top of each serving, and sprinkle with chopped cilantro. Serve with the fresh fruit salad and warmed flour tortillas on the side.

Nutritional Profile per Serving: Calories—541; calories from fat—63; fat (gm)—7 or 11% daily value; saturated fat (gm)—2; sodium (mg)—427; cholesterol (mg)—3; carbohydrates (gm)—108; dietary fiber (gm)—15

⌘ NORA'S SPICY BLACK BEANS ON A VEGETABLE PLATE

At Nora Pouillon's organic, multi-ethnic restaurant in Washington, D.C., she serves a different combination of vegetables every night, sometimes as many as 10 different kinds. Nora says she has one customer who lost 20 pounds in one year by eating the vegetarian menu twice a week at Restaurant Nora. *This dish is the Vegetarian Plate served at the restaurant and has fantastic eye appeal: a veritable rainbow of vegetables. Nora encourages you to alternate vegetables with the season—butternut squash purée, yellow beans, and broccoli are just a few warm colors and soothing textures you might add. It's your choice.*

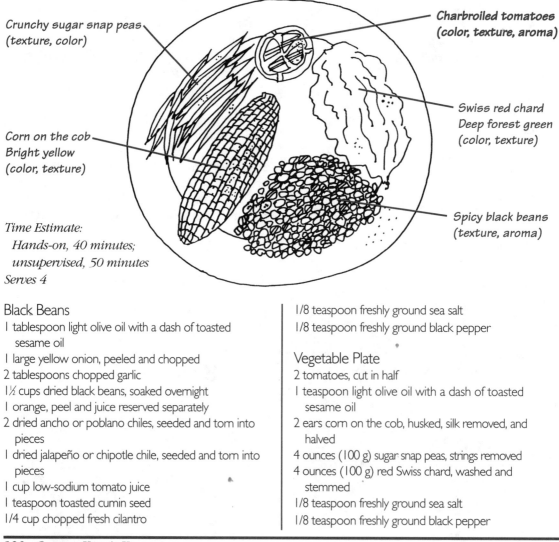

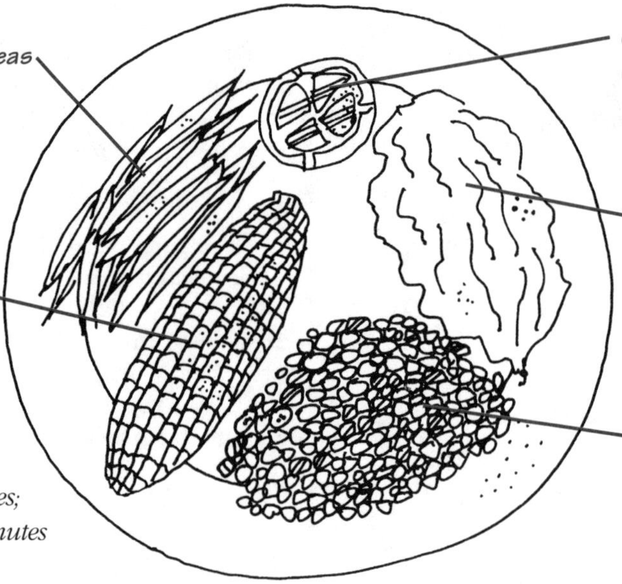
Crunchy sugar snap peas
(texture, color)
Charbroiled tomatoes
(color, texture, aroma)
Swiss red chard
Deep forest green
(color, texture)
Corn on the cob
Bright yellow
(color, texture)
Spicy black beans
(texture, aroma)

Time Estimate:
Hands-on, 40 minutes;
unsupervised, 50 minutes
Serves 4

Black Beans

- 1 tablespoon light olive oil with a dash of toasted sesame oil
- 1 large yellow onion, peeled and chopped
- 2 tablespoons chopped garlic
- 1½ cups dried black beans, soaked overnight
- 1 orange, peel and juice reserved separately
- 2 dried ancho or poblano chiles, seeded and torn into pieces
- 1 dried jalapeño or chipotle chile, seeded and torn into pieces
- 1 cup low-sodium tomato juice
- 1 teaspoon toasted cumin seed
- 1/4 cup chopped fresh cilantro
- 1/8 teaspoon freshly ground sea salt
- 1/8 teaspoon freshly ground black pepper

Vegetable Plate

- 2 tomatoes, cut in half
- 1 teaspoon light olive oil with a dash of toasted sesame oil
- 2 ears corn on the cob, husked, silk removed, and halved
- 4 ounces (100 g) sugar snap peas, strings removed
- 4 ounces (100 g) red Swiss chard, washed and stemmed
- 1/8 teaspoon freshly ground sea salt
- 1/8 teaspoon freshly ground black pepper

Nora Pouillon is recognized as one of the most talented and successful chefs in the United States. Her two restaurants in Washington, D.C., Restaurant Nora and City Café, are frequently named among Washington's best.

Nora is an advocate for increasing the quality and nutritional value of our food supply. "Beginning with pesticide and chemical-free ingredients, we prepare food in a simple, healthful manner, inspired by culinary traditions from around the world. Fifteen years ago, this was a radical concept. Now more and more people realize that there is a direct link between the food we eat and our physical, emotional, and mental well-being. Making the decision to eat healthy food is the most important thing a person can do for him or herself."

Born in Vienna, Nora says, "I was introduced to beans upon coming to the United States, and I find the variety just unbelievable. Black beans are my favorite, but since they take so long to cook, I always make double what the recipe calls for. That way, there are plenty cooked and ready for other things—like a black bean and papaya relish to go on grilled fish or chicken. Other healthy ways to eat black beans are in a Jamaican dirty rice with cilantro and cumin; sprinkled on a romaine salad with some feta cheese;or with some steamed butternut squash in a quesadilla.

The black beans: Heat the olive oil in a large skillet and fry the onion and garlic until softened, about 2 minutes. Drain the black beans and add to the onion with enough fresh water to cover them by 2 inches (6 cm). Stir in the orange peel, orange juice, chiles, tomato juice, and toasted cumin. Bring to a boil, reduce the heat, cover, and simmer until the beans are tender, the liquid is absorbed, and the chiles have disintegrated, about 1½ hours. Stir in the cilantro, salt, and pepper and keep warm.

The vegetable plate: While the beans are cooking, prepare the vegetable plate. Brush the tomatoes with the olive oil and broil or grill, very close to the heat source, until they are quite brown, about 5 minutes. Fill a medium saucepan three-quarters full with water and bring to a boil. Add the corn and cook until tender, about 4 minutes. Place the sugar snap peas and Swiss chard in a steamer and cook for 2 minutes. The snap peas and chard will still be bright green and red, but slightly softened.

To serve: Spoon a large portion of the black beans onto each plate and arrange the tomatoes, corn, sugar snap peas, and Swiss chard artfully around them. Serve immediately.

MEET AN ANCHO AND CHIPOTLE

Anchos are dried poblano chiles and they vary in hotness. If you grind them, you get the chili powder used to make the famous Southwestern and Tex-Mex chili con carne. Chipotles are dried and smoked jalapeño chiles. They are always hot and add a great smoky flavor to any dish. Chipotle tomato sauce is one of Nora's favorites, and she thinks it's "perfect" for Southwestern or Mexican foods.

Nutritional Profile per Serving			
	Classic	Springboard	Daily Value
Calories	339	417	
Calories from fat	135	63	
Fat (gm)	15	7	20%
Saturated fat (gm)	6	1	5%
Sodium (mg)	1239	205	9%
Cholesterol (mg)	30	0	0%
Carbohydrates (gm)	34	75	25%
Dietary fiber (gm)	10	18	72%
Classic compared: Casserole of Red Beans			

14 PASTRY CRUSTS

A lower-fat pastry crust, both tender and flaky, can grace all your classic preparations, both sweet and savory.

L et's start out by saying that what we want from a pastry crust is tenderness, but not so much that it falls apart almost by looking at it.

Until now sugar and fat helped flour to hang together tenderly. There is now a third helper: I call it skill . . . and enough patience to read this chapter and try the recipes. That's the only way I know of developing skill.

Is it worth trying our new pie crust version compared with the classic? Just consider fat and calories and I think you'll rush to freeze your margarine.

BASIC PASTRY CRUST
Yields two 8-inch (20-cm) crusts

1½ cups cake flour
1 teaspoon sugar
1/8 teaspoon salt
2 tablespoons light olive oil
4 tablespoons (1/2 stick) margarine or butter,
    frozen for 15 minutes
1 teaspoon distilled vinegar
4 tablespoons ice water
2 tablespoons 2-percent-fat milk

Nutritional Profile per Serving		
	Classic	**Springboard**
Calories	338	186
Fat (gm)	27	10
Saturated fat (gm)	11	1

Put the flour, sugar, and salt in a large mixing bowl, drizzle evenly with the oil, and whisk together with a fork until it has a fine sandy texture.

Remove the margarine from the freezer and slice it into 1/8-inch (0.5-cm) pieces. Stir it into the flour mixture just enough to coat the margarine and keep the pieces from sticking together. Sprinkle with the vinegar and water, then use two knives cutting in a crisscross motion to work the dough just until all the liquid is absorbed. Shape into a ball, put in a small bowl, cover with plastic, and refrigerate for 10 minutes before rolling. The longer it sits, the more the liquid will spread throughout the dough, making it easier to roll. Brush with milk after rolling.

Tips and Hints

Lower-fat pastry crusts

- Use cake flour. It has less protein than all-purpose flour, which reduces the production of gluten and makes for a more tender crust.
- For an even tenderer crust, remove 1 tablespoon of each cup of flour and replace with 1 tablespoon cornstarch. This reduces the protein yet again.
- For sweeter crusts, add more sugar or very sweet fruit purée (like prunes). The sugar prevents gluten from forming by keeping two of the proteins from combining.
- Since my family is trying not to have saturated fat, I use a good solid stick margarine; not the soft tub, which has added water and is difficult to cut into uniform pieces.

✖ Smoked Pork and Apple Tiddy Oggy

A Tiddy what? In England, a "tiddy" is a potato. When the potato pasty, or potpie, became the standard working man's lunch, it was simply called a tiddy oggy. This recipe was created for Olga Lundstrom, who indicated on her Food Preference List that she liked steak and kidney pie and was a real meat lover. This recipe gives you the satisfaction of eating savory pork chops, but in smaller quantities (just look at the nutritional comparison with the classic to see exactly how much the risk has decreased).

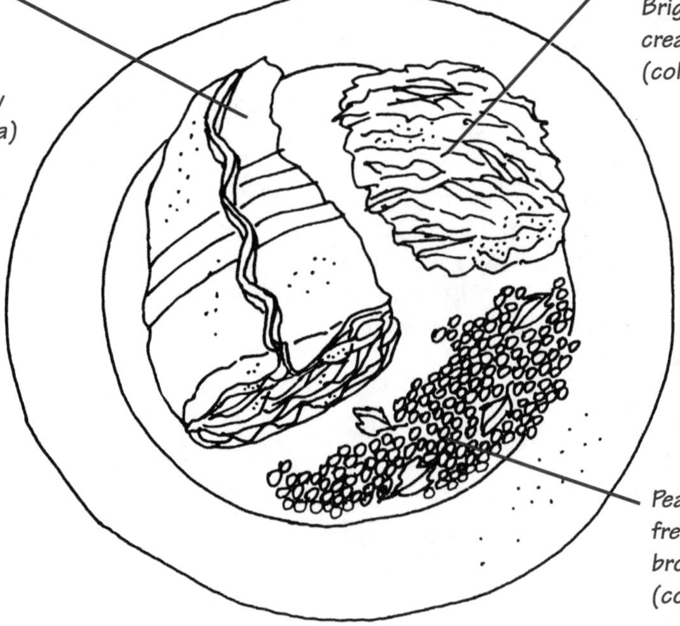

Tiddy Oggy:
Light flaky pastry
filled with smoked
loin of pork, apple,
and french mustard
Golden brown, glossy
(texture, color, aroma)

Carrot and parsnip
cottage mash
Bright carrot with
creamy parsnips
(color, texture, aroma)

Peas cooked in
fresh mint and
brown sugar
(color, aroma, texture)

Time Estimate:
Hands-on, 40 minutes;
unsupervised, 30 minutes
Serves 4

Tiddy Oggy

1 recipe Basic Pastry Crust (page 123)
2 teaspoons Dijon mustard
4 ounces (100 g) steamed sweet potato, chopped fine
4 ounces (100 g) smoked pork chop, fat removed, chopped fine
4 ounces (100 g) apple, cored, peeled, and chopped
2 tablespoons 2-percent-fat milk (for glaze)

Cottage Mashed Parsnip, Carrot, and Peas

1 pound (450 g) parsnips, peeled and roughly chopped
1 pound (450 g) carrots, peeled and roughly chopped
1/8 teaspoon freshly ground sea salt
Freshly ground white pepper to taste
Freshly grated nutmeg to taste
1/4 cup water
1/4 cup whole mint leaves
2 tablespoons brown sugar
2 cups fresh or frozen peas

Make the pastry crust and put in the refrigerator to chill. Mix together the mustard, sweet potato, smoked pork, and apple, tossing until well coated with the mustard.

Preheat the oven to 425°F (220°C). Remove the dough from the refrigerator and divide it into 4 parts. Flour your hands and lightly shape each part into a ball. Dust a clean surface with a small amount of flour and roll out each pastry ball into a circle roughly 7 inches (18 cm) in diameter. Then cut out an exact 6-inch (15-cm) circle, with a plate or bowl as a guide, and trim the excess.

Put an even amount of the filling mixture into the center of each pastry round. Use a pastry brush dipped in cold water to wet the edges. Enclose the filling by folding the rounds in half to resemble a turnover. Seal the edges by pressing together firmly and crimping with your fingers or the tines of a fork. Brush the pasties with the milk, place on a lightly greased baking sheet, and bake for 30 minutes or until the crust is golden brown. Remove from the oven and let cool for 5 minutes.

The vegetables: Place the parsnips in a steamer tray and steam for 8 minutes. Add the carrots and steam for 10 minutes. Transfer the parsnips and carrots from the steamer to a warm bowl and roughly mash. Season with the salt, pepper, and nutmeg and set aside. In a medium saucepan, bring the water, mint, and sugar to a boil, add the peas, and simmer until they are tender, about 5 to 10 minutes for fresh, 3 minutes for frozen.

To Serve: Serve one tiddy oggy on each plate with the mashed vegetables and peas on the side.

⌗ EXTRA MEAL

This low-fat pie crust freezes well. Cut a piece of cardboard about 10 inches wide and fit it into a gallon-size plastic freezer bag. Roll out two 10-inch (25-cm) diameter circles. Place the first crust directly on the cardboard, cover with waxed paper or parchment paper, and slip the second crust on top. Press out the air and freeze solid. To thaw, take a crust out of the bag and lay it on the kitchen counter with a towel over it. A frozen pie crust makes the recipe for potpie on the next page especially easy.

Nutritional Profile per Serving			
	Classic	**Springboard**	**Daily Value**
Calories	1369	475	
Calories from fat	702	117	
Fat (gm)	78	13	20%
Saturated fat (gm)	41	2	10%
Sodium (mg)	1313	753	31%
Cholesterol (mg)	210	15	5%
Carbohydrates (gm)	137	77	25%
Dietary fiber (gm)	15	12	48%
Classic compared: Tiddy Oggy			

✖ POTPIE

*I love savory meat pies. Yes, they're a part of
my English heritage, but I also think a
creamy meat filling nestled in a tender flaky
crust is universal comfort food. If you freeze
one of my basic pastry crusts (see page 125),
you can whip this up in a flash whenever
you, or one of your family members, need a
little extra comfort.*

Time Estimate:
  Hands-on, 10 minutes;
  unsupervised, 1 hour
Serves 4

Leftover low-fat stew (see reduced Oxtail Soup on page
    166)
1 recipe Basic Pastry Crust (page 123), thawed

   Preheat the oven to 350°F (180°C). Transfer a
previously made stew or perhaps the reduced
Oxtail Soup (page 166) to a 9-inch (23-cm) pie
dish. Lay the rolled-out crust over the top and
prick with a fork to let the steam escape while
cooking. Bake for 30 to 50 minutes, depending
on how much gravy is in the stew and how crisp
you like the crust.

Nutritional Profile per Serving: Calories—277; calories from
fat—36; fat (gm)—4 or 5% daily value; saturated fat (gm)—
1; sodium (mg)—155; cholesterol (mg)—1; carbohydrates
(gm)—59; dietary fiber (gm)—12

❖ CHERRY COBBLER

Fruit cobbler is one of America's favorite desserts: bursting with fruit that can vary with the best in season, paired with an irresistibly crumbly topping and whipped cream. I think my springboard version has all of the classic's original comforts. It was based upon a recipe sent to me by Joanne Galloway. Joanne reports that "our family thought your recipe was great." Hope your family likes it, too. It's particularly simple when you use the canned sour cherries.

Time Estimate:
  Hands-on, 30 minutes;
  unsupervised, 40 minutes
Serves 6

Filling
2 (16-ounce) (450-g) cans pitted sour cherries, in juice
3/4 cup sugar
1/4 cup freshly squeezed lemon juice
1 tablespoon plus 1 teaspoon cornstarch
1/4 teaspoon almond extract

Topping
3/4 cup unbleached all-purpose flour
1 tablespoon plus 1/2 teaspoon sugar
1/2 teaspoon soda
3/4 teaspoon baking powder
1 tablespoon cold stick margarine
6 tablespoons 1-percent-fat buttermilk
1 teaspoon light olive oil

1½ cups frozen nonfat vanilla yogurt

The filling: Preheat the oven to 350°F (180°C). Spray an 8-inch (20-cm) pie dish with vegetable oil cooking spray. Discard 1/2 cup of the cherry juice. In a large bowl combine the rest of the juice, cherries, sugar, lemon juice, cornstarch, and almond extract. Pour into the prepared pie dish.

The topping: In a small bowl, combine the flour, 1 tablespoon of the sugar, and the baking powder. Cut in the margarine with a fork or pastry blender until it's the consistency of coarse meal. Make a well in the center, pour in the buttermilk and oil, and mix lightly until just moistened. Drop the topping in large spoonfuls over the cherries and sprinkle with the remaining 1/2 teaspoon of sugar. Bake for 40 minutes. The top will be nice and brown. Remove from the oven and let cool for 15 minutes. Cut into wedges and top each serving with 1/4 cup of the frozen yogurt.

Nutritional Profile per Serving: Calories—277; calories from fat—36; fat (gm)—4 or 6% daily value; saturated fat (gm)—1; sodium (mg)—155; cholesterol (mg)—1; carbohydrates (gm)—59; dietary fiber (gm)—1

✳ Spiced Apple Pie with Cashew Pastry Crust

Terri Berkey has created one of the best apple pies I've ever tasted—and that includes the fatty ones, too. The crust is a lovely crusty rich warm brown, encompassing the apples like velvet.

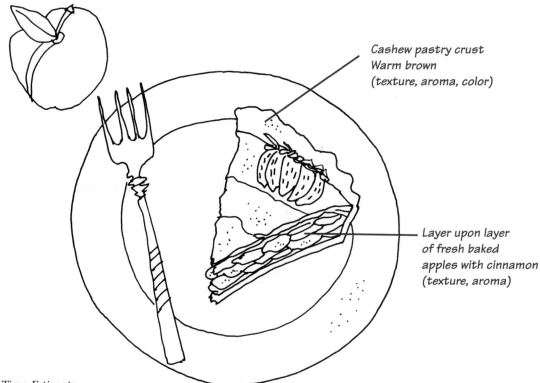

Cashew pastry crust
Warm brown
(texture, aroma, color)

Layer upon layer
of fresh baked
apples with cinnamon
(texture, aroma)

Time Estimate:
  Hands-on, 35 minutes;
  unsupervised, 1 hour 20 minutes
Serves 8 to 10

Crust
1/2 cup roasted unsalted cashews
1 cup cake flour (*not* self-rising)
1½ cups all-purpose flour
1/2 teaspoon freshly ground sea salt
3/4 teaspoon ground allspice
1/4 teaspoon baking soda
1½ tablespoons freshly squeezed lemon juice
6 tablespoons light corn syrup
1½ to 2 tablespoons ice water

Filling
9 cups peeled, cored, and sliced apples (a combination of 4 Granny Smith and 3 Golden Delicious apples works well)
5 tablespoons all-purpose flour
3 tablespoons dark brown sugar
3/4 teaspoon ground cinnamon
2 teaspoons freshly squeezed lemon juice

I have a very healthy admiration (no pun intended) for **Terri Berkey's** work. She works with health and fitness spas to transform basic nutritional principles into fine dining, and consults with restaurants to communicate nutrition information about their food without spoiling the dining environment.

Because her clients live in the New York City and Boston area, Terri must make her food compete with that of some of the most extraordinary restaurants in the world, and do it with much less fat.

"The simple solution," she told me, "is to displace meat, fish, and poultry as the centerpiece and focus instead on foods we used to consider as side dishes: whole grains and vegetables."

The biggest problem she faces is unrealistic expectations when people change their diet. "We become accustomed to a certain comfort zone of food, traditional appearances and tastes. I have to remind people that different tastes do not mean inferior, just different."

Although we live three thousand miles apart, Terri and I are of one mind.

NOBODY LIKES A SOGGY CRUST

Store the leftover apple pie in a loosely covered container. Covering tightly will cause the crust to become soggy.

The crust: Place the cashews in a food processor and process to a fine powder, stopping before the nuts begin to release their oils and become cashew butter. In a medium bowl, combine the cake flour, all-purpose flour, salt, allspice, baking soda, and ground cashews until well mixed. In a small bowl combine the lemon juice, corn syrup, and 1½ tablespoons of ice water, stirring to blend. (Note: the corn syrup will not blend well with the other liquids, but this is all right.) Add the liquid mixture to the dry mixture, stirring to mix evenly and moisten all the dry ingredients. The dough will be quite stiff. If more liquid is needed, add an extra 1/2 tablespoon of ice water. Gather the dough into a ball, wrap in plastic, and chill at least 30 minutes. (This may be made up to 1 day ahead and chilled; let rest at room temperature for 5 minutes before rolling.)

The filling: Toss the apples with all the remaining ingredients.

Preheat the oven to 350°F (180°C). Remove the crust from the refrigerator. Generously flour a piece of waxed or parchment paper. Roll two-thirds of the dough on a floured surface until it is 2 inches (6 cm) larger than a 9-inch (27-cm) deep-dish pie plate. The dough is very solid and will take some work to roll evenly. Rub the deep-dish pie plate very lightly with vegetable oil, wiping any excess with a paper towel. Carefully transfer the pastry to the prepared pie plate and fill with the apple mixture. Repeat the rolling procedure with the remaining dough and place on top of the filling. Trim, crimp, and decorate the top as desired, being sure to pierce the top crust in several places to create steam vents. Bake in the preheated oven until golden brown, about 1 hour. Cool on a wire rack. When well cooled, cut with a serrated knife.

Nutritional Profile per Serving			
	Classic	**Springboard**	**Daily Value**
Calories	401	310	
Calories from fat	171	45	
Fat (gm)	19	5	8%
Saturated fat (gm)	3	.88	4%
Sodium (mg)	376	148	6%
Cholesterol (mg)	.78	0	0%
Carbohydrates (gm)	55	66	22%
Dietary fiber (gm)	4	6	24%
Classic compared: Apple Pie			

15 RICE AND CHEESE CRUSTS

Crisp rice and cheese crust is another lower-fat alternative for savory quiches and pies.

As an alternative to traditional pastry crusts for savory pies, the rice and cheese crust provides a curious combination of taste, texture, and appearance as it reduces fat. I haven't yet taken it into the realm of legume or other grain crusts, but it doesn't seem too unlikely—a couscous crust or well-cooked wheat berry feels like a great idea, especially with a pinch of cumin seed?

BASIC RICE AND CHEESE CRUST

Yields one 8-inch (20-cm) crust

3 cups water
2/3 cup uncooked white rice, rinsed ·
1/4 cup freshly grated Parmesan cheese
1/8 teaspoon freshly ground sea salt
1/4 teaspoon freshly ground white pepper
1 lightly beaten egg white

Pour the water into a medium saucepan, bring to a boil, add the rice, and boil for 10 minutes. Drain through a metal hand sieve or colander. Pour about 2 inches (5 cm) of water into the same saucepan, bring to a boil, set the sieve of rice on top, cover, and let steam for 5 minutes. Transfer the rice to a bowl and immediately stir in the remaining ingredients, blending thoroughly. Place the mixture in a nonstick 9-inch (23-cm) pie pan. Press it firmly into the shape of a crust, starting at the center and moving out. Raise the sides about 1/2 inch (1.5 cm) above the pan rim. It's ready to be filled.

Tips and Hints

- The rice (or other grains or legumes) must be precooked so that the texture remains slightly undercooked. If the grain is mushy, it won't work well.
- Prevent your fingers from sticking to the rice mixture as you press it into the pie pan by having a bowl of cold water on the side and wetting your fingers.
- When it's time to add the filling, pour in two-thirds of the custard and let it partially bake. Then pour in the rest of the custard and finish baking. This helps to set the custard and provide a great-looking full-to-the-brim top. The Cornquichetador recipe that follows is a good example.

✛ CORNQUICHETADOR

JoAnne Davis sent me a recipe for one of her favorite vegetarian entrees, hoping I could lessen the fat. We changed the original's Bisquick to a rice and cheese crust, the eggs to liquid egg substitute, and reduced the cheese by 75 percent. But the thing I think I like the most about the new version is the corn purée in the quiche filling—a creamy texture with almost no fat and nice added nutrition. This is a super brunch or lunch dish.

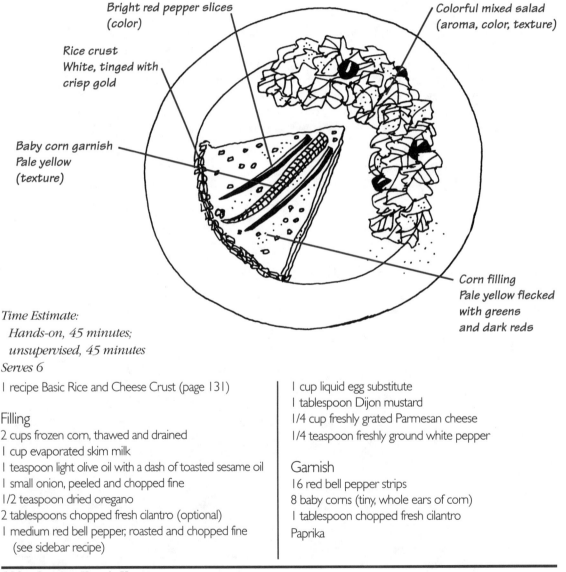

Bright red pepper slices (color)

Colorful mixed salad (aroma, color, texture)

Rice crust White, tinged with crisp gold

Baby corn garnish Pale yellow (texture)

Corn filling Pale yellow flecked with greens and dark reds

Time Estimate:
  Hands-on, 45 minutes;
  unsupervised, 45 minutes
Serves 6

1 recipe Basic Rice and Cheese Crust (page 131)

Filling
2 cups frozen corn, thawed and drained
1 cup evaporated skim milk
1 teaspoon light olive oil with a dash of toasted sesame oil
1 small onion, peeled and chopped fine
1/2 teaspoon dried oregano
2 tablespoons chopped fresh cilantro (optional)
1 medium red bell pepper, roasted and chopped fine
   (see sidebar recipe)

1 cup liquid egg substitute
1 tablespoon Dijon mustard
1/4 cup freshly grated Parmesan cheese
1/4 teaspoon freshly ground white pepper

Garnish
16 red bell pepper strips
8 baby corns (tiny, whole ears of corn)
1 tablespoon chopped fresh cilantro
Paprika

ROASTED RED PEPPERS

Position a cooking rack 2 inches (5 cm) from the broiling heat source. Cut the top and bottom off the peppers, deseed, and cut each one into 4 large flat pieces. Place on a baking sheet, skin side up, and press to flatten. Broil until blistered and black, about 10 minutes. Remove from the oven and immediately transfer to a paper bag. Seal well and let peppers steam for 20 minutes. Pinch-peel off the charred skin and you're ready to cook.

When you don't have time to roast, use the roasted sweet red peppers bottled in glass jars. They are very rustic with charred flecks on the flesh, but they taste wonderful and cost only a fraction more than roasting your own in season.

⬚ EXTRA MEAL

Make an extra rice and cheese crust and freeze it to use on another day, perhaps for the Ham Sandwich Pie recipe that follows. Press the extra crust into another 9-inch (23-cm) pie pan. Slip the crust, pan and all, into a gallon-size resealable freezer bag. Exhaust the air, place in the freezer, and use within 2 months.

Prepare the rice and cheese crust and press it into a 9-inch (23-cm) pan. Set aside.

The filling: In a food processor, purée the corn and 1/8 cup of the milk for 5 minutes. Strain, pressing hard to extract the liquid. Discard the solids and reserve the purée.

Preheat the oven to 350°F (180°C). Pour the

JoAnne Davis first served her corn quiche as a vegetarian entree for a family reunion. She was really hoping I could "fix it," because she is trying to lose weight and get relief from gallstones.

The ingredient that caught her eye in the revised Conquichetador was the roasted peppers, "I knew that these would be fantastic." JoAnne says the thing that helps her most in attaining her diet goals is studying the nutritional analysis of each recipe. She says she "can't ignore what's in black and white."

oil into a large skillet over medium heat and fry the onion and oregano for 5 minutes. Remove from the heat, stir in the cilantro and chopped roasted pepper, and sprinkle the filling over the prepared crust. In another bowl, combine the egg substitute, remaining evaporated milk, corn purée, mustard, Parmesan cheese, and white pepper. Pour this custard gently over the filling until it's just about 1/2 inch from the top. Reserve the remaining custard. Bake for 5 minutes. Pour in the rest of the custard and bake for 15 minutes.

Remove from the oven and gently lay the baby corns alternating with the red pepper strips around the top. Put back in the oven for 25 minutes, until the custard is just set. Remove from the oven and let stand 10 minutes before slicing. Garnish with the cilantro and a sprinkling of paprika and bring to the table to cut and serve.

Nutritional Profile per Serving			
	Classic	Springboard	Daily Value
Calories	272	218	
Calories from fat	135	36	
Fat (gm)	15	4	6%
Saturated fat (gm)	7	2	10%
Sodium (mg)	684	405	17%
Cholesterol (mg)	174	8	3%
Carbohydrates (gm)	22	33	11%
Dietary fiber (gm)	1	3	12%
Classic compared: Corn Quiche			

❧ Ham Sandwich Pie

I used a frozen rice and cheese crust to make this pie. A piece of it can go from a brunch buffet to a brown-bag lunch. It's filling, it's satisfying, and the flavors are everyone's favorites.

Time Estimate:
 Hands-on, 20 minutes;
 unsupervised, 55 minutes
Serves 6

Corn Custard
2 cups fresh or frozen whole-kernel corn
1 cup evaporated skim milk
1 cup liquid egg substitute

1 recipe Basic Rice and Cheese Crust (page 131)

Filling
2 ounces (50 gm) French baguette, sliced very thin
1/2 teaspoon Dijon mustard
1 ounce (25 g) Canadian bacon, sliced paper thin
1/4 cup freshly grated Parmesan cheese
1 cup roasted red peppers
Paprika

The custard: Preheat the oven to 350°F (180°C). In a food processor, purée the corn and 1/8 cup of the milk for 5 minutes. Strain, pressing to extract all the liquid. Mix the corn purée with the rest of the milk and the egg substitute. Pour half of the custard into the rice crust.

The filling: Spread half the bread slices on one side with mustard and place on top of the custard in the pie crust. Add a layer of Canadian bacon and a sprinkle of Parmesan cheese. Pour on half the remaining custard, all the roasted red peppers, and the remaining bread. Top with the remaining custard and Parmesan cheese and bake for 45 minutes. Remove from the oven and let stand for 10 minutes before slicing with a very sharp knife. Serve garnished with a sprinkle of paprika.

Nutritional Profile per Serving: Calories—149; calories from fat—18; fat (gm)—2 or 3% daily value; saturated fat (gm)—1; sodium (mg)—321; cholesterol (mg)—7; carbohydrates (gm)—22; dietary fiber (gm)—2

❖ DUNGAREE PIE

Now, this is a hearty beef pie that you can eat in your cowboy boots and most faded dungarees—at least that's what we infer from its colorful name, Dungaree Pie. It's based on a recipe sent to us from Lynda Otte. Lynda's new vocation as a full-time mom has made cooking her creative outlet. She says that family health problems have inspired her to "create healthy alternatives that taste good." Lynda reported that her taste testing of our springboard version "worked great. The substitution of a rice crust with the beans in the filling worked better than my pastry crust that included rice and beans." Thank you, Lynda.

Time Estimate:
  Hands-on, 25 minutes;
  unsupervised, 20 minutes
Serves 6

Filling

1 Rice and Cheese Crust (page 131), in a 9-inch (23-cm) pie dish
1/2 teaspoon light olive oil with a dash of toasted sesame oil
1/4 pound (100 g) extra lean ground beef
2 tablespoons low-sodium tomato paste
1/2 medium onion, peeled and chopped
1 clove garlic, bashed, peeled, and chopped
1 teaspoon ground cumin

1½ teaspoons chili powder
1/2 teaspoon dried basil
1/2 teaspoon dried oregano
1/2 cup chopped celery
1/2 large green bell pepper, seeded and chopped
1/2 pound (227 g) Roma tomatoes, peeled, seeded, and diced
1 cup low-sodium kidney beans, well rinsed
1 cup frozen corn
1/2 cup low-sodium beef stock (page 231)
1 tablespoon red wine vinegar
1/4 cup freshly grated Parmesan cheese

Preheat the oven to 350°F (180°C). Prepare the crust and set aside. Pour half the oil into a large high-sided skillet on high heat and brown the meat. Push it to one side of the pan, reduce the heat to medium, and cook the tomato paste until it darkens. Push the tomato sauce aside into the meat, add the remaining oil, and fry the onion and garlic until they start to wilt. Stir in the cumin, chili powder, basil, oregano, celery, green pepper, and tomatoes. Cover and simmer for 5 minutes. Add the beans, corn, beef stock, and vinegar, bring to a boil, and cook for 3 minutes. Pour the filling into the prepared rice and cheese crust, sprinkle evenly with the Parmesan cheese, and bake for 20 minutes. Cut into 6 wedges and serve.

Nutritional Profile per Serving: Calories—229; calories from fat—54; fat (gm)—6 or 9% daily value; saturated fat (gm)—3; sodium (mg)—373; cholesterol (mg)—18; carbohydrates (gm)—32; dietary fiber (gm)—5

✖ RUSSIAN SALMON PIE

Suzanne Thostensen, my senior food associate, took my basic Rice and Cheese Crust and gave it some more visual interest and texture with the addition of wild rice. This elegant salmon dish is a modification of coulibiac, an ultra-rich Russian recipe. When she served it for two artists (her husband, Jeff, and friend, Ed) these two discerning eyes proclaimed this pie, layered with pink salmon and green asparagus, tangy with lemon juice and fragrant with dill, "a feast to celebrate the spring!" Try it and you'll see what they mean.

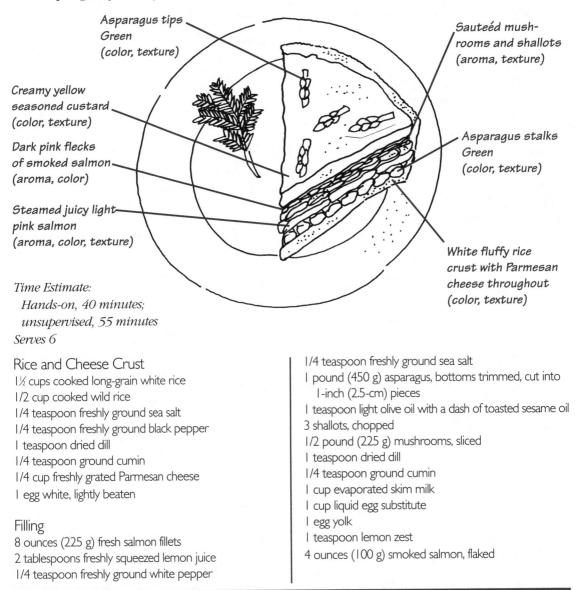

Asparagus tips
Green
(color, texture)

Sautéed mush-
rooms and shallots
(aroma, texture)

Creamy yellow
seasoned custard
(color, texture)

Dark pink flecks
of smoked salmon
(aroma, color)

Steamed juicy light
pink salmon
(aroma, color, texture)

Asparagus stalks
Green
(color, texture)

White fluffy rice
crust with Parmesan
cheese throughout
(color, texture)

Time Estimate:
  Hands-on, 40 minutes;
  unsupervised, 55 minutes
Serves 6

Rice and Cheese Crust
1½ cups cooked long-grain white rice
1/2 cup cooked wild rice
1/4 teaspoon freshly ground sea salt
1/4 teaspoon freshly ground black pepper
1 teaspoon dried dill
1/4 teaspoon ground cumin
1/4 cup freshly grated Parmesan cheese
1 egg white, lightly beaten

Filling
8 ounces (225 g) fresh salmon fillets
2 tablespoons freshly squeezed lemon juice
1/4 teaspoon freshly ground white pepper

1/4 teaspoon freshly ground sea salt
1 pound (450 g) asparagus, bottoms trimmed, cut into
    1-inch (2.5-cm) pieces
1 teaspoon light olive oil with a dash of toasted sesame oil
3 shallots, chopped
1/2 pound (225 g) mushrooms, sliced
1 teaspoon dried dill
1/4 teaspoon ground cumin
1 cup evaporated skim milk
1 cup liquid egg substitute
1 egg yolk
1 teaspoon lemon zest
4 ounces (100 g) smoked salmon, flaked

And now please meet my real-life heroine, **Suzanne Thostensen**. She has worked with me as my senior food associate for two books and three years of television programs. She's one of those people who is easy to honor: a talented cook who has worked in restaurants for many years and a well-respected caterer in the Skagit Valley area of Washington State.

"Many of the clients I've worked with don't know how to ask for lower-fat treatment of their food. People need to be encouraged or somehow informed how to ask for what they need."

For healthy eating to become truly popular, Suzanne sees the need for strong leadership. "Like clothes fashions, food is fickle. We need to always promote, model, and teach healthier cooking techniques to the people around us."

The rice crust: Combine all the ingredients, press into a 9-inch (23-cm) glass or ceramic pie dish, and set aside.

The filling: Pour water into a steamer pot and bring to a boil. Place the salmon fillets on a steamer tray, sprinkle with 1 teaspoon of the lemon juice, the pepper and salt, and steam for 5 minutes. The salmon will still be raw, but will finish cooking later in the pie. Remove from the heat and set aside. When cool, remove and discard the skin.

Place the asparagus pieces in a steamer tray, keeping the tips and stalks separate. Steam for 2 minutes; the stalks should be bright green and still crisp. Remove from the heat and set aside.

Pour the oil into a medium skillet on medium heat and fry the shallots until they start to wilt, about 2 minutes. Add the mushrooms, sprinkle with the remaining lemon juice, and fry for 5 minutes.

In a small bowl, combine the dill, cumin, milk, egg substitute, and egg yolk. Whisk well and set the custard mixture aside.

To assemble: Preheat the oven to 350°F (180°C). Put the steamed asparagus stalks in the bottom of the prepared rice crust and sprinkle with the lemon zest. Spread the salmon out on top. The cooked mushrooms and shallots are the next layer, with the flaked smoked salmon scattered on top. Pour the seasoned custard mixture over all. Garnish the top with the steamed asparagus tips. Bake until the custard is set, about 35 to 45 minutes. Remove from the oven and let sit for 10 minutes before cutting. Cut into wedges and present with a salad and bread on the side.

Nutritional Profile per Serving			
	Classic	**Springboard**	**Daily Value**
Calories	265	219	
Calories from fat	171	54	
Fat (gm)	19	6	9%
Saturated fat (gm)	6	3	15%
Sodium (mg)	734	523	22%
Cholesterol (mg)	240	61	20%
Carbohydrates (gm)	14	21	7%
Dietary fiber (gm)	1	2	8%
Classic compared: Fish Pie			

16
BREAD CRUSTS

A low-fat bread crust adds texture, nutrients and comfort, often as simple as hollowing out a large crusty loaf of bread.

There is something especially comforting about hot foods served in a crust: pies, pastries, sausage rolls, vol-au-vents, quiche, even potstickers and potato-topped casseroles, browned in the oven or under the grill. Perhaps it's the notion of sealed-in aromatic goodness just waiting to be released?

One such comforting tradition has its roots in New Orleans, where the mediatrice (peacemaker) was a loaf of bread hollowed out and filled with hot fried oysters. Presumably, late-night revelers brought this home as a gift of reconciliation.

Way back in 1960 I upgraded this idea for New Zealand television viewers, and made it even richer for the Galloping Gourmet television series in 1970. But during these Minimax days, I've used the basic idea of hollowed-out loaves of bread for a French rarebit, using Yukon Gold potatoes flavored with cheese in a long French bread loaf; in place of the puff pastry for Chicken Yankova; and as an alternative to the vol-au-vent pastry case for a wild mushroom in cream sauce appetizer. . . . And now for the latest peacemaker. There is almost no savory food that cannot be used as a filling.

Tips and Hints

- Find a local bakery that sells uncut bread loaves, especially the crusty long French sticks called baguettes (pronounced ba-GET). Also look for the fatter, shorter Italian breads, about 12 inches (30 cm) long and about 5 inches (13 cm) wide, plain or sour- dough. For a main dish, one loaf will serve 6 adults.
- Inspect the loaf to find its smooth side; this will form the hinge. You cut into the bread from the opposite side, stopping just before the smooth side. Now

A Baguette is not a small bag.

tunnel out the soft doughy interior, leaving about a 1/2 inch (0.75 to 1.5 cm) insulated wall. This depends upon how deeply fissured the crust is.
- Keep the crumbs for stuffing, adding to soups, or for bread crumbs.

☒ THE PEACEMAKER
(OYSTER AND BACON LOAF)

When Lorraine Haley sent me her Peacemaker recipe to "fix," I was already familiar with the recipe, as I had used it when I had a cooking television series in New Zealand in 1969. Lorraine reports that this lightened version is "delicious—even better than the original." I hope you agree.

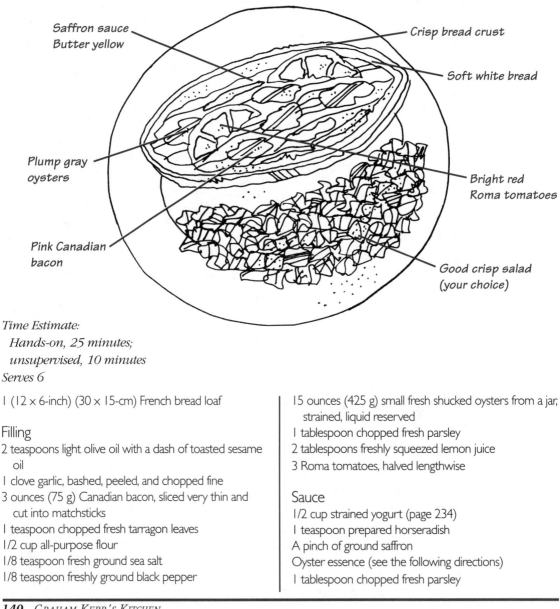

Saffron sauce
Butter yellow

Crisp bread crust

Soft white bread

Plump gray
oysters

Bright red
Roma tomatoes

Pink Canadian
bacon

Good crisp salad
(your choice)

Time Estimate:
  Hands-on, 25 minutes;
  unsupervised, 10 minutes
Serves 6

1 (12 x 6-inch) (30 x 15-cm) French bread loaf

Filling
2 teaspoons light olive oil with a dash of toasted sesame oil
1 clove garlic, bashed, peeled, and chopped fine
3 ounces (75 g) Canadian bacon, sliced very thin and cut into matchsticks
1 teaspoon chopped fresh tarragon leaves
1/2 cup all-purpose flour
1/8 teaspoon fresh ground sea salt
1/8 teaspoon freshly ground black pepper

15 ounces (425 g) small fresh shucked oysters from a jar, strained, liquid reserved
1 tablespoon chopped fresh parsley
2 tablespoons freshly squeezed lemon juice
3 Roma tomatoes, halved lengthwise

Sauce
1/2 cup strained yogurt (page 234)
1 teaspoon prepared horseradish
A pinch of ground saffron
Oyster essence (see the following directions)
1 tablespoon chopped fresh parsley

Lorraine Haley grew up in a family where her Irish mother cooked "very, very heavy food" and her own cooking favored fat-laden Southern U.S.A. food.

But after her mother died of a stroke, and her husband died unexpectedly of a heart attack, Lorraine was ready for a change. For the past 15 years she has cut back on fat: no frying, no salt, no "cooked-to-death vegetables." The result? Today Lorraine is 70 years old and, in her own words, "healthy as I could be."

Slice open the French bread loaf down one side, leaving a hinge on the least cracked side of the bread. Scoop out the soft center, leaving 1/2 inch (1.5 cm) of bread all around. (You should have about 6 ounces (170 g) of good bread crumb material that you can dry out, freeze, and use later.)

The filling: Pour the oil into a large skillet and fry the garlic on medium heat for 30 seconds. Add the bacon and fry for 1 minute. Stir in the tarragon and remove from the heat.

Preheat the oven to 450°F (230°C). Measure the flour, salt, and pepper into a plastic resealable bag and shake to mix well. Put about 3 oysters into the bag at a time, shake until well coated, then lay on top of the cooked bacon mixture. When all the oysters are coated and in the skillet, return to the heat and fry for 3 minutes on each side. Sprinkle with the parsley, lemon juice, and a small amount of pepper. Spoon into one side of the hollowed-out bread loaf.

In the same skillet, fry the tomatoes for 1 minute on each side—just to soak up the pan juices. Place the tomatoes on top of the oysters, cut side down. Top the filled loaf with its lid, wrap with aluminum foil quite tightly, making sure it's covered well, place on a baking sheet, and bake for 10 minutes. Open the foil and bake for 5 minutes to crisp the bread.

The sauce: While the loaf is baking, deglaze the skillet with the reserved oyster juices, making sure to scrape up any bits from the bottom and sides of the pan. Strain this into a small bowl and mix together with the strained yogurt, horseradish, and saffron. It should be the same color as mayonnaise.

Remove the loaf from the oven and place on a carving board. Open the bread lid, pour in the sauce, and close. Cut into 6 slices and serve on individual plates, garnished with the parsley. It can be served warm or cold.

✂ EXTRA MEAL

When you make the Peacemaker, prepare two, leaving out the tomatoes and the sauce in the second one. Slice the one you are going to freeze in 6 pieces, cutting not quite through the bottom. Place a piece of wax paper between each slice, wrap tightly in plastic, and place in a resealable freezer bag. The frozen Peacemaker should be used within 2 months. When you are ready to use it, let it thaw in the refrigerator. Wrap the thawed Peacemaker in foil and bake at 300°F (150°C) for 1 hour. If you are using just one serving slice, bake it for 15 minutes.

Nutritional Profile per Serving			
	Classic	**Springboard**	**Daily Value**
Calories	600	315	
Calories from fat	297	54	
Fat (gm)	33	6	9%
Saturated fat (gm)	11	2	10%
Sodium (mg)	1055	774	32%
Cholesterol (mg)	152	27	22%
Carbohydrates (gm)	49	45	15%
Dietary fiber (gm)	3	2	8%
Classic compared: The Peacemaker, Oyster and Bacon Loaf			

✖ PIZZA WITH ROASTED EGGPLANT AND PEPPER*

You've seen him profiled on the public broadcasting science series Nova, *interviewed by Bill Moyers, and now here's his bread crust recipe: pizza! Dean Ornish, M.D., serves this pizza at his Preventive Medicine Research Institute in Sausalito, California. Dr. Ornish has long held my respect for his clinical research over the past 17 years, demonstrating—for the first time—that lifestyle changes may begin to reverse coronary heart disease. The recipe was developed by the Institute's chef, Jean-Marc Fullsack. At 377 calories and 2 grams of fat per serving, it's an incredible contrast to the classic pepperoni pizza's 615 calories per serving and 48 grams of fat.*

Time Estimate:
  Hands-on, 35 minutes;
  unsupervised, 20 minutes
Serves 8

Dough
1 tablespoon active dry yeast
4 cups organic unbleached all-purpose flour
1½ cups warm water
1 teaspoon honey
1/2 teaspoon salt

Pizza Sauce
1 cup sliced roasted onion
1 cup tomato purée
1/8 teaspoon salt (optional)
1/4 teaspoon sugar (optional)
1 teaspoon dried thyme
1 teaspoon chopped fresh basil
1 teaspoon dried oregano
1 teaspoon finely chopped garlic
1 teaspoon freshly ground black pepper

Topping
1 medium eggplant, sliced thick
1 red bell pepper, seeded and sliced into 4 large flat pieces
2 tablespoons chopped fresh oregano
1 tablespoon chopped garlic
6 ounces grated nonfat mozzarella cheese

The dough: In a large bowl, mix the yeast, 4 teaspoons of the flour, the warm water, and honey. Cover and let rest for 30 minutes in a warm place. Beat in the rest of the flour and salt. Turn the dough out on a floured surface and knead for about 10 minutes, or until smooth and elastic, sprinkling with a little more flour if the dough seems excessively sticky. Cover and let sit in a warm place for 1 to 1½ hours, until the dough doubles in volume. Punch down and roll out onto a 12- to 16-inch (30- to 40-cm) pizza pan.

The pizza sauce: In a small saucepan on medium heat combine all the ingredients and heat through. Remove from the heat and set aside.

The topping: Arrange a rack about 4 inches (10 cm) from the broiler heating element. Place the red pepper pieces skin side up on a baking sheet along with the eggplant slices and broil until the pepper's skin is blistered and blackened, about 10 minutes. Remove from the oven. When cool enough to handle, peel and roughly chop the eggplant. Slice the red pepper into thin strips.

Preheat the oven to 450°F (250°C). Spread a thin layer of pizza sauce on the rolled-out pizza dough. Sprinkle evenly with the topping ingredients, finishing with the cheese on top. Bake in the preheated oven until the crust is brown, about 15 to 20 minutes.

Nutritional Profile per Serving: Calories—377; calories from fat—18; fat (gm)—2 or 3% daily value; saturated fat (gm)—0.4; sodium (mg)—599; cholesterol (mg)—1; carbohydrates (gm)—77; dietary fiber (gm)—10

* Recipe by Jean-Marc Fullsack; copyright Dean Ornish, M.D.

PAISANO SANDWICH

The Italian submarine sandwich is indisputably fast food: whipped up in minutes at delicatessens around the United States as layers of Italian ham and cheese drenched in vinaigrette. Fast, perhaps, but not your first choice on a low-fat diet.

Enter Susan Modica. She is a busy woman: between her three loves—art, animals, and work—she's often too tired to even "flick on my Cuisinart." But she does enjoy getting in the kitchen for some creative cookery and presenting her husband with a great dish—and Susan thinks this recipe is "wonderful." So this one's for all you Italian submarine sandwich lovers and too-little-time-to-cook people out there—take heart!

Time Estimate: Hands-on, 30 minutes
Serves 4

1 (1-pound) (450-gm) Italian bread loaf
1 clove garlic, smashed and peeled
1/2 recipe Garbanzo Cheese (page 116)
1 teaspoon chopped fresh basil
1/4 teaspoon freshly ground black pepper
1 teaspoon light olive oil with a dash of toasted sesame oil
1 ounce (25 g) Canadian bacon, cut into small chunks
10 ounces (280 g), fresh spinach washed, stemmed, and cut into thin strips
2 tablespoons balsamic vinegar
2 Roma tomatoes, sliced
10 to 12 fresh basil leaves
2 tablespoons Parmesan cheese

Cut the bread in half lengthwise and pull out a little of the soft middle. Place under the broiler to toast lightly on the cut side. Remove from the oven and rub lightly with the smashed garlic clove.

Mix the garbanzo cheese with the basil and pepper.

Heat the oil in a large skillet, add the bacon, and fry until it starts to brown. Add the spinach, cooking and tossing until it wilts. Stir in the vinegar and remove from the heat.

Assemble and serve: Spread the garbanzo cheese mixture on both sides of the prepared bread. Set under the broiler to warm the cheese. Remove from the oven and cover one side with the spinach mixture, sliced tomatoes, basil leaves, and Parmesan cheese. Close the sandwich and press down to distribute the flavors. Slice into four pieces and dig in!

Nutritional Profile per Serving: Calories—368; calories from fat—54; fat (gm)—6 or 9% daily value; saturated fat (gm)—2; sodium (mg)—727; cholesterol (mg)—10; carbohydrates (gm)—61; dietary fiber (gm)—6

✖ TORTA RUSTICA

Jenny Steinle says this dish—layers of colorful roasted vegetables and egg custard in a bread crust—is beautiful enough to present as a centerpiece at an informal luncheon, but so good chilled that you can easily take it along on a picnic outing. While the preparation is a bit long, you can make it ahead of time. It keeps well in the refrigerator for 4 days.

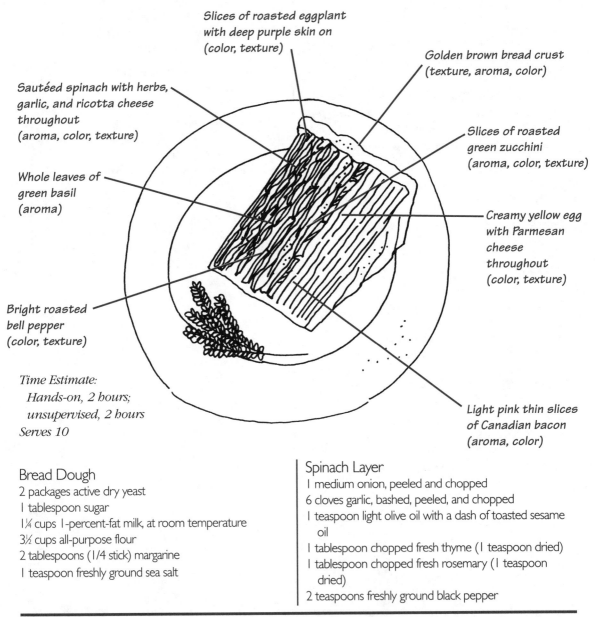

Slices of roasted eggplant with deep purple skin on (color, texture)

Golden brown bread crust (texture, aroma, color)

Sautéed spinach with herbs, garlic, and ricotta cheese throughout (aroma, color, texture)

Slices of roasted green zucchini (aroma, color, texture)

Whole leaves of green basil (aroma)

Creamy yellow egg with Parmesan cheese throughout (color, texture)

Bright roasted bell pepper (color, texture)

Time Estimate:
Hands-on, 2 hours;
unsupervised, 2 hours
Serves 10

Light pink thin slices of Canadian bacon (aroma, color)

Bread Dough
2 packages active dry yeast
1 tablespoon sugar
1¼ cups 1-percent-fat milk, at room temperature
3½ cups all-purpose flour
2 tablespoons (1/4 stick) margarine
1 teaspoon freshly ground sea salt

Spinach Layer
1 medium onion, peeled and chopped
6 cloves garlic, bashed, peeled, and chopped
1 teaspoon light olive oil with a dash of toasted sesame oil
1 tablespoon chopped fresh thyme (1 teaspoon dried)
1 tablespoon chopped fresh rosemary (1 teaspoon dried)
2 teaspoons freshly ground black pepper

1 (10-ounce) (300-g) package frozen chopped spinach, thawed and squeezed dry
Juice of 1/2 lemon
1 (15-ounce) (425-g) carton part-skim ricotta cheese

Custard
2 cups liquid egg substitute
1/4 cup freshly grated Parmesan cheese

Roasted Vegetables
1 large eggplant, sliced lengthwise into 1/4-inch (0.75-cm) slices

2 zucchini, sliced lengthwise into 1/4-inch (0.75-cm) slices
1 teaspoon light olive oil with a dash of toasted sesame oil
2 large red bell peppers, roasted (see page 133 or use roasted peppers from the jar)
1/2 pound (225 g) Canadian bacon, sliced whisper thin
1 cup fresh whole basil leaves
1 beaten egg white

The bread dough: In a small bowl, mix the yeast, half the sugar, and half the milk and let stand for 5 minutes, or until creamy.

Put 3 cups of the flour into a large mixing bowl and cut in the margarine with a knife or fork. Make a well, add the yeast mixture, the rest of the milk, sugar, and salt. Work together, first with a spatula and then your hands, until the dough forms a cohesive mass. Turn out onto a floured surface and knead until smooth and elastic, about 10 minutes, adding flour as necessary to prevent sticking. Place in a greased bowl, cover with a towel, and let rise about 1 hour, or until doubled. Punch down and let rise again.

The spinach mixture: In a large skillet on medium heat fry the onion and garlic in the oil for 2 minutes. Add the thyme, rosemary, and pepper and fry until the onion is translucent, about 5 minutes. Remove from the heat and stir in the spinach and lemon juice. Fold in the ricotta cheese and set aside.

The custard: Preheat the oven to 350°F (180°C). Spray two 9-inch (23-cm) nonstick pie pans with a little vegetable oil cooking spray. Pour 1 cup of the liquid egg substitute into each pan and sprinkle each with 2 tablespoons of the Parmesan cheese. Bake until the egg sets, about 5 to 10 minutes. Remove from the oven and let cool. Slide a rubber spatula around the edges and underneath to release the cooked custard rounds from the pans onto plastic wrap or wax paper. Set aside.

The roasted vegetables: Adjust an oven rack 2 inches (5 cm) below the heating element and preheat the broiler. Lightly rub the surface of the eggplant and zucchini with the oil, lay the slices on a roasting rack, and broil until they darken, about 5 to 10 minutes on each side. Remove from the oven and set aside.

To assemble: Preheat the oven to 350°F (180°C) and spray a 9-inch (23-cm) springform pan with vegetable oil cooking spray. On a lightly floured surface, roll the bread dough out into a circle that is large enough to line the prepared pan and extend 2 to 3 inches (5 to 8 cm) over the edge. Transfer the dough to the pan, making sure it's pressed into the bottom edges. Layer in this order: half the Canadian bacon, half the custard, half the roasted zucchini, half the bell pepper, half the basil leaves, half the spinach filling, half the roasted eggplant. Then repeat with the remaining halves.

Close the top by taking hold of an edge of the dough, stretching it away, pulling up toward you, and bringing it over the center

And now for someone completely different: **Jenny Steinle** has worked with me as my second food assistant for the food in this book and my most recent public broadcasting television series. Although only in her early twenties, Jenny is an excellent cook with a palate well beyond her years.

Jenny is a recent graduate of culinary school, where she says she wasn't taught a great deal on low-fat cooking. I asked her if her personal food style had changed after our work together. "Yes," she smiled. "But it's been a slow process for me since I was so used to the French cuisine I was taught in school. I realize now that less can be more, as long as it has the freshest ingredients."

Nutritional Profile per Serving			
	Classic	**Springboard**	**Daily Value**
Calories	663	438	
Calories from fat	279	90	
Fat (gm)	31	10	15%
Saturated fat (gm)	13	4	20%
Sodium (mg)	1030	634	31%
Cholesterol (mg)	232	27	9%
Carbohydrates (gm)	44	64	21%
Dietary fiber (gm)	4	6	24%
Classic compared: Classic Torta Rustica			

of the filling. Then take hold of an edge about 3 inches (8 cm) away and repeat to overlap onto the first part. Repeat the process four or five times around the pan to create a series of overlapping folds across the top, crimping with your fingers to hold the edges together. Secure the tip of the last fold by twisting and pinching the center piece of dough in order to seal. To make an air vent you may either make a small round incision in the top's center or slits around the perimeter of the top. Cover lightly with foil, and bake for 1 hour. Turn the heat up to 400°F (205°C) and bake for another 30 minutes. Remove the foil, brush the top with the beaten egg white, and continue baking for 30 more minutes—the top will be nice and brown. Remove from the oven and let cool in the pan for 2 hours. Then place in the refrigerator overnight to let the layers set.

To serve: Run a knife along the outer edges to loosen and then release the springform sides. Slice the torta into 10 wedges and serve with a chilled glass of de-alcoholized wine and fresh fruit.

Graham's favorite part of this recipe is the assembly . . .

17

STACK 'N STEAM

Layers of steamer trays cook everything from side vegetables to main dishes to textural perfection, all at the same time.

Cooking and storing cookware in the modest galley of my 36-foot sailboat is especially challenging. This explains how I became inspired by the vision of a stack 'n steam cooking system. Here you can take advantage of one stovetop burner and steam various levels of vegetables, fish, and poultry, which all require differing lengths of cooking, all at the same time. The steaming racks that I eventually was able to design and have manufactured are the one piece of equipment we take everywhere and use all the time—at sea and at home.

The stack 'n steam is the best way to cook the freshest

and best vegetables you can find in season, beautifully garnished and seasoned with the highest-quality ingredients. Believe me, please, that you
will be delighted with your stack-and-steam meals, gaining a variety of
vegetable colors, textures, aromas, micronutrients, and delicious mouth-
watering taste experiences.

Tips and Hints
- Cut vegetables into even-sized pieces according to their degree of density and fiber.
- Group vegetables with similar cooking times on the same tray.
- Season each vegetable just the way you like it. Experiment with a wide
  array of citrus juices, fresh herbs like lemon thyme and
  rosemary, spices like nutmeg and cardamon.
- Always have your steaming water at a
  full boil when you start cooking.
- Remember to start a timer when
  you commence steaming, removing
  trays of more quickly cooked
  vegetables when they're
  ready, leaving the others
  to continue the process.

SAUNA

SMOKED TURKEY–STUFFED PEPPERS LAMBERT

Many people don't think of steaming for their main dish, but it works perfectly here. Jolynn Lambert came up with a wonderful version of stuffed peppers that made even me overcome a long-held prejudice. If you've been persecuted by awful stuffed pepper recipes, please don't miss out . . . this one is well worth the effort.

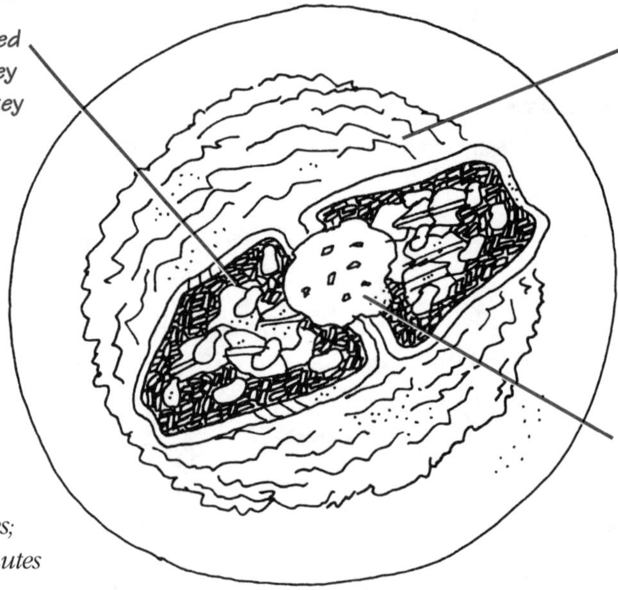

Steamed peppers stuffed with white rice, red kidney beans, and smoked turkey
Bright red, white, pinks, green flecks
(color, texture, aroma)
Steamed kale garnished with flecks of vivid red and white
Deep green
(texture, color)
Cilantro yogurt sauce
White with flecks of green and yellow
(texture, color)

Time Estimate:
Hands-on, 20 minutes; unsupervised, 25 minutes
Serves 4

4 large red bell peppers

Stuffing

1 teaspoon light olive oil with a dash of toasted sesame oil
1/2 cup finely chopped onion
2 cloves garlic, bashed, peeled, and chopped
1/4 cup finely chopped celery
1/4 cup finely chopped jicama
1 jalapeño pepper, seeded and diced fine
1/2 teaspoon ground cumin
Cayenne pepper to taste (optional)
1 cup uncooked long-grain white rice, rinsed
2 cups low-sodium chicken stock (page 231)
8 ounces (225 g) smoked turkey, cut into 1/4-inch (0.75-ml) dice
1/2 cup low-sodium red kidney beans, drained and rinsed

Vegetable

1 (10-ounce or 300-g) bunch kale, trimmed and rinsed
2 tablespoons chopped red bell pepper trimmings (from above)
2 tablespoons chopped jicama
1/8 teaspoon freshly ground sea salt
1/8 teaspoon freshly ground black pepper
1/4 teaspoon chopped fresh cilantro

Sauce

1/2 cup strained yogurt (page 234)
1 tablespoon chopped fresh cilantro
1/8 teaspoon freshly ground white pepper
1 tablespoon freshly grated Parmesan cheese

Garnish

4 teaspoons freshly grated Parmesan cheese
Paprika
4 teaspoons chopped fresh cilantro

Jolynn Lambert and her husband, Ron, are both into health and fitness. Neither of them has any health problems to combat; they just want to cook low-fat as part of their overall lifestyle. However, they found that many low-fat, low-cholesterol cookbooks were "so bland." Jolynn says she searches for new aroma, color, and texture combinations that can make her cooking exciting.

She urges people to "put aside their biases" and go for the gusto in trying new ingredients. "I loved butter, used to put it on anything. Now I eat bread plain, and taste the food instead of piling stuff on top. You just have to make the decision to change in your own mind."

EXTRA MEAL

Make an extra recipe of the pepper stuffing and freeze it to use in the recipe for stuffed chard leaves that follows. It can be frozen in a gallon-size resealable freezer bag. Flatten the bag, letting out the air in the process. Label, date, and freeze flat. Use within 3 months.

WOULD YOU KNOW A JICAMA IF YOU SAW ONE?

They're sold in the stores as whole light-brown tubers, about 6 inches (15 cm) in diameter. When you cut inside you find the treasure: a crunchy white flesh, just slightly sweet, quite similar to water chestnuts. Jicama is a good source of vitamin C, a delightful addition to your fresh salads. They'll stay stored in your refrigerator for up to 2 weeks.

Cut the tops off the peppers and slice off just enough at the bottom to allow them to stand up straight, reserving the trimmed scraps for use in the Vegetable (see above). Remove the seeds and core.

The stuffing: Pour the oil into a high-sided skillet on medium heat and fry the onion, garlic, celery, jicama, and jalapeño for 2 minutes. Stir in the cumin, the cayenne pepper, rice, and stock. Bring to a boil, cover, lower the heat, and simmer for 15 minutes. Stir in the turkey and the beans, remove from the heat, and set aside.

Put at least 3 inches (8 cm) of water in your steamer pot and bring to a boil. Stuff the bell peppers, pressing the stuffing down firmly with the back of a spoon and filling completely to the top. Put the peppers on the steamer tray, cover, and steam for 15 minutes. Remove from the heat and set aside.

The vegetable: Layer all the vegetable ingredients into another steamer tray, with the kale on the bottom, bell pepper, jicama, salt, pepper, and cilantro on top. Stack over the stuffed pepper tray, return the steamer to the heat, and steam for 5 minutes.

The sauce: Measure the yogurt, cilantro, pepper, and Parmesan into a bowl and mix well.

To serve: Split the cooked stuffed peppers down the middle from top to bottom and place on a bed of the steamed kale on individual serving plates. Top with the rest of the steamed vegetables, ladle sauce over everything, and garnish with a sprinkling of the Parmesan cheese, paprika, and cilantro.

Nutritional Profile per Serving			
	Classic	**Springboard**	**Daily Value**
Calories	311	420	
Calories from fat	153	45	
Fat (gm)	17	5	8%
Saturated fat (gm)	8	2	10%
Sodium (mg)	537	905	38%
Cholesterol (mg)	156	27	9%
Carbohydrates (gm)	24	69	23%
Dietary fiber (gm)	4	7	28%
Classic compared: Green Peppers Stuffed with Meat and Rice			

STUFFED SWISS CHARD LEAVES

The stuffing for this delicious meal comes from the preceding recipe for stuffed peppers Lambert. I hope you like Swiss chard as much as I do: not only are its colors a wonderful addition to your plate, it is also a terrific source of vitamins A and C and the mineral iron.

Time Estimate:
Hands-on, 20 minutes;
unsupervised, 45 minutes
Serves 4

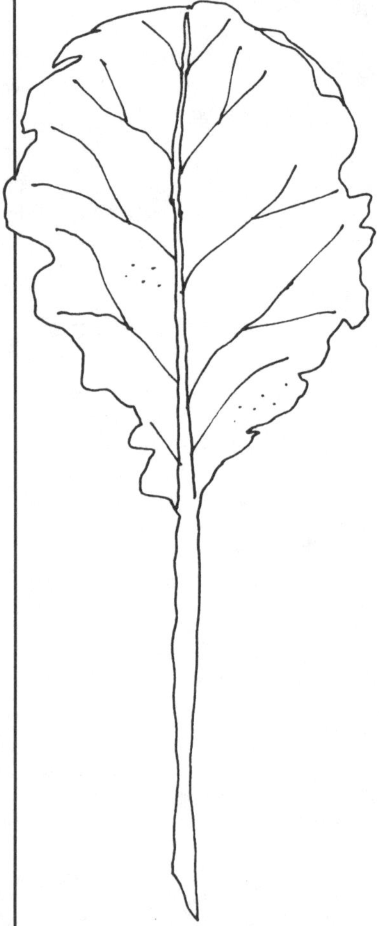

2 bunches Swiss chard, washed and trimmed
1 recipe stuffing from Smoked Turkey–Stuffed Peppers Lambert, thawed if frozen
1 (11-ounce) (300-g) can low-sodium vegetable juice
2 tablespoons chopped fresh parsley

Preheat the oven to 350°F (180°C). Steam the Swiss chard leaves for 4 minutes and rinse with cold water. Lay 2 of the steamed leaves in a dry 1-cup measuring cup, overlapping each other. Pack with about 3/4 cup of the stuffing mixture. Fold the ends together and transfer to an 8 x 8-inch (20 x 20-cm) casserole dish. Pour the vegetable juice over the bundles and bake for 45 minutes. Serve with a scattering of the parsley.

Nutritional Profile per Serving: Calories—349; calories from fat—36; fat (gm)—4 or 6% daily value; saturated fat (gm)—0.9; sodium (mg)—842; cholesterol (mg)—23; carbohydrates (gm)—59; dietary fiber (gm)—5

✖ STEAMED APPLES JULIE

"I have always enjoyed cooking, and I'm afraid my poor husband shows it," writes Julie Faulk. "I've won many ribbons at the fair here for my cookies. But I've had to learn to cook all over again since my triple-bypass surgery two years ago."

Julie says that "everyone who tried these apples thought they had lots of calories. The maple syrup is a marvelous idea for flavor— my husband went wild over it." Because Julie is a borderline diabetic, she substituted brown Sweet 'n Low and nutmeg in the yogurt topping. Julie also had the great idea of toasting the nuts to give them extra flavor, making them in big batches, and freezing them.

Time Estimate:
 Hands-on, 15 minutes;
 unsupervised, 15 minutes
Serves 4

4 Jonagold or Granny Smith apples
2 tablespoons chopped walnuts
1/4 cup raisins
4 gingersnap cookies or graham crackers, roughly
  crushed
1/2 teaspoon ground cinnamon
1/4 teaspoon ground allspice
1/2 cup strained yogurt (page 234)
1 tablespoon maple syrup
1 teaspoon vanilla extract
Freshly grated nutmeg

Wash the apples and cut off the stem ends. Scoop out the pulp, hollowing each apple about 3/4 of its length, making sure to get all the core, and leaving a good 1/2 inch (1.5 cm) of sturdy wall. Keep the pulp and discard the core and seeds.

Preheat the oven to 350°F (180°C). Toast the walnuts on a baking sheet until lightly brown, about 10 minutes.

Pour about 2 inches (5 cm) of water into your steamer pot and bring to a boil. In a small bowl, mix the reserved apple pulp, raisins, crushed gingersnaps, cinnamon, allspice, and toasted walnuts. Stuff the hollowed-out apples, packing firmly, and place in a steamer tray. Stack into the steamer pot, cover, and steam until soft, about 15 minutes. Remove from the tray and let cool for 10 minutes.

In a small bowl mix the yogurt, maple syrup, and vanilla.

To serve: Transfer the apples to serving plates, top with a dollop of the creamy yogurt topping and a sprinkle of the fragrant nutmeg, and enjoy!

Nutritional Profile per Serving: Calories—262; calories from fat—4; fat (gm)—4 or 6% daily value; saturated fat (gm)—1; sodium (mg)—91; cholesterol (mg)—1; carbohydrates (gm)—55; dietary fiber (gm)—6

✖ TWIN FILLETS OF ORANGE ROUGHY AND SALMON

Here is a synergy in the stack 'n steamer: all the juices steaming off the fish, basil, and vegetables are captured in the sauce below and all the flavor of rosemary and cumin in the sauce below is captured by the fish! My thanks to Diana Armstrong for this sumptuous dinner for two.

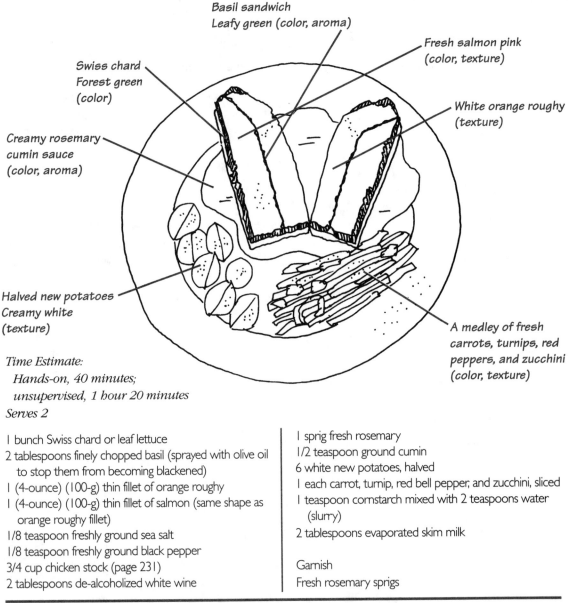

Basil sandwich
Leafy green (color, aroma)

Fresh salmon pink
(color, texture)

Swiss chard
Forest green
(color)

White orange roughy
(texture)

Creamy rosemary
cumin sauce
(color, aroma)

Halved new potatoes
Creamy white
(texture)

A medley of fresh
carrots, turnips, red
peppers, and zucchini
(color, texture)

Time Estimate:
  Hands-on, 40 minutes;
  unsupervised, 1 hour 20 minutes
Serves 2

1 bunch Swiss chard or leaf lettuce
2 tablespoons finely chopped basil (sprayed with olive oil to stop them from becoming blackened)
1 (4-ounce) (100-g) thin fillet of orange roughy
1 (4-ounce) (100-g) thin fillet of salmon (same shape as orange roughy fillet)
1/8 teaspoon freshly ground sea salt
1/8 teaspoon freshly ground black pepper
3/4 cup chicken stock (page 231)
2 tablespoons de-alcoholized white wine

1 sprig fresh rosemary
1/2 teaspoon ground cumin
6 white new potatoes, halved
1 each carrot, turnip, red bell pepper, and zucchini, sliced
1 teaspoon cornstarch mixed with 2 teaspoons water (slurry)
2 tablespoons evaporated skim milk

Garnish
Fresh rosemary sprigs

Originally from South Africa, **Diana Armstrong** teaches cooking both nationally and internationally, has published a cookbook and coauthored a nutritional analysis software program. Diana believes that it is necessary for people to "change their wants" rather than "want to change." It is with this in mind that she coordinates and selects classes taught at University Synergy, so that low-fat cooking can become part of an exciting, colorful, and realistic everyday routine for the patients and community members who attend the school.

Diana is a self-professed "herb nut" and a "color-in-cooking freak." She favors pure simplicity. "One day we are all going to wake up and really taste the pure deliciousness of single foods. We'll ponder on the flavor of a carrot as though it were a truffle, but until then, let's make the mélange of low-fat foods into an evening of fireworks!"

I want to personally thank Diana for her work in editing the professional chef recipes that were contributed to this book—a synergistic collaborator and a charming energetic new friend indeed.

The day before, choose the best leaves from the Swiss chard and blanch for 30 seconds in boiling water. Lay between 2 kitchen towels and press down to remove excess moisture.

Spread the basil on one side of the orange roughy fillet and top with the salmon fillet, with the basil spread between fish. Lay out a large piece of plastic wrap, spread overlapping blanched Swiss chard leaves evenly on top, and set the fish in the middle. Sprinkle with salt and pepper. First wrap the fish in the Swiss chard leaves and then in the plastic wrap. Refrigerate for at least 1 hour or preferably overnight so that the parcel of fish becomes firm and easier to handle.

In the bottom of a steamer, pour the chicken stock, wine, rosemary, and cumin. On the first steamer rack, place the prepared fish and surround with the potatoes, carrots, and turnips, and put it in your steamer pot. On the second steamer rack, place the red pepper and zucchini and put that on top of the first steamer rack. (If you don't have a stack 'n steam, put all the vegetables around the fish on one layer.) Cover the entire combination and cook slowly on medium heat. When the juices have begun to simmer, reduce the heat to low and steam very gently for 10 to 15 minutes. Switch off the heat and set aside, still covered, for 10 minutes.

Remove the two stacks from the steamer and set aside. Now make the sauce. Remove the rosemary from the pan juices and return the pan to the heat. Stir in the cornstarch slurry and bring to a boil, stirring constantly until thickened, about 1 minute. Remove from the heat and gently stir in the evaporated skim milk.

To Serve: Pool the sauce onto two warm plates. Cut the fish into four serving pieces and place carefully on the sauce, surrounded by the vegetables. Garnish with the fresh rosemary.

Nutritional Profile per Serving			
	Classic	**Springboard**	**Daily Value**
Calories	986	488	
Calories from fat	639	36	
Fat (gm)	71	4	6%
Saturated fat (gm)	41	1	5%
Sodium (mg)	966	490	20%
Cholesterol (mg)	284	65	22%
Carbohydrates (gm)	14	82	27%
Dietary fiber (gm)	2	10	40%
Classic compared: Salmon with White Wine Sauce, Truffles, and Madeira			

18

ROASTED VEGETABLES

A few minutes under the broiler or on the grill transforms familiar vegetables into smoky-sweet tasting sensations.

When I eat out and have to order from a menu, my eye flicks over the pages to find evidence of roasted or broiled vegetables.

There is something earthy and real about the way natural sugars caramelize in a hot oven or under a radiant grill. Add some robust herbs and each vegetable begins to transfer its flavor oils to the common good. Wow, that's eating!

Tips and Hints

- Use only fresh, seasonal, local vegetables. Cut them into even sizes, according to fiber and density. A good start is with cored and seeded sweet bell peppers, eggplant, zucchini, sweet onions, green and red tomatoes, fennel bulbs, sweet potatoes.
- Lay fresh herbs and spices on top: lemon thyme, rosemary, garlic, gingerroot, cardamom, cumin.
- Garnish with fresh herbs: basil, mint, cilantro, a dusting of Parmesan cheese and black pepper, even a sprinkle of vinegar—ah, I can smell and see and taste it now!

Graham earns his "roasted vegetable" badge.

✜ LINGUINI WITH SCALLOPS, SHRIMP, AND ROASTED VEGETABLES

You can thank Lars Ryssdol for this lovely combination of ingredients for pasta—they were selected based on the Food Preference List he sent me. The thing Lars likes about roasting vegetables is "the metabolic change that happens. Specifically with garlic, roasting changes the acids to sugars, takes away the bitterness, adding sweetness and carmelization." The whole dish is just super (Lars has even cooked it twice!).

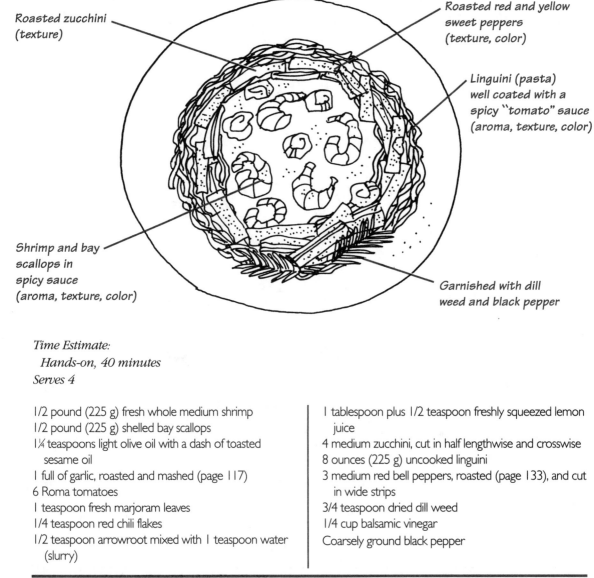

Roasted zucchini (texture)

Roasted red and yellow sweet peppers (texture, color)

Linguini (pasta) well coated with a spicy "tomato" sauce (aroma, texture, color)

Shrimp and bay scallops in spicy sauce (aroma, texture, color)

Garnished with dill weed and black pepper

Time Estimate:
  Hands-on, 40 minutes
Serves 4

1/2 pound (225 g) fresh whole medium shrimp
1/2 pound (225 g) shelled bay scallops
1¼ teaspoons light olive oil with a dash of toasted sesame oil
1 full of garlic, roasted and mashed (page 117)
6 Roma tomatoes
1 teaspoon fresh marjoram leaves
1/4 teaspoon red chili flakes
1/2 teaspoon arrowroot mixed with 1 teaspoon water (slurry)

1 tablespoon plus 1/2 teaspoon freshly squeezed lemon juice
4 medium zucchini, cut in half lengthwise and crosswise
8 ounces (225 g) uncooked linguini
3 medium red bell peppers, roasted (page 133), and cut in wide strips
3/4 teaspoon dried dill weed
1/4 cup balsamic vinegar
Coarsely ground black pepper

"Stop, look, and listen" is how **Lars Ryssdol** describes his cooking style. "I want to apply my tastes to what I see and hear and find." Lars has no health reasons for cooking low fat; he just generally approves of that lifestyle. "I just try to omit fat and include flavor." Lars told me about adding dried cherries to a pork, onion, and mushroom dish he did—what a bright note! Lars also does a pesto from the dried cherries to serve with grilled meats—a great idea.

Peel, clean, and remove the tails from the shrimp. Remove the muscle from the scallops (if taken whole from the shell) and pat the scallops dry with a paper towel.

Pour 1/2 teaspoon of the oil into a small skillet and fry the garlic for 1 minute. Place the tomatoes in a plastic bag and press gently until squished. Add the tomatoes, marjoram, and red chili flakes to the garlic and cook, covered, for 8 minutes. Remove from the heat and mash through a sieve—a nice, spicy, marinara sauce. Transfer to a saucepan, bring to a boil, remove from the heat, stir in the arrowroot slurry, return to the heat, and bring to a boil to thicken and clear, about 30 seconds. Stir in 1 tablespoon of the lemon juice and keep the sauce warm.

Lay the zucchini on a roasting rack, skin side down, and broil for 10 minutes. Flip them over and broil 3 more minutes. Remove from the oven, cut in half again lengthwise, cover, and keep warm.

Cook the linguine according to package directions just before you go to the next step. Drain and keep warm.

Pour 1/2 teaspoon of the oil into a large skillet and get it smoking hot. Add the shrimp, toss until an even pink throughout, then transfer to a plate. Pour 1/4 teaspoon of the oil into the same skillet on high heat and fry the scallops for 1 minute. Add the cooked shrimp, 1/2 teaspoon of the dill weed, the remaining 1/2 teaspoon lemon juice, and the roasted pepper strips. Toss well.

To serve: Make a small linguine nest in the middle of each serving plate. Arrange the scallops and shrimp inside and the vegetables around the outside. Spoon an even amount of sauce over each serving and sprinkle with the remaining 1/4 teaspoon dill weed, the balsamic vinegar, and freshly ground pepper.

Nutritional Profile per Serving			
	Classic	**Springboard**	**Daily Value**
Calories	748	428	
Calories from fat	396	45	
Fat (gm)	44	5	8%
Saturated fat (gm)	13	1	5%
Sodium (mg)	783	235	10%
Cholesterol (mg)	129	71	24%
Carbohydrates (gm)	51	70	23%
Dietary fiber (gm)	7	8	32%
Classic compared: Three-Green Pasta with Scallops and Pesto Sauce			

HAM AND CHEESE SANDWICH WITH ROASTED PEPPERS

This is one of my favorite sandwiches. I especially love it when I'm videotaping my television series, and need a pick-me-up kind of experience: the smoky taste from the roasted red bell peppers, vibrant colors, and crunchy textures are just the thing.

When you find bell peppers on sale, especially the sweet red variety, or find lots of them ripe in your garden, roast as many as you can at one time. After they're roasted and peeled, lay them on a wax paper–covered baking sheet and set them in the freezer. They will freeze hard in 2 to 3 hours. Store the frozen peppers in resealable freezer bags, separated by wax paper. Thaw as many as you need a couple of hours before you want to use them.

Time Estimate:
Hands-on, 10 minutes
Serves 4

8 slices Italian bread
4 teaspoons Dijon mustard
4 ounces (125 g) lean smoked ham, trimmed of all visible fat
4 ounces (125 g) low-fat Swiss cheese
8 long fresh basil leaves, cut into thin strips
2 roasted bell pappers (page 133)
4 large lettuce leaves, preferably Boston or butter lettuce

Spread the mustard on one side of all the bread slices. Layer half with one slice of the ham and cheese, a sprinkle of basil, the roasted peppers, and a lettuce leaf, then top each with the rest of the crusty Italian bread slices.

Nutritional Profile per Serving: Calories—247; calories from fat—63; fat (gm)—7 or 11% daily value; saturated fat (gm)—3; sodium (mg)—759; cholesterol (mg)—26; carbohydrates (gm)—27; dietary fiber (gm)—2

ROASTED VEGETABLE LASAGNE

Karen VandenBrink says she raised her (now grown) son on pasta, particularly lasagne. That's why she was so pleased when I created this much healthier version, chock-full of hearty roasted vegetables. Karen reports that it was "delicious, much lighter than my original recipe." She does suggest adding the meaty flavor of a little fennel seed and some added body with tomato paste—over to you now for your own experiments.

Time Estimate:
Hands-on, 1 hour;
unsupervised, 1 hour 15 minutes
Serves 6

Vegetable Mixture

1/2 pounds (225 g) red bell peppers, seeded and chopped into 1/2-inch (1.5-cm) dice
1 carrot, cut into matchsticks
2 zucchini, cut into 1/2-inch (1.5-cm) thick half-moons
1 eggplant, cut into 1/2-inch (1.5-cm) chunks
1 onion, peeled and chopped
1 teaspoon light olive oil with a dash of toasted sesame oil
1 teaspoon whole cumin seed
1/4 teaspoon freshly ground black pepper
6 cloves garlic, peeled and wrapped in foil

Tomato Sauce

1/2 teaspoon light olive oil with a dash of toasted sesame oil
1/2 onion, peeled and chopped
2 cloves garlic, bashed, peeled, and chopped
1 teaspoon dried oregano
1 teaspoon dried basil
2 (14-ounce) (400-g) cans low-sodium diced tomatoes, in juice
2 teaspoons arrowroot mixed with 1 tablespoon water (slurry)

Spinach Layer

1/2 teaspoon light olive oil with a dash of toasted sesame oil

8 medium mushrooms, sliced thick

1/2 pound (225 g) raw spinach, cut into strips

1/4 cup basil leaves, cut into strips

1/4 teaspoon freshly ground black pepper

6 curly lasagne noodles, cooked according to package directions

1/2 cup freshly grated Parmesan cheese

The vegetables: Preheat the oven to 400°F (200°C). Toss the peppers, carrot, zucchini, eggplant, and onion with the oil. Spread out on a large baking sheet and sprinkle with the cumin and pepper. Set the foil-wrapped garlic on one corner of the pan. Bake for 30 minutes; stir to make sure the vegetables are cooking evenly and bake for 15 minutes more. Remove from the oven and transfer all the vegetables to a large bowl. Squeeze the baked garlic cloves into the bowl and mix well.

The tomato sauce: Pour the oil into a medium saucepan and fry the chopped onion and garlic until it starts to wilt. Add the oregano and basil and cook for 2 more minutes. Pour in the tomatoes and cook, uncovered, for 20 minutes. Remove from the heat, stir in the slurry, return to the heat to thicken and clear.

The spinach layer: Pour the oil into a large frying pan on medium heat and fry the mushrooms until they start to brown. Add the spinach, basil, and pepper and cook just until the spinach wilts. Transfer the cooked vegetables to a sieve and press out the excess liquid.

To assemble: Spoon a little sauce into an 8 x 8-inch (20 x 20-cm) baking dish. Lay 3 noodles on the bottom, trimmed to size. Cover with 1/3 of the sauce, the cooked mushrooms and spinach, and a sprinkle of the cheese. Cover with the noodle trimmings, 1/3 of the sauce, the roasted vegetables,

and a sprinkle more of the cheese. Cover with the last 3 noodles, the remaining sauce, and sprinkle with the remaining cheese. Bake at 400°F (200°C) 30 minutes. Remove from the oven and let sit for 15 minutes. Cut into 6 portions and serve.

Nutritional Profile per Serving: Calories—234; calories from fat—45; fat (gm)—5 or 8% daily value; saturated fat (gm)—2; sodium (mg)—209; cholesterol (mg)—7; carbohydrates (gm)—40; dietary fiber (gm)—7

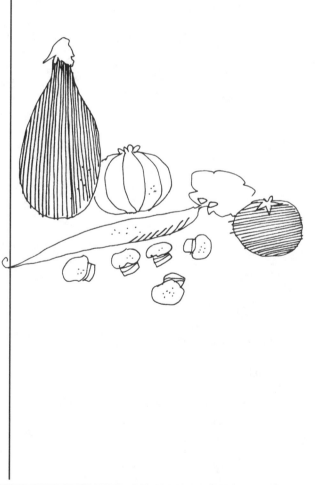

✖ STRIPED BASS WITH ROASTED VEGETABLES

The roasted vegetables in this dish by Matt Stein are a meal all by themselves, but with the striped bass and paprika sauce, you have a party on your hands.

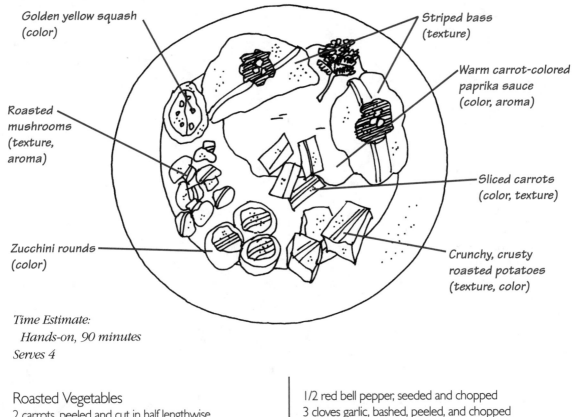

Golden yellow squash (color)

Striped bass (texture)

Warm carrot-colored paprika sauce (color, aroma)

Roasted mushrooms (texture, aroma)

Sliced carrots (color, texture)

Zucchini rounds (color)

Crunchy, crusty roasted potatoes (texture, color)

Time Estimate:
  Hands-on, 90 minutes
Serves 4

Roasted Vegetables
2 carrots, peeled and cut in half lengthwise
1 leek, cleaned, cut in half lengthwise, and tied together with string
3 cloves garlic, peeled
2 shallots, peeled and halved
4 potatoes, peeled and cut into 2-inch (5-cm) chunks
2 zucchini, cut into 2-inch (5-cm) pieces
2 yellow squash, cut into 2-inch (5-cm) pieces
10 mushrooms
A spritz of olive oil spray

Paprika Sauce
4 cups fish or vegetable stock (page 233)
2 onions, peeled and chopped
1/4 carrot, chopped

1/2 red bell pepper, seeded and chopped
3 cloves garlic, bashed, peeled, and chopped
2 teaspoons paprika
1/4 teaspoon caraway seeds
1/4 teaspoon red chili flakes
2 medium tomatoes, peeled and chopped
1/2 cup de-alcoholized white wine
1 tablespoon cornstarch mixed with 2 tablespoons de-alcoholized white wine (slurry)
2 tablespoons cream
1/8 teaspoon freshly ground sea salt
1/8 teaspoon freshly ground black pepper

Fish
1 teaspoon olive oil
4 (4-ounce) (125-g) triangular pieces of striped bass

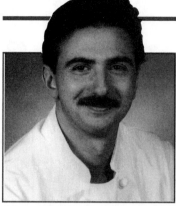

Matt Stein is an executive chef who is part of a creative team that births brand-new restaurants, and therefore has to have a very clear focus on today's restaurant patrons.

At the Clearwater Café, Matt planned an entire section of the menu as vegetarian, with a daily changing soup and several entree salads that also had a choice of three low-fat or nonfat dressings. Matt notes that "The low-fat dressings are very popular, as are all the pastas with fresh vegetables and the mixed grain risottos."

There is nothing held back in Matt's view of restaurants in the year 2000, "By then everything we eat will have to be evaluated nutritionally."

Now that's quite a thought, and if the information is provided in a way that doesn't spoil the restaurant's ambience, I think it will be good news for all restaurant patrons.

A Sauce for Your Freezer

Vegetable sauces such as this Paprika Sauce freeze well. Transfer it to a resealable plastic bag, seal, label, and date, and lay flat in the freezer. If you need only a little bit of sauce to spice up a dish, simply break off a piece from the flat frozen slab. It will keep, airtight, for up to 6 months. When ready to use, gently heat on top of the stove or zap it in the microwave.

The roasted vegetables: Heat the oven to 450°F (230°C). Blanch the carrots, leek, and garlic by plunging them into boiling water to cover for 1 minute; drain at once and pat dry. Place all the vegetables in a roasting pan, give them a small spritz of olive oil spray, and roast for 45 minutes, or until they are a warm brown color and the potatoes are cooked through.

The paprika sauce: Pour 1 tablespoon of the fish or vegetable stock into a medium skillet on low heat and add the onions, carrot, red bell pepper, and garlic. Cook for 10 minutes without letting them brown. Sprinkle in the paprika, caraway, and chili flakes and cook for 5 more minutes. Stir in the tomatoes and cook for 5 minutes. Pour in the white wine and cook for 5 minutes. Pour in the remaining fish stock and boil, uncovered, about 15 minutes, until the liquid is reduced to about two-thirds of its original volume. Remove from the heat, add the cornstarch slurry, return to the heat, and boil until thickened and clear, about 1 minute. Stir in the cream, salt, and pepper. Strain and keep warm.

The fish: Just before serving, pour the olive oil into a medium skillet on high heat. When hot, add the bass, skin side down, and fry until brown, about 5 minutes on each side, depending on the thickness. Divide the sauce among the plates, top with the bass, and surround with the vegetables.

Nutritional Profile per Serving			
	Classic	**Springboard**	**Daily Value**
Calories	560	440	
Calories from fat	315	90	
Fat (gm)	35	10 ·	15%
Saturated fat (gm)	18	3	15%
Sodium (mg)	511	438	18%
Cholesterol (mg)	149	64	21%
Carbohydrates (gm)	36	59	20%
Dietary fiber (gm)	6	10	40%
Classic compared: Sea Bass with Vegetables and Hungarian Paprika Sauce			

19

MEAT IN THE MINOR KEY

Smaller portions of meat are supplemented with delicious vegetables and creative whole-grain presentations.

This chapter is for the dedicated meat eater: those who dream of slicing into a thick charbroiled porterhouse steak. The good news is that meat can be part of a creative and health diet—just use less of it.

Changing fatty flesh proteins, like red meat, from a major chord in your cooking to a minor key is a gradual process. For instance, I've slowly but steadily changed my meat-eating habits from a 32-ounce (900-g) porterhouse steak in 1958 to a 16-ounce (450-g) strip sirloin in 1978 to a 2-ounce (50-g) pork tenderloin in 1994—that's a 30-ounce reduction (almost 900g) in serving size that took me 36 years.

The right amount of meat in your diet all depends upon where you are in your search for good health and a sense of well being. If you have no known health risks, then a 6-ounce steak is fine, provided that's the total meat you eat for one day. But if you know that you, or your loved ones who watch you, are somehow at risk, and you want to prevent disease, then the steak needs to shrink to not more than 3½ to 4 ounces (100 g)—about the size of a deck of playing cards. Then, if someone's at high risk, 2 ounces (50 g) or less on an occasional basis would be your target.

Now, I don't expect you to be convinced by me to simply walk away from your favorite steak because of one short chapter . . . but on the other hand—you might!

Tips and Hints

- When you begin to move your meat portion into a minor key, it's absolutely vital to make a list of the fruits, vegetables, and whole grains that you really enjoy and can successfully use to fill its place. The trick is to replace 1 ounce (25 g) of meat with up to 4 ounces (100 g) of a well-loved and healthy alternative. Choose a 6-ounce (125-g) boneless pork loin chop and serve it smothered in 4 ounces (100 g) of shallow fried peaches and, say, a mustard sauce?

You must remember this, vegetables make a great main dish.

Meat in the Minor Key

- When you get down to a 2-ounce (50-g) meat portion, you've made a dramatic change and should look for around 24 ounces (700 g) of vegetables, fruit, and whole grains as a complement. Perhaps sweet potato, braised leeks or onions, a large broiled beefsteak tomato, and some vivid green peas?

�֎ OXTAIL AND BARLEY SOUP

Virginia Bacon Peterson's husband, Peter, has a problem with blood pressure and cholesterol, so she's always looking for food that's "low fat but wonderfully tasty with spices." She indicated in her Food Preference List that she had become interested in the meat-in-the-minor-key concept. I suggested that we use the unique flavor of oxtail and pair it up with barley and shiitake mushrooms to make a hugely aromatic soup.

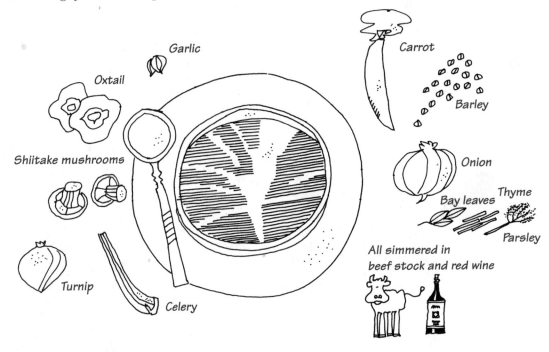

Garlic
Carrot
Oxtail
Barley
Shiitake mushrooms
Onion
Thyme
Bay leaves
Parsley
All simmered in beef stock and red wine
Turnip
Celery

Time Estimate:
  Hands-on, 30 minutes;
  unsupervised, 2 hours
Serves 4

2 pounds (900 g) oxtail, cut into sections
1 teaspoon light olive oil with a dash of toasted sesame oil
1 large onion, peeled and diced
3 cloves garlic, bashed, peeled, and chopped
1 large carrot, peeled and diced into 1/2-inch (1.5-cm) pieces
2 stalks celery, diced into 1/2-inch (1.5-cm) pieces
3 tablespoons low-sodium tomato paste
2 (14-ounce) (400-g) cans low-sodium beef stock
1 cup de-alcoholized red wine

1/2 teaspoon whole black peppercorns
10 sprigs fresh parsley
6 sprigs fresh thyme
2 bay leaves
6 cups water
1/2 cup pearl barley
2 large carrots, peeled and diced into 1/4-inch (0.75-cm) pieces
1 cup diced turnips (1/4 inch/0.75 cm pieces)
4 ounces shiitake mushrooms, stems removed, chopped

"This version of oxtail soup," reported **Virginia Peterson**, "is the best ever! I wondered why the shiitake mushrooms until I tasted them, then, voilà! I found them to be chewy, not tough, not crispy, just marvelous!

"Nothing was too strong in texture or flavor—truly a marvelous tasting soup. We thought we might try it with a soup bone and top sirloin chunks next time—would you approve?" Wholeheartedly, ma'am!

Blanch the oxtail in boiling water for 3 minutes, just enough to take the red color away from surface. Drain, put the oxtail pieces on a rack in a roasting pan, and place under the broiler for 15 minutes on each side until nice and brown.

Pour the oil into a large saucepan on medium heat and fry the onion and garlic for 3 minutes. Add the carrot and celery and fry for 5 minutes. Stir in the tomato paste, coat the vegetables well, and cook until the paste darkens. Add the stock, wine, oxtails, peppercorns, parsley, thyme, and bay leaves. Cover and simmer for 2 hours.

During the last half hour of simering, pour the 6 cups of water into a large soup pot, bring to a boil, stir in the barley, and boil for 25 minutes. Add the carrots and turnips and boil for 15 minutes. Drain, reserving 1 cup of the cooking liquid, and set aside.

Transfer the cooked oxtail to a cutting board. Remove the meat from the bones, keeping it in fairly large chunks, discarding any visible fat. Strain the stock into another saucepan, discarding the solids. Add the meat, turn the heat to medium-high, add the vegetable-barley mixture, the shiitake mushrooms, and the 1 cup of reserved vegetable-barley water and just heat through.

✂ EXTRA MEAL

Double this whole recipe except for the shiitake mushrooms. Dip out half of the soup before adding the mushrooms and barley water. Cool in the refrigerator and then pour into a gallon-size resealable freezer bag. Flatten the bag, expelling all the air, label, and date. This can be kept frozen for up to 6 months. It goes well in the potpie recipe on page 126 and the Cottage Pie recipe that follows.

Nutritional Profile per Serving			
	Classic	**Springboard**	**Daily Value**
Calories	291	296	
Calories from fat	126	108	
Fat (gm)	14	12	18%
Saturated fat (gm)	5	4	20%
Sodium (mg)	142	115	5%
Cholesterol (mg)	30	45	15%
Carbohydrates (gm)	17	27	9%
Dietary fiber (gm)	1	5	20%
Classic compared: Oxtail Soup			

✄ COTTAGE PIE

This is a much loved dish passed on from generation to generation in my family. In fact, my mother, Mardi, asked for Cottage Pie instead of birthday cake on her ninetieth birthday. Having the previously made Oxtail Soup on hand will make things go quite easily.

Time Estimate:
  Hands-on, 15 minutes;
  unsupervised, 1 hour 20 minutes
Serves 6

1 recipe Oxtail and Barley Soup (page 166)
2 pounds (900 g) russet potatoes, peeled and quartered
1 cup 1-percent-fat buttermilk
1/8 teaspoon freshly grated nutmeg
1/4 teaspoon freshly ground white pepper
1/8 teaspoon freshly ground sea salt

Bring the oxtail soup to a boil in a heavy pan. Turn the heat down to medium and continue to boil, allowing much of the liquid to evaporate until it's thick like a stew. This will take about 1 hour of gentle, steady boiling.

Boil the potatoes for 30 minutes, pour off the water, return the potatoes to the pot, cover with a clean dish towel, and let sit on low heat to dry out for 5 minutes. Transfer to a large bowl and mash with the buttermilk, nutmeg, pepper, and salt.

Pour the thickened oxtail-barley mixture into a 9 x 13-inch (23 x 33-cm) baking dish. Spread the potatoes over the filling to cover. Bake for 30 minutes at 350°F (180°C). Make long stripes in the potato crust with a fork and slide under the broiler for 5 minutes to brown.

Nutritional Profile per Serving: Calories—370; calories from fat—81; fat (gm)—9 or 14% daily value; saturated fat (gm)—3; sodium (mg)—224; cholesterol (mg)—32; carbohydrates (gm)—56; dietary fiber (gm)—8

Monterey Casserole

Natasha DelaCruz calls the springboarded version of her original Monterey casserole recipe "purely magnificent!" She goes on to say, "I thought I would miss the chewy, cheesey texture, but the beans and corn tortillas are just as delicious."

Natasha and her husband are both engineers and they have a young son. She says that "the stress of having an infant and a very demanding job drove me to snack." In mid-1992 she started reading about exercise and low-fat food alternatives to improve her health. Seven months later she had lost 40 pounds and reduced her cholesterol from 165 to 119. Natasha says, "To this day, my permanent change in lifestyle has kept me in the best physical condition I've ever experienced."

Time Estimate:
Hands-on, 30 minutes;
unsupervised, 1½ hours
Serves 6

1/2 pound (225 g) extra-lean ground beef
1 small onion, peeled and chopped fine
1 clove garlic, bashed, peeled, and chopped fine
1/8 teaspoon cayenne pepper
1/2 teaspoon ground cumin
3 cups low-sodium refried beans, preferably homemade
2 medium zucchini, cut in 1-inch (2.5-cm) dice
4 fresh jalapeño peppers, seeded and sliced
1 (14-ounce) (400-g) can low-sodium tomato sauce
1 (14-ounce) (400-g) can low-sodium diced tomatoes
6 corn tortillas, torn in large pieces
1 (10-ounce) (300-g) carton frozen corn kernels
14 medium black olives, halved
1½ cups strained yogurt (page 234)
1/2 cup chopped fresh cilantro

Preheat the oven to 350°F (180°C). In a very hot nonstick skillet, brown the ground beef for 3 minutes. Reduce the heat to medium and fry the onion, garlic, cayenne, and cumin for 3 minutes.

To assemble: Layer a medium casserole with 1/4 of the refried beans, all the zucchini, 1/2 of the jalapeños, 1/4 each of the tomato sauce and the diced tomatoes, and 1/3 of the tortillas. The next layer should have 1/4 of the beans, all the meat, 1/4 of the tomato sauce and diced tomatoes, and 1/3 of the tortillas. The next layer should have 1/4 of the beans, all the corn, the remaining jalapeños, olives, 1/4 each of the tomato sauce and diced tomatoes, and the remaining tortillas. Top with the remaining beans, tomato sauce, and diced tomatoes. Cover lightly with foil and bake for 1½ hours.

To serve: Cut into six wedges and garnish with the strained yogurt and chopped cilantro.

Nutritional Profile per Serving: Calories—388; calories from fat—72; fat (gm)—8 or 12% daily value; saturated fat (gm)—2; sodium (mg)—626; cholesterol (mg)—25; carbohydrates (gm)—59; dietary fiber (gm)—11

DAVID'S CHICKEN PICCATA

Chef David Glynn tries to keep flavors and recipes simple, allowing the food and its quality to speak for itself. This recipe is a great example—the medley of flavors is so attractive I don't think you'll notice that the serving size of the chicken is only 2 ounces!

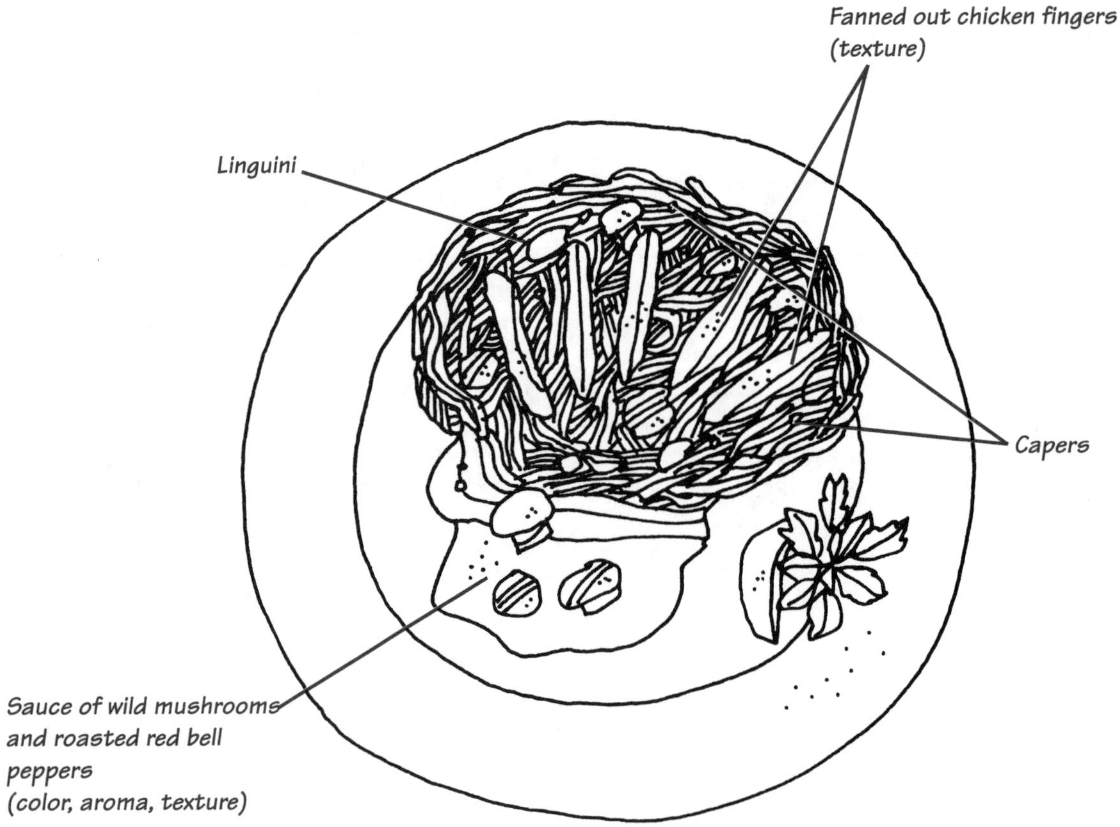
Fanned out chicken fingers (texture)
Linguini
Capers
Sauce of wild mushrooms and roasted red bell peppers (color, aroma, texture)

Time Estimate:
Hands-on, 35 minutes
Serves 6

4 (3-ounce) (100-g) chicken breasts or pieces, boneless with skin on
1/8 teaspoon freshly ground sea salt
Freshly ground black pepper to taste
1 cup low-fat chicken stock (page 231)
3 cloves garlic, bashed, peeled, and minced
4 cups sliced assorted wild mushrooms (oyster, shiitake, crimini, portobello)
1/2 cup green onions, sliced fine
1/2 cup purée of roasted red peppers (page 133)
3 tablespoons de-alcoholized white wine or sherry
1 tablespoon capers
Juice of 1 lemon
12 ounces uncooked linguine

On a recent visit to Dayton, Ohio, I had the pleasure of working with chef **David Glynn** of the Peasant Stock restaurant. David prepared an entire multi-course dinner from my book *Creative Choices* for a special seating in his excellent establishment and it went very well.

At his own restaurant, David says, "You'll find great vegetarian dishes and very popular combination entrees with rice and pasta. You'll also find a chef who wants to feed your mind, body, and soul."

I found that David had compelling personal reasons to change his diet. His wife had a serious cholesterol problem and David's father had a heart attack followed by quadruple heart bypass surgery. "I worked to create dishes that are not only low in calories but have a heavy emphasis on small amounts of meat, avoiding dairy products if possible, and using natural sauces."

When "Dried" Is a Dream

David Glynn always prefers to use imported dried pastas as opposed to fresh pasta for three reasons. Imported dried pastas are:

• generally made from 100 percent durum semolina flour
• easy to handle and store
• naturally able to absorb sauces

Heat the oven to broil. When the heat is really high, broil the chicken breasts, skin side up, until well browned. Turn the heat off and leave the chicken for 5 minutes. Remove the chicken, take off the skin, and pat off any extra fat with a paper towel. Season lightly with the salt and pepper.

Pour 1/4 cup of the chicken stock into a large hot skillet, add the garlic, and simmer for 1 minute. Add the mushrooms and another 1/4 cup of chicken stock; shake the mushrooms back and forth as they simmer. As they begin to cook through, add the green onions and shake-cook for another minute. Add the red pepper purée, the remaining stock, wine, and capers and simmer until slightly thickened. Adjust the reasoning with the lemon juice.

While the mushroom mixture is simmering, cook the pasta according to package directions.

To serve: Slice the chicken into fingers. Pile the pasta on individual plates, ladle with the mushrooms and sauce, and fan a few chicken fingers over the top.

Nutritional Profile per Serving			
	Classic	**Springboard**	**Daily Value**
Calories	819	105	
Calories from fat	504	18	
Fat (gm)	56	2	3%
Saturated fat (gm)	12	.55	3%
Sodium (mg)	1085	181	8%
Cholesterol (mg)	202	29	10%
Carbohydrates (gm)	23	8	3%
Dietary fiber (gm)	1	3	12%
Classic compared: Chicken Supremes with Piquant Caper Sauce			

20

GROUND MEATS

The freshest, lowest-fat, tastiest ground meat for your dishes is possible when you grind your own.

From hamburgers to spaghetti and meatballs, gefilte fish to quenelles, so many of our favorite ethnic dishes use qround meat or fish as an ingredient. To make it the freshest, most flavorful, and leanest meat possible, I recommend you use the information in this chapter to grind your own.

This technique is not limited to ground beef. As you'll see from the recipes that follow, chicken, turkey, seafood and pork are all great basic grinding material.

Tips and Hints
All Meats

- Reduce the fat by removing all the skin and visible fat before grinding.
- Cut the meat into equal-sized small chunks for ease in grinding.
- Grind small amounts.
- Pulse the food processor so the meat won't turn into a thick paste.
- Don't throw your seasonings after the meat into the grinder. You will maintain more interesting texture if you hand-chop the vegetables and seasonings and mix them by hand with the ground meat.
- All parents will rejoice when I point out that you can sneak in nutritious vegetables for fussy children (and adults) by mixing them with the ground meats. Meatballs and meat loaves can also include potatoes, carrots, and spinach that will fool even the pickiest eater—a great place to springboard!

Poultry

- Control the fat content by keeping the white and dark meat separate. Dark meat increases flavor, but has much more fat than white. I grind them separately and use about 1 part dark meat to 3 parts light meat. This gives you roughly 2 grams of fat for a 3½–ounce serving.
- Use a fresh or frozen bird. To avoid bacterial contamination, thaw the bird in the refrigerator and keep it there until ready to use. Put it back in the refrigerator between stages. Always cook the ground meat to 160°F.
- Because poultry is mild in flavor, remember that it takes flavors from aromatic vegetables, herbs, and spices very easily.

Fish

- Use the freshest fish possible or buy quick frozen. Avoid contamination by keeping fish refrigerated as much as possible and cooking it as quickly as possible.
- Fish will take on seasonings and flavoring from aromatic vegetables quite easily.

�֍ TURKEY MEATBALLS AND MUSHROOMS IN A SWEET AND SPICY SAUCE

Richard Schwartz is a keen cook in a family that really watches what they eat. We springboarded on Richard's original recipe for Sweet and Sour Turkey Meatballs. We had some negotiations: Richard eats no sugar ever, so where I would have used red currant jelly, I've agreed to his "all fruit" grape jelly; and he has been gracious enough to permit our using vegetable juice to replace his favored "Westbrae Natural Catsup" that we could not find in the Pacific Northwest (Richard does recommend looking for the Natural Unketchup, though, which is thick, gooey, salt free, and sugar free).

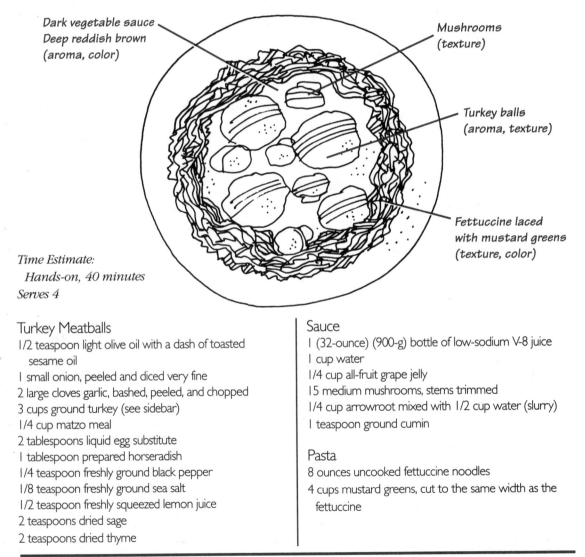

Dark vegetable sauce
Deep reddish brown
(aroma, color)

Mushrooms
(texture)

Turkey balls
(aroma, texture)

Fettuccine laced
with mustard greens
(texture, color)

Time Estimate:
 Hands-on, 40 minutes
Serves 4

Turkey Meatballs

1/2 teaspoon light olive oil with a dash of toasted
 sesame oil
1 small onion, peeled and diced very fine
2 large cloves garlic, bashed, peeled, and chopped
3 cups ground turkey (see sidebar)
1/4 cup matzo meal
2 tablespoons liquid egg substitute
1 tablespoon prepared horseradish
1/4 teaspoon freshly ground black pepper
1/8 teaspoon freshly ground sea salt
1/2 teaspoon freshly squeezed lemon juice
2 teaspoons dried sage
2 teaspoons dried thyme

Sauce

1 (32-ounce) (900-g) bottle of low-sodium V-8 juice
1 cup water
1/4 cup all-fruit grape jelly
15 medium mushrooms, stems trimmed
1/4 cup arrowroot mixed with 1/2 cup water (slurry)
1 teaspoon ground cumin

Pasta

8 ounces uncooked fettuccine noodles
4 cups mustard greens, cut to the same width as the
 fettuccine

Richard Schwartz says, "Your taste buds get used to low-fat cooking. I started when my wife and I went to a health spa. We thought it would take a lot of getting used to, but it didn't; it's just a matter of getting it straight in your head.

"I look for anything that will add flavor without fat to my cooking. I love the strained yogurt for the richness it adds and I use a flavor injector needle — I gave everybody one of those for Christmas!"

To Grind Your Own Fresh Turkey Meat

Buy a half or a 10- to 12-pound turkey. Using a good sharp knife, remove the wing, thigh, leg, and breast. Save the wing and leg for soup, like the turkey tomato soup that follows. Remove all the skin from the breast and the thigh and cut away the meat from the bones. Pulse the dark and white meat separately in a food processor about 24 times each. Spread the breast meat out on a cutting board, cover with the dark meat, and chop with the back of a knife or bash and chop the two together until they become an even mix. Measure the amount of meat you will need for this recipe and freeze the rest for later use.

⊠ Extra Meal

Use the turkey legs and wings left over from grinding your own meat for turkey tomato soup.

The turkey meatballs: Pour the oil into a small skillet on medium heat and fry the onion and garlic for 2 minutes. Put the ground turkey in a large bowl, add the cooked onions and garlic, the matzo meal, egg substitute, and seasonings, and mix well. Use 1/4 cup of the mixture to make each meatball. Set aside.

The sauce: In a small Dutch oven, mix the V-8 juice, water, and grape jelly and bring to a boil. Add the meatballs and the mushrooms and simmer for 20 minutes. Remove from the heat, stir in the arrowroot slurry, return to the heat, and bring to a boil to thicken and clear, about 30 seconds. Season with the sage and cumin and keep warm.

The pasta: Cook the fettuccine according to package directions, drain, transfer to a large warm bowl, and toss with the uncooked greens.

To serve: Make a fettuccine nest on each individual plate, nestle in 3 each of the turkey meatballs and 3 or 4 mushrooms, and ladle 1/2 cup of the sauce over the top.

Nutritional Profile per Serving			
	Classic	**Springboard**	**Daily Value**
Calories	733	572	
Calories from fat	333	126	
Fat (gm)	37	14	22%
Saturated fat (gm)	10	4	20%
Sodium (mg)	858	231	10%
Cholesterol (mg)	224	116	39%
Carbohydrates (gm)	69	81	27%
Dietary fiber (gm)	8	9	36%
Classic compared: Sweet and Sour Meatballs			

✖ TURKEY TOMATO SOUP

I use the leftover turkey legs and wings from making the turkey meatballs in the preceding recipe for this wonderful soup. It has a lovely rich color, and the curry gives it a lively flavor. Remember that the legs and wings are high-fat parts of the bird, so it's important to skim off the fat that rises to the top of the soup.

Time Estimate:
  Hands-on, 20 minutes;
  unsupervised, 2 or 3 hours
Serves 8

1 tablespoon light olive oil with a dash of toasted sesame oil
2 medium onions, peeled and sliced
1 clove garlic, bashed, peeled, and sliced
2 tablespoons curry powder
2 turkey legs
2 turkey wings
1 (32-ounce) (900-g) bottle low-sodium vegetable juice, such as V-8
4 cups water
4 bay leaves
1 tablespoon dried thyme
3 sprigs fresh parsley
12 whole black peppercorns
6 whole cloves
4 cups cooked long-grain white rice
1/4 cup chopped fresh parsley or cilantro

Pour the oil into a medium stockpot and fry the onion and garlic over medium heat for 2 minutes. Stir in the curry and cook for 2 minutes. Add the turkey parts, juice, water, and spices, bring to a boil, and boil for 5 minutes. Lower the heat, cover, and simmer for 2 hours.

Strain the broth into a container, pressing firmly to get all the juice and flavor. Set the turkey parts aside and discard the cooked vegetable pulp. Pour the broth into a fat strainer cup, then pour the defatted broth into a medium saucepan. Take all the skin and fat off the turkey and discard. Pull the meat from the bones, leaving it in nice large chunks, discarding the bones. Stir the turkey meat into the broth and heat through. Ladle the warm soup over 1/2 cup of rice in each soup bowl and garnish with a sprinkle of parsley or cilantro.

Nutritional Profile per Serving: Calories—263; calories from fat—63; fat (gm)—7 or 11% daily value; saturated fat (gm)—2; sodium (mg)—80; cholesterol (mg)—50; carbohydrates (gm)—30; dietary fiber (gm)—2

❌ Sweet and Sour Surprise Meatballs

These ground-pork meatballs are based upon the Food Preference List sent to me by Linda Storey, a college student in Illinois. I love the tiny pineapple surprise in the middle of each meatball. Once you catch on to the concept, you can see that the possibilities for your own surprise meatballs are endless.

Time Estimate:
  Hands-on, 45 minutes
Serves 6

Meatballs

1½ cups uncooked long-grain white rice
1 pound (450 g) lean pork
2 tablespoons finely chopped green onions, green and white parts
1/2 teaspoon finely chopped fresh gingerroot
1 teaspoon garlic, bashed, peeled, and chopped
1/4 cup liquid egg substitute
2 teaspoons low-sodium soy sauce
2 (8-ounce) (225-g) cans pineapple chunks, juice reserved
1 teaspoon light olive oil with a dash of toasted sesame oil
2 carrots, cut into 1/8-inch (0.5-cm) thick pieces on the diagonal.
1 green bell pepper, cut into 1-inch (2.5-cm) squares

Sauce

1/2 cup reserved pineapple juice (see above)
1/4 cup water
2 tablespoons rice wine vinegar
2 tablespoons sugar
2 tablespoons ketchup
1/2 teaspoon finely chopped fresh gingerroot
1 teaspoon garlic, bashed, peeled, and chopped
1/4 teaspoon cayenne pepper (optional)
2 tablespoons reserved pineapple juice (see above) mixed with 1 tablespoon cornstarch (slurry)

The meatballs: Cook the rice according to package directions. Set 1/3 cup of the cooked rice aside for the meatballs. Put the rest in a metal sieve, place over the saucepan containing a tiny bit of simmering water, cover, and keep warm until ready to serve with the final dish.

Grind the pork in a processor and transfer to a large bowl. Add the green onions, ginger, garlic, egg substitute, soy sauce, and the 1/3 cup reserved rice. Mix until just well blended.

Take about 1/8 cup of the pork mixture and flatten it in your hand. Place a chunk of pineapple in the center and enclose it in the meat. Repeat with the remaining pork. You should have 24 golf-ball-size meatballs. Set aside.

The sauce: In a medium bowl, mix all the sauce ingredients except the slurry, stirring until the sugar dissolves. Set aside.

Pour the oil into a large nonstick skillet and fry the meatballs untl brown on all sides. Add the sauce, cover and simmer for 10 minutes. Stir in the carrots and green pepper and simmer 5 minutes more. Remove from the heat, stir in the cornstarch slurry, return to the heat, and bring to a boil for 1 minute to thicken and clear. Stir in any extra pineapple chunks.

To serve: Mound some rice on each serving plate, make a well in the center, and fill it with the meatballs and sauce.

Nutritional Profile per Serving: Calories—405; calories from fat—81; fat (gm)—9 or 14% daily value; saturated fat (gm)—3; sodium (mg)—200; cholesterol (mg)—63; carbohydrates (gm)—52; dietary fiber (gm)—2

✛ AHI BURGER WITH MUSTARD ICE CREAM

Chef Jean Pierre Lemanissier's seafood burger is fragrant, even refreshing, with bao syang *(see page 83) from the pungent* wasabi *(a horseradish paste found in the Asian section of the supermarket) and pickled ginger. The mustard ice cream is the perfect accent. It all makes for perfectly delicious summer barbecue fare.*

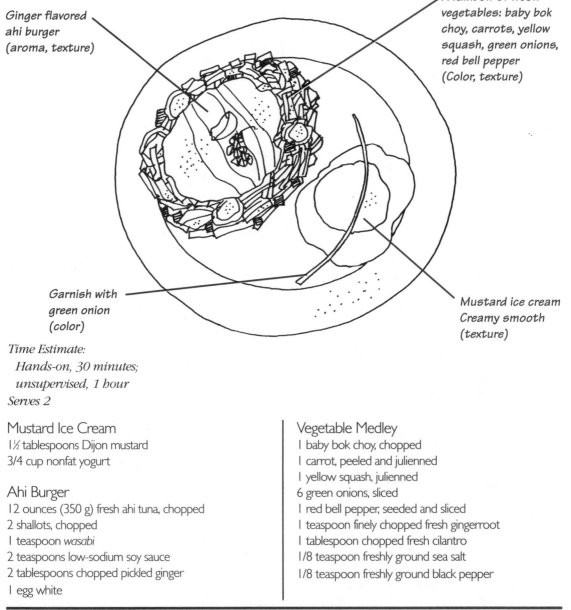

Ginger flavored
ahi burger
(aroma, texture)

A rainbow of fresh
vegetables: baby bok
choy, carrots, yellow
squash, green onions,
red bell pepper
(Color, texture)

Garnish with
green onion
(color)

Mustard ice cream
Creamy smooth
(texture)

Time Estimate:
  Hands-on, 30 minutes;
  unsupervised, 1 hour
Serves 2

Mustard Ice Cream
1½ tablespoons Dijon mustard
3/4 cup nonfat yogurt

Ahi Burger
12 ounces (350 g) fresh ahi tuna, chopped
2 shallots, chopped
1 teaspoon *wasabi*
2 teaspoons low-sodium soy sauce
2 tablespoons chopped pickled ginger
1 egg white

Vegetable Medley
1 baby bok choy, chopped
1 carrot, peeled and julienned
1 yellow squash, julienned
6 green onions, sliced
1 red bell pepper, seeded and sliced
1 teaspoon finely chopped fresh gingerroot
1 tablespoon chopped fresh cilantro
1/8 teaspoon freshly ground sea salt
1/8 teaspoon freshly ground black pepper

As chef de cuisine of Restaurant Antoine at Le Meridien in Newport Beach, California, **Jean Pierre Lemanissier** serves cuisine with a traditional French approach, broadened to develop his own lighter, more inventive "California cuisine."

Jean Pierre's restaurant is one of the few places I know that have a *prix fixe* (fixed price) menu for a three-course vegetarian meal, changed every day to ensure that only the freshest and best seasonal vegetables are included.

Jean Pierre told me that "More and more people want to know the nutritional information about the foods they eat." In response, his kitchen is cooking with less fat, trimming more fat off cuts of meat, and lightening sauces as well. Jean Pierre says his most successful dish at Restaurant Antoine has been a grilled vegetable terrine, which he also likes to prepare at his cooking classes.

The mustard ice cream: Combine the mustard and yogurt and place in an ice cream machine or freezer until frozen but not too hard.

The ahi burger: Mix all the ingredients in a bowl and form into two patties. Fry the patties in a nonstick skillet on medium heat for 2 minutes until brown on both sides—do not overcook. Remove from the heat, cover, and keep warm.

The vegetable medley: In a nonstick skillet on medium heat, fry all the vegetables, ginger, cilantro, and seasonings until the vegetables are lightly cooked but still crisp. Remove from the heat and set aside.

To serve: Spoon a good portion of vegetables onto a plate, top with the ahi burger, and garnish with an ice cream scoop of the mustard ice cream on the side.

Nutritional Profile per Serving			
	Classic	Springboard	Daily Value
Calories	661	300	
Calories from fat	351	27	
Fat (gm)	39	3	5%
Saturated fat (gm)	13	.70	4%
Sodium (mg)	1220	901	38%
Cholesterol (mg)	163	95	32%
Carbohydrates (gm)	51	24	8%
Dietary fiber (gm)	4	5	20%
Classic compared: Cheeseburger with Potato Salad			

21

*T*HE *M*AILLARD *R*EACTION

Browning tomato paste turns starch to sugar, develops depth of flavor, and adds rich color to all your savory cooking.

How can a single ingredient, heated in a little oil, become a bouquet of aromas, adding color and depth to dozens of dishes? This occurs every time you brown tomato paste, called "the Maillard reaction," named after Dr. Louis Camille Maillard, who discovered it in 1912. When heated, the plant proteins in the tomato paste darken and the tomato sugars caramelize—a good, clean taste intensified by a simple heating process.

In my search for a creative alternative that helps bring depth of color and taste to cooking with the least amount of fat, I have found no equal to the Maillard reaction. Use the Maillard reaction's mysterious smoky taste in all deep brown stews, soups, casseroles, sauces, pot roasts, and braised meats.

Tips and Hints

The challenge with any form of darkening is to avoid actually burning the food, especially when there is lots of volatile natural sugar present.

- Heat the tomato paste in a heavy-based pan
- Keep the heat no higher than medium.
- Stir constantly during the cooking process to prevent scorching. It should darken, but not burn.

How a single ingredient, heated in a little oil, can become a bouquet of aromas.

✠ PERUVIAN CHICKEN

Consuelo Ledesma and I went back and forth on my Minimax of a favorite family dish from Peru. In this final edition, I use the Maillard reaction of tomato paste to deepen the flavors of the sauce, which usually relies on as much as 1/3 cup of oil. In the classic recipe, the gizzards are eaten. You may wish to set them aside, but please don't leave them out of the pot, as they contribute to the unique flavor.

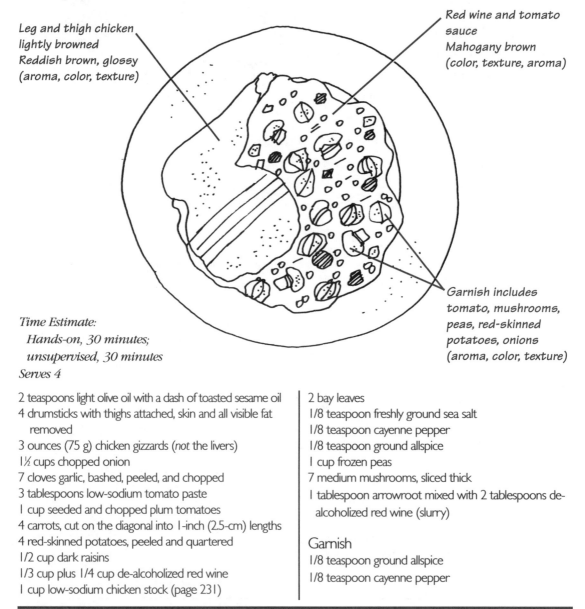

Leg and thigh chicken lightly browned
Reddish brown, glossy
(aroma, color, texture)

Red wine and tomato sauce
Mahogany brown
(color, texture, aroma)

Garnish includes tomato, mushrooms, peas, red-skinned potatoes, onions
(aroma, color, texture)

Time Estimate:
  Hands-on, 30 minutes;
  unsupervised, 30 minutes
Serves 4

2 teaspoons light olive oil with a dash of toasted sesame oil
4 drumsticks with thighs attached, skin and all visible fat removed
3 ounces (75 g) chicken gizzards (*not* the livers)
1½ cups chopped onion
7 cloves garlic, bashed, peeled, and chopped
3 tablespoons low-sodium tomato paste
1 cup seeded and chopped plum tomatoes
4 carrots, cut on the diagonal into 1-inch (2.5-cm) lengths
4 red-skinned potatoes, peeled and quartered
1/2 cup dark raisins
1/3 cup plus 1/4 cup de-alcoholized red wine
1 cup low-sodium chicken stock (page 231)

2 bay leaves
1/8 teaspoon freshly ground sea salt
1/8 teaspoon cayenne pepper
1/8 teaspoon ground allspice
1 cup frozen peas
7 medium mushrooms, sliced thick
1 tablespoon arrowroot mixed with 2 tablespoons de-alcoholized red wine (slurry)

Garnish
1/8 teaspoon ground allspice
1/8 teaspoon cayenne pepper

Peruvian-born *Consuelo Ledesma* shared a Peruvian chicken stew recipe with me out of her rich culinary heritage. She wants low-fat cooking to "both taste and look good." Like so many of us, she is searching for ways to retain in her cooking what she knows is going to please her friends, but she doesn't want to rely upon salt, oils, and sugar to do the trick.

It's this kind of thoughtfulness that makes her an attractive friend, and her hospitality a gracious mix of pleasing and caring.

✂ EXTRA MEAL

For an extra meal that can be frozen for use in the future, double the Peruvian Chicken with a few special instructions: double the chicken, salt, onion, cayenne pepper, chicken stock, and wine, including the tomato paste browning, but no added vegetables. After the chicken has cooked for 30 minutes, remove all the pieces from the pan. Set half the chicken pieces aside and place in a flat plastic container with 3/4 cups of the strained cooking juices. Then return the rest of the chicken to the pan and continue the cooking process. Label, date, and freeze until ready for use.

To defrost, let thaw in the refrigerator overnight, or place in the microwave for 4 minutes, until the sauce has released from the sides of the bag. Transfer the chicken and sauce to a saucepan and simmer over a low heat until heated through, about 10 minutes. This is the time to add extra-fresh vegetables that you have on hand.

Pour 1 teaspoon of the oil into a high-sided skillet on medium heat and lightly brown the legs and gizzards. Remove from the pan and set aside.

Pour the remaining teaspoon of oil into the same skillet and fry the onion until limp, about 5 minutes. Add the garlic and tomato paste and cook on medium heat until the tomato paste darkens, about 10 minutes, stirring constantly to prevent scorching. Add the tomatoes, carrots, potatoes, raisins, and 1/3 cup of the wine and stir well. Return the browned chicken and gizzards to the skillet and add the bay leaves, pushing them down into the sauce. Sprinkle with the salt, pepper, and allspice, cover, reduce the heat, and simmer for 30 minutes.

Remove the chicken legs and set aside. Discard the bay leaves. Stir in the peas, mushrooms, and remaining 1/4 cup of the wine. Bring to a boil, remove from the heat, and stir in the arrowroot slurry. Return to the heat and bring to a boil to thicken and clear, about 30 seconds. If desired, snip off the exposed leg bones on the chicken with a pair of poultry shears. Return the chicken to the skillet to heat through.

To serve: If you have a decorative skillet you can take it to the table; or you may transfer to a casserole dish. Just before serving, dust the surface with the allspice and cayenne pepper.

Nutritional Profile per Serving			
	Classic	**Springboard**	**Daily Value**
Calories	743	571	
Calories from fat	234	108	
Fat (gm)	26	12	19%
Saturated fat (gm)	7	3	15%
Sodium (mg)	439	269	11%
Cholesterol (mg)	420	136	45%
Carbohydrates (gm)	74	79	26%
Dietary fiber (gm)	8	9	26%
Classic compared: Peruvian Chicken Stew			

The Maillard Reaction

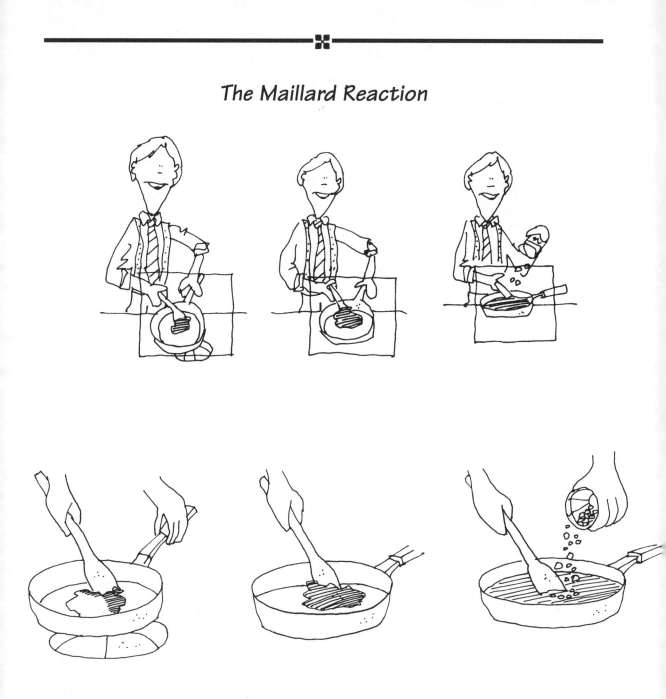

⌘ Creole Chicken

Diane Lorentson was "very excited" to receive this recipe because her husband is on a low-fat diet. The result, she said, was "absolutely fabulous" and "my kids even liked it!" This 32-year-old mother of two girls said she used to weigh just over 200 pounds. She put herself on a very low-fat diet and started working out three times a week. Within two months, Diane tells us she lost 45 pounds, and two years later, she has maintained that weight.

Time Estimate:
Hands-on, 30 minutes;
unsupervised, 20 minutes
Serves 6

2 large chicken breasts, skinned, boned, and cut into large chunks
2 large chicken legs and thighs, skinned and boned
1/2 teaspoon light olive oil with a dash of toasted sesame oil
2 tablespoons low-sodium tomato paste
1 cup chopped onion
3 cloves garlic, bashed, peeled, and chopped
1 ounce (25 g) Canadian bacon, chopped
1/2 cup diagonally sliced celery
1 large green bell pepper, seeded and cut in strips
1 teaspoon paprika
1 teaspoon dried thyme
1 pinch saffron
1/4 teaspoon red chili flakes
1 bay leaf
2 teaspoons filé powder
1 (28-ounce) (800-g) can low-sodium crushed tomatoes
4½ cups cooked rice

Brown the chicken pieces in a medium nonstick skillet over medium heat, remove from the pan, and set aside. Pour the oil into the same pan and fry the tomato paste until the color darkens, stirring to prevent scorching, about 5 minutes. Stir in the onion and garlic and cook for 2 minutes. Stir in the Canadian bacon, celery, green pepper, and all the seasonings and cook for 3 more minutes. Add the tomatoes and the browned chicken, bring to a slow boil, and simmer gently for 20 minutes. Serve over the cooked rice.

Filé Powder

This condiment is basic to the Southeastern United States' traditional Creole cookery. The Chocotow Indians from that region first made it from the dried leaves of the sassafras tree and used it as a thickening agent. Be careful not to boil your dish after adding the filé powder, because it tends to become stringy.

Nutritional Profile per Serving: Calories—355; calories from fat—54; fat (gm)—6 or 9% daily value; saturated fat (gm)—2; sodium (mg)—506; cholesterol (mg)—64; carbohydrates (gm)—46; dietary fiber (gm)—4

The Mallard Reaction
!?!?!

❖ ROASTED EGGPLANT CURRY WITH RED POTATOES

So satisfying, so filling, it's almost impossible to believe that this is a meatless meal—it's certainly not a wishy-washy veggie creation! Chef Neela Paniz utilizes the Maillard reaction in this recipe by roasting fresh tomatoes instead of pan-frying tomato paste. The resulting hearty flavor will please the staunchest meat-and-potatoes advocate.

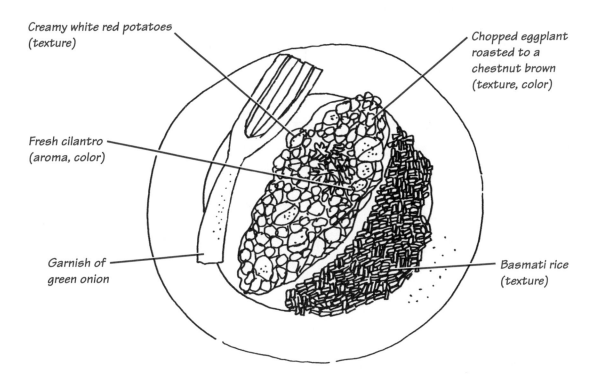

Creamy white red potatoes (texture)

Chopped eggplant roasted to a chestnut brown (texture, color)

Fresh cilantro (aroma, color)

Garnish of green onion

Basmati rice (texture)

Time Estimate:
  Hands-on, 45 minutes
Serves 4

1 large eggplant, peeled and quartered
2 large yellow onions, peeled and halved
4 tomatoes, cut into quarters
Vegetable oil cooking spray
3 red-skinned new potatoes, peeled, cut into 3/4-inch (2-cm) cubes, and parboiled
1 tablespoon ground coriander
2 serrano chiles, seeded and finely chopped

1 (2-inch) (5-cm) piece gingerroot, peeled and chopped fine
1/4 teaspoon cayenne powder
1 teaspoon ground cumin
1 cup low-sodium tomato sauce
1/4 teaspoon freshly ground sea salt
Chopped fresh cilantro

Within weeks of **Neela Deva Paniz's** opening Bombay Café and Catering in Los Angeles, the *Los Angeles Times* was raving about the food. Neela's rich culinary heritage grew out of her childhood in India: picking cherries in the Kulu Valley and watching Chandan, the family cook, grind masalas (what we know as "curry powders") sitting on the kitchen floor in Delhi. But the supreme cook, her mother, "abhorred oily or fatty food. She always set a dinner table that boasted of the freshest and most flavorful light foods in town."

Although Neela reports that most Indians are vegetarians, she admits that Indian food is traditionally high-fat. "This has led to my creating a number of dishes that are lighter and not necessarily fried, or fried in the least amount of oil, and that taste as light as possible. I find that the fresh lightness is one of the reasons why our customers enjoy the food much more than at the usual Indian restaurant."

THE VEGETARIAN WONDER

Roasted eggplant is a great meat substitute, but barbecued eggplant is a vegetarian wonder. Cut an eggplant (with skin on) into 1-inch (2.5-cm) thick slices. Brush with a little oil, sprinkle very liberally with fresh oregano, thyme, or marjoram, and a little salt and pepper. Cook on the grill until well browned, almost charred on both sides. Wrap in foil and return to the grill until the eggplant is cooked through, about 5 minutes.

Preheat the oven to 400°F (200°C). Place the eggplant, onions, and tomatoes in a roasting pan and spray with oil. Roast until the eggplant is almost charred and the onions and tomatoes are a deep rich brown color, about 40 minutes. Chop all the vegetables roughly, stir in the potatoes, and transfer to a medium saucepan. Add the coriander, chiles, ginger, cayenne, cumin, tomato sauce, and salt. Simmer gently until the potatoes are just cooked, about 15 minutes. Garnish with the cilantro and serve with basmati rice, Indian chapati, or pita bread.

Nutritional Profile per Serving			
	Classic	**Springboard**	**Daily Value**
Calories	105	225	
Calories from fat	63	18	
Fat (gm)	7	2	3%
Saturated fat (gm)	1	0.3	1%
Sodium (mg)	539	179	7%
Cholesterol (mg)	0	0	0%
Carbohydrates (gm)	11	51	17%
Dietary fiber (gm)	3	9	36%
Classic compared: Eggplant Sauté			

ÉTOUFFÉE

Shallow frying in a touch of oil, and then simmering in a little flavored liquid, covered, creates low-fat, moist, tender meals.

É touffée means "shallow fried with moist aromatics in a covered pan," and I think the entire principle of Minimax—minimum risk, maximum creativity—is summed up in this technique. It allows for lowered risk by fat reduction and increased creativity by its extremely flexible use of aroma, color, and texture, within a virtually foolproof and fast cooking method.

Essentially, étouffée is shallow-fried food surrounded by aromatic enhancements, like onions, shallots, leeks, garlic, and gingerroot, and a teaspoon of oil to release volatile oils. Add moisture to this, either stock, reduced stock, de-alcoholized wine, fruit juice, beer, vinegar, Worcestershire sauce, fish sauce, etc. Then season with fresh or dried herbs or freshly ground spices.

With the lid fixed tightly in place, the original shallow fry has now become part poach, part steam, but all flavor. You end up with perfectly moist fish, poultry, pork, beef, or lamb and the collection of aromatics and seasonings, that, with an extra dash of wine or stock, can be either a cooked "salsa" condiment or a garnished sauce, thickened with a little arrowroot.

Tips and Hints

JUMBO POTSTICKERS

I've always enjoyed potstickers, but in their classic form, these little bundles of dough filled with pork can run as high as 40 percent calories from fat. I created this Springboard version using the étouffée cooking technique to meet the needs of Kay Reid. With shrimp as its filling, only 11 percent of its calories come from fat. I've also made the dumplings double the usual size in order to cut down on labor in the kitchen. All you need to complete your meal is a stir-fry of your favorite vegetables.

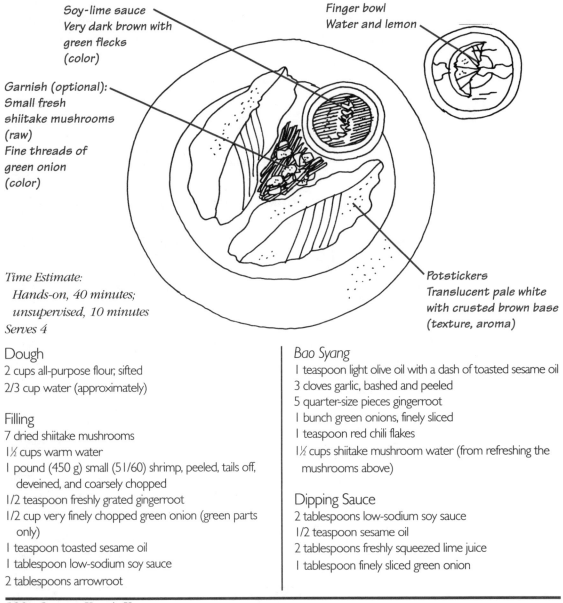

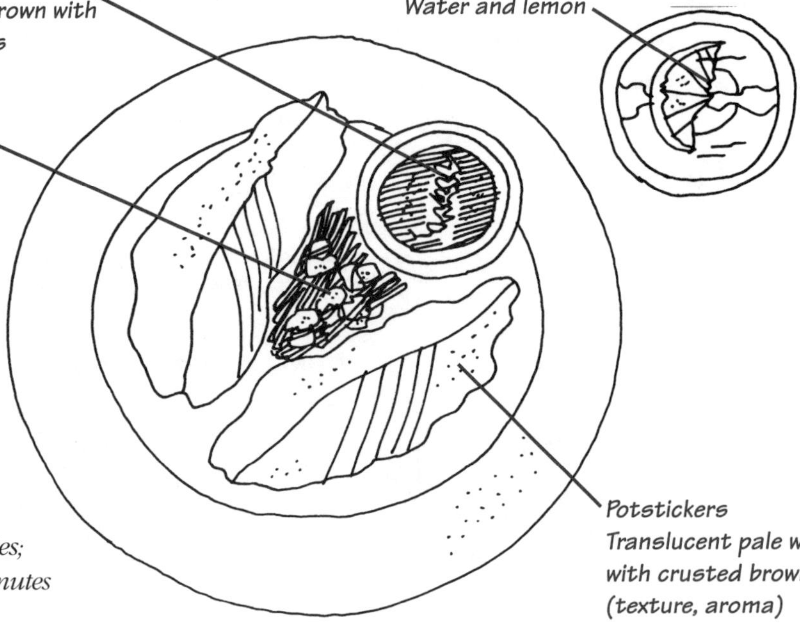
Soy-lime sauce
Very dark brown with green flecks (color)
Finger bowl
Water and lemon
Garnish (optional):
Small fresh shiitake mushrooms (raw)
Fine threads of green onion (color)
Potstickers
Translucent pale white with crusted brown base (texture, aroma)

Time Estimate:
Hands-on, 40 minutes; unsupervised, 10 minutes
Serves 4

Dough
2 cups all-purpose flour, sifted
2/3 cup water (approximately)

Filling
7 dried shiitake mushrooms
1½ cups warm water
1 pound (450 g) small (51/60) shrimp, peeled, tails off, deveined, and coarsely chopped
1/2 teaspoon freshly grated gingerroot
1/2 cup very finely chopped green onion (green parts only)
1 teaspoon toasted sesame oil
1 tablespoon low-sodium soy sauce
2 tablespoons arrowroot

Bao Syang
1 teaspoon light olive oil with a dash of toasted sesame oil
3 cloves garlic, bashed and peeled
5 quarter-size pieces gingerroot
1 bunch green onions, finely sliced
1 teaspoon red chili flakes
1½ cups shiitake mushroom water (from refreshing the mushrooms above)

Dipping Sauce
2 tablespoons low-sodium soy sauce
1/2 teaspoon sesame oil
2 tablespoons freshly squeezed lime juice
1 tablespoon finely sliced green onion

SHIITAKE MUSHROOMS

These dried, dark-brown Chinese mushrooms have a deep, earthy flavor and meaty texture—an excellent addition to stir-fries and soups. You can find them in plastic packages in the Asian section of many grocery stores or any Asian specialty food store.

A DUMPLING OR WON TON PRESS

If you develop a fondness for potstickers, you'll make the process go much quicker with a dumpling or won ton press, which can be found in most housewares shops. You simply put the rolled-out dough in the center of the press, put in the filling, brush the edges with a small amount of cold water, and close the press together to seal.

✕ EXTRA MEAL

Leftover potstickers can be used in the Thai hot and sour soup that follows. Double the dough and filling parts of the potsticker recipe. Lay the extra potstickers on a greased cookie sheet and freeze solid, about 2 hours. Remove from the sheet, lay in a gallon-size resealable freezer bag, and use within 2 months.

The dough: Put the sifted flour into a large food processor, switch on, and *slowly* add water. Very suddenly it will turn into a ball. Transfer to a floured board and knead for 2 or 3 minutes. Place in a bowl, cover with plastic, and let rest for 30 minutes.

The filling: Soak the dried mushrooms in warm water for 20 minutes. Strain, reserving the mushrooms and soaking water separately. Remove and discard the mushroom stems; coarsely chop the rest. On a large, flat surface, spread out each of the ingredients evenly in the following order: shrimp, shiitakes, ginger, onion, sesame oil, soy sauce, and arrowroot. Use a chopping motion with a chef's knife or a cleaver to mix all the ingredients together on the cutting board.

To assemble: Divide the dough into eight 2-ounce (50-g) pieces. You may have a little dough left over. Roll each piece into a ball and then roll out into a very thin (1/16-inch or 0.25-cm) 6-inch (15-cm) circle. Put 2 rounded tablespoons of the filling in the center of the circle. Fold in half, making a half-moon shape, and crimp the edges firmly. Repeat for the remaining dough.

The **bao syang***:* Pour the oil into a high-sided skillet and fry the potstickers with the garlic, ginger, onions, and chili flakes, without turning, until the potsticker bottoms are brown. Pour the reserved soaking liquid in, cover, and pan-steam (étouffée) for 10 minutes.

The sauce: Mix the soy sauce, sesame oil, lime juice, and onion together in a large bowl or pour into individual dipping bowls.

To serve: Place 2 potstickers on each individual plate and serve with the dipping sauce. I suggest you also give your guests a small bowl of water and a piece of lemon so that they can wash their fingers when the dunking is over.

Nutritional Profile per Serving			
	Classic	Springboard	Daily Value
Calories	266	346	
Calories from fat	108	36	
Fat (gm)	12	4	6%
Saturated fat (gm)	3	1	5%
Sodium (mg)	1161	580	24%
Cholesterol (mg)	45	107	36%
Carbohydrates (gm)	29	56	19%
Dietary fiber (gm)	2	3	12%
Classic compared: Potstickers			

✖ JUMBO POTSTICKER DISKS IN THAI HOT AND SOUR SOUP

Four leftover potstickers form the basis for this aromatic soup. The lemon grass, Kaffir lime leaves, galangale, and chili paste are highly aromatic Asian seasonings that lift this ordinary chicken soup to new heights. Perhaps it's time to visit an Asian specialty grocery and get a few of them in your kitchen cupboard?

Time Estimate:
  Hands-on, 35 minutes
Serves 4

1/2 recipe frozen jumbo potstickers (page 190) (4 jumbo potstickers)
4 cups low-sodium chicken stock (page 231)
1 lemon grass stalk, crushed and cut into 1-inch (2.5-cm) pieces
3 Kaffir lime leaves
2 slices galangale
1 teaspoon chili paste (caution: this is *hot* stuff!)
2 tablespoons fish sauce (*nam pla*)
1½ tablespoons freshly squeezed lemon juice
1 green onion, sliced on the diagonal
1 cup quartered mushrooms
1 tablespoon fresh cilantro leaves
2 cups diced chicken (preferably leg and thigh meat)

Cut each of the frozen potstickers into 5 pieces, discarding the end pieces of dough.

Pour the chicken stock into a large saucepan with the lemon grass, Kaffir lime leaves, and galangale. Bring to a boil, cover, and boil for 5 minutes. Stir in the chili paste, fish sauce, lemon juice, green onion, mushrooms, cilantro, and chicken, and bring to a boil. Add the potsticker slices, bring back to a boil, reduce the heat, and simmer gently for 5 minutes. Serve in deep soup bowls, making sure to divide the potsticker slices equally.

Nutritional Profile per Serving: Calories—516; calories from fat—99; fat (gm)—11 or 17% daily value; saturated fat (gm)—3; sodium (mg)—698; cholesterol (mg)—170; carbohydrates (gm)—60; dietary fiber (gm)—5

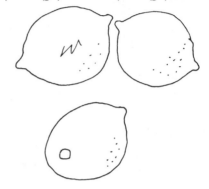

✖ CHUNKY CHICKEN CURRY

Braiden Rex-Johnson tells me that she has been a proponent of low-fat cooking for 10 years, since her husband, Spencer, was diagnosed with high blood pressure. Now she says foods prepared with large amounts of fat, butter, and cream "really do not taste good." Braiden has also lost 20 pounds, which she has successfully kept off for many years.
We went back and forth from Braiden's original curry recipe, both of us loving the fresh pineapple but Braiden noting that many people might have to work up to the level I liked of fresh ginger. Braiden is the author of the Pike Place Market Cookbook, *and she can be found at that market several times a week shopping for the freshest produce, fish, and dairy products.*

Time Estimate:
  Hands-on, 20 minutes;
  unsupervised, 30 minutes
Serves 6

2 pound butternut squash, halved and seeded
2 tablespoons low-sodium tomato paste
2 tablespoons de-alcoholized dry white wine
1½ tablespoons curry powder (see sidebar)
1/4 teaspoon freshly ground sea salt
1/2 teaspoon red chili flakes
I pound (450 g) boneless, skinless chicken breasts
I teaspoon light olive oil with a dash of toasted sesame oil
1/2 cup chopped onion
2 cloves garlic, bashed, peeled, and chopped fine
I tablespoon finely chopped fresh ginger
1/2 pound (225 g) fresh pineapple, roughly chopped, or
   I (8-ounce) (225-g) can crushed pineapple in
   unsweetened juice
2 medium carrots, cut into matchsticks
2 small zucchini, cut into matchsticks
I tablespoon cornstarch mixed with 2 tablespoons water
   (slurry)
1/2 cup nonfat plain yogurt
3 cups cooked rice

Invert 1/2 butternut squash on a baking sheet and heat at 350°F (180°C) for 45 minutes. Keep warm. Save the other half for another recipe.

In a large bowl, combine the tomato paste, wine, curry powder, salt, and red chili flakes. Cut each chicken breast once lengthwise, then across in 1/2-inch (1.5-cm) slices. Mix with the tomato paste mixture, cover, and let marinate in the refrigerator for at least 30 minutes.

Pour the oil into a high-sided skillet over medium-high heat and fry the onion, garlic, and ginger for 2 minutes. Add the fresh pineapple (or the canned pineapple with its juice) and carrots and cook for 5 minutes. Add the chicken and marinade mixture, cover, and simmer for 20 minutes. Stir in the zucchini and allow to heat through. Remove from the heat, stir in the cornstarch slurry, return to the heat, and bring to a boil for 3 minutes. Stir a little of the hot sauce into the yogurt, then stir all the yogurt back into the dish. Don't boil; otherwise the sauce will curdle.

To serve: Place a slice of the cooked squash in the middle of each serving plate, top with 1/2 cup of the cooked rice and equal portions of the chicken curry.

Nutritional Profile per Serving: Calories—313; calories from fat—36; fat (gm)—4 or 6% daily value; saturated fat (gm)—1; sodium (mg)—165; cholesterol (mg)—42; carbohydrates (gm)—48; dietary fiber (gm)—6

HOMEMADE CURRY POWDER

Commercial curry powder is a mixture of spices that you might want to vary to suit your personal tastes by making at home. here's a basic recipe.

1/2 teaspoon coriander seed
1/4 inch (0.75 cm) cinnamon stick
1/2 teaspoon cumin seed
3 whole cloves
1/4 teaspoon cardamom seed
I teaspoon curry powder
1/2 teaspoon turmeric

Place all the spices in a small electric coffee grinder and whiz for 4 minutes. Transfer the powder to a small metal sieve and shake to let the powders fall through. Toss out the gritty remains.

✖ Pan-Seared Mahimahi with Cockles and Mussels

Rick Moonen loves the poetry of this dish with cockles and mussels. But if you can't get cockles, don't be put off. Instead, use clams as a substitute. The mahimahi with the fresh vegetables and fragrant seasonings makes this a truly outstanding sensory experience—a great example of étouffée.

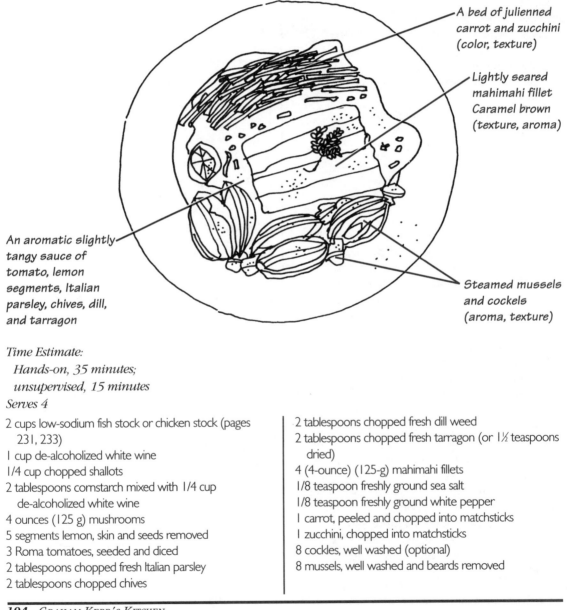

A bed of julienned carrot and zucchini (color, texture)

Lightly seared mahimahi fillet Caramel brown (texture, aroma)

An aromatic slightly tangy sauce of tomato, lemon segments, Italian parsley, chives, dill, and tarragon

Steamed mussels and cockels (aroma, texture)

Time Estimate:
  Hands-on, 35 minutes;
  unsupervised, 15 minutes
Serves 4

2 cups low-sodium fish stock or chicken stock (pages 231, 233)
1 cup de-alcoholized white wine
1/4 cup chopped shallots
2 tablespoons cornstarch mixed with 1/4 cup de-alcoholized white wine
4 ounces (125 g) mushrooms
5 segments lemon, skin and seeds removed
3 Roma tomatoes, seeded and diced
2 tablespoons chopped fresh Italian parsley
2 tablespoons chopped chives

2 tablespoons chopped fresh dill weed
2 tablespoons chopped fresh tarragon (or 1½ teaspoons dried)
4 (4-ounce) (125-g) mahimahi fillets
1/8 teaspoon freshly ground sea salt
1/8 teaspoon freshly ground white pepper
1 carrot, peeled and chopped into matchsticks
1 zucchini, chopped into matchsticks
8 cockles, well washed (optional)
8 mussels, well washed and beards removed

Rick Moonen's restaurant, the Water Club in New York City, is actually a permanently moored converted barge. Critics describe his food as a "seafood-slanted all-American menu that is flat out fresh, light yet zesty, preferring distilled flavor essences to the classic butter and cream." When you've got the time, it's a great destination and the food is wonderful.

Rick explains, "I alter the menu seasonally. As the weather warms up, I reduce butter and cream and replace them with salsas, vinaigrettes, and infusions. My grill becomes the focal point, and that allows me to marinate fresh items and quickly finish them to order."

Rich has a wonderful specialty that's always available, rain or shine: steamed spaghetti squash. There is also a crisp basil polenta served with grilled vegetables and a fresh tomato sauce. "I don't believe that a customer should be forced to order a dull steamed vegetable plate."

I do like this man.

MAHIMAHI EN PAPILLOTE

The mahimahi can also be presented en papillote by preparing 4 individual aluminum foil pockets and placing the raw fish and a quarter of the remaining ingredients in each. Bake at 375°F (180°C) for 20 minutes.

Place the fish stock, white wine, and shallots in a medium pan and boil about 15 minutes, until the liquid is reduced to approximately 2 cups. Remove from the heat, stir in the cornstarch slurry, return to the heat, and boil about 3 minutes. (While you are reducing the stocks, sear the mushrooms in a small frying pan with a spritz of olive oil.) Allow the liquid to cool, then add the lemon segments, tomatoes, mushrooms and chopped herbs.

In a large nonstick skillet over medium heat sear the mahimahi, which has been lightly salted and peppered, until lightly browned, about 2 minutes on each side. Place the carrot and zucchini in the bottom of a large, heavy-based skillet, cover with the seared mahimahi, and pour the sauce over the fish. Carefully place the cockles and mussels on top, cover, and cook over a gentle heat for 10 minutes.

To serve: Bow-tie pasta will help soak up some of the delicious juices that come from this carousel of fish, seafood, vegetables, and fresh herbs.

Nutritional Profile per Serving	Classic	Springboard	Daily Value
Calories	350	225	
Calories from fat	171	18	
Fat (gm)	19	2	3%
Saturated fat (gm)	3	.27	1%
Sodium (mg)	616	179	14%
Cholesterol (mg)	114	90	30%
Carbohydrates (gm)	8	19	6%
Dietary fiber (gm)	2	3	12%
Classic compared: Hellenic Seafood Stew			

23
POULTRY SKIN ON

Cook meat and fish with the skin on to keep it moist and tender; remove before eating to get rid of the fat.

When you look at the nutritional numbers, it's obvious that poultry makes excellent low-fat eating—but only when the fat and skin are removed. Equally obvious is the fact that all dry-heat methods of cooking (pan-frying, broiling, roasting, grilling) tend to make meat drier, even stringy, if *cooked* without the skin. It is not a matter of whether you should *cook* with the skin on, but rather *when* you should take it off.

My research shows that the answer depends on the method of cooking. You can safely leave the skin on for all dry-heat cooking and remove it before serving. But for moist-heat methods, like braising, étouffée, stewing, casseroles, the skin fat can accumulate in the final dish. In any dish that includes grains (like my wife Treena's favorite, vegetable and barley soup), the grain will soak up the fat from the meat like a sponge. In all these cases, you will have to take the skin off before cooking or, for the leanest final dish, cook the meat separately. However, there is an exception for poaching, boiling, or steaming, where a thin broth develops and vegetables that are used for seasoning are later discarded. In this latter case, whatever fat is released will float to the surface, where it can be removed.

Tips and Hints

- As always, buy the best and freshest. At peak freshness, poultry is plump and firm. They should have no pinfeathers and no odor. You may like to try free-range chickens, which are mostly hormone free and antibiotic free, and sample their much touted flavor (the fat will be quite yellow).

- A whole chicken is the best buy; you yourself can cut off the breast meat for dry-heat dishes and the legs for moist-heat uses. When handling the raw birds, always wash your hands, knives, and cutting board in hot soapy water to prevent possible bacterial contamination of other food.

Poultry with the skin off.

- Fry poultry breasts skin side down to release a little fat, then flip them over to seal. When cooked, remove the breast and blot the pan dry with a paper towel to remove most of the excess fat. Now you can continue with your recipe using the same skillet.

✖ STIR-FRIED DUCK AND LYCHEES

"I always remove the skin after I cook poultry; to lose that juice is nonsense." Those are the words of Chester Jaro. He is one of our rare birds: he indicated a preference for duck as a favorite main dish and "stir-fry" as his number-one preferred cooking method—so this elegant stir-fry is your dish, Chester.

If you buy a whole duck, you can use the breasts for this recipe and save the legs to use in *Braised Duck with Pineapple and Peppers (page 200)*. You will also have a carcass to make the stock that adds so much flavor to both dishes.

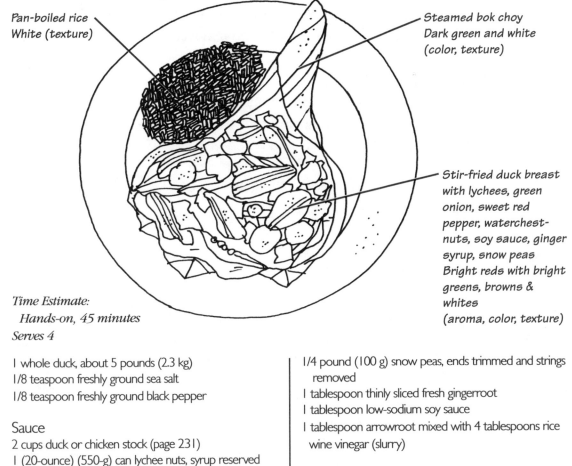

Pan-boiled rice
White (texture)

Steamed bok choy
Dark green and white
(color, texture)

Stir-fried duck breast
with lychees, green
onion, sweet red
pepper, waterchest-
nuts, soy sauce, ginger
syrup, snow peas
Bright reds with bright
greens, browns &
whites
(aroma, color, texture)

Time Estimate:
  Hands-on, 45 minutes
Serves 4

I whole duck, about 5 pounds (2.3 kg)
1/8 teaspoon freshly ground sea salt
1/8 teaspoon freshly ground black pepper

Sauce
2 cups duck or chicken stock (page 231)
I (20-ounce) (550-g) can lychee nuts, syrup reserved
I teaspoon light olive oil with a dash of toasted sesame oil
I bunch green onions, white and green parts separated
1/2 medium red bell pepper, seeded and cut into 1/2-inch (1.5-cm) strips
I (8-ounce) (225-g) can water chestnuts, drained, each chestnut cut into 3 pieces

1/4 pound (100 g) snow peas, ends trimmed and strings removed
I tablespoon thinly sliced fresh gingerroot
I tablespoon low-sodium soy sauce
I tablespoon arrowroot mixed with 4 tablespoons rice wine vinegar (slurry)

Bok Choy
4 small heads bok choy
1/8 teaspoon freshly ground sea salt
1/8 teaspoon freshly ground black pepper

4 cups cooked long-grain white rice

⊠ EXTRA MEAL

After cutting the breasts off a whole duck, and using the carcass for duck stock, you can use the duck legs for the braised duck with pineapple and peppers (recipe follows). To freeze the legs, take the skin and fat off, wrap each leg in plastic wrap, and freeze in a quart-size resealable plastic bag. Don't forget to label and date the bag.

And don't throw away that skin and fat from the legs. It will impart enormous flavor to the duck stock and you can skim off excess fat from the top later.

Disjoint the duck (or have your butcher do this), cutting it up as you would a chicken. You will use only the breast for this recipe; set aside the remainder for another use.

Preheat the oven to 350°F (180°C). Put the duck breast halves in a small ovenproof skillet on medium heat and fry skin side down for a few minutes to render the fat. Sprinkle with the salt and pepper, turn over, and brown the other side for 1 minute. Wipe any fat out of the pan, return the duck, place in the oven, and bake for 20 minutes. The internal temperature should read 160°F (71°C). Transfer the duck to a cutting board and keep warm.

The sauce: Pour all the pan juices into a saucepan with the duck stock and the lychee syrup. Boil until reduced to 1½ cups, about 15 minutes. Pour into a fat strainer, then pour the defatted stock back into the saucepan and set aside.

Pour the oil into a large skillet on medium-high heat and fry the white parts of the green onions and the bell pepper for 1 minute. Add the water chestnuts, snow peas, ginger, and green onion parts. Deglaze the pan with the defatted stock mixture, then stir in 16 lychees and the soy sauce. Bring to a boil, remove from the heat, stir in the arrowroot slurry, return to the heat, and boil until thickened, about 30 seconds.

The bok choy: Wash the stems carefully. Place the heads in a steamer tray, cover, and steam for 3 minutes. Season lightly with salt and pepper.

To serve: Remove and discard the heavy fat and skin from the duck, then cut each breast across the grain into 1/4-inch (0.75-cm) slices—you should have about 20 slices. Place a steamed bok choy head in the middle of each plate and fan out the leaves. Spoon the duck and the sauce onto the leaves and serve the rice on the side.

Nutritional Profile per Serving			
	Classic	Springboard	Daily Value
Calories	857	544	
Calories from fat	459	99	
Fat (gm)	51	11	17%
Saturated fat (gm)	9	3	15%
Sodium (mg)	1529	418	17%
Cholesterol (mg)	70	55	18%
Carbohydrates (gm)	68	87	29%
Dietary fiber (gm)	5	6	24%
Classic compared: Duck Salad			

✖ Braised Duck with Pineapple and Peppers

Duck has the unique quality of being elegant enough for guests but definitely comfortable enough to serve for the family. This colorful braise can be made with the duck legs left over from making stir-fried duck and lychees, in the preceding recipe.

Time Estimate:
Hands-on, 20 minutes;
unsupervised, 1 hour
Serves 4

3 cups low-fat duck or chicken stock (page 231)

2 duck legs (drumsticks and thighs), stripped of skin and fat

1 teaspoon light olive oil with a dash of toasted sesame oil

1 tablespoon freshly grated gingerroot

1/2 each green, red, and yellow bell pepper, seeded and cut into 1-inch (2.5-cm) pieces

1½ cups fresh pineapple, cut into 1-inch (2.5-cm) chunks

1 cup unsweetened pineapple juice

1 cup reserved low-fat duck stock (used in cooking the legs)

2 tablespoons arrowroot mixed with 2 tablespoons low-sodium soy sauce and 2 tablespoons unsweetened pineapple juice (slurry)

4 cups cooked rice

2 heads bok choy, cut thinly on the diagonal and lightly steamed

Pour the duck stock into a large pot, add the duck legs, and gently simmer for 1 hour. Transfer the duck legs to a plate and, when cool, strip the meat from the bones and cut into large chunks. Pour 1 cup of the stock used in cooking into a fat strainer and set aside. Freeze the rest for another recipe.

Pour the oil into a large skillet on medium heat and fry the ginger for 1 minute. Add all the peppers and fry for 3 minutes. Stir in the pineapple chunks and just heat through. Deglaze the pan with the pineapple juice and duck stock and bring to a boil. Remove from the heat, stir in the arrowroot slurry, return to the heat, and stir until thickened and clear, about 30 seconds. Stir in the cooked duck meat and heat through. Spoon the stew over the cooked rice and serve with lightly steamed bok choy on the side.

Nutritional Profile per Serving: Calories—387; calories from fat—45; fat (gm)—5 or 7% daily value; saturated fat (gm)—2; sodium (mg)—380; cholesterol (mg)—21; carbohydrates (gm)—70; dietary fiber (gm)—3

✠ Dijon Chicken

I springboarded this recipe with Cindy Durkin, who says "It's even better than my original!" Cindy and her husband both have "hectic" jobs at Microsoft Computers. "Cooking healthy is very important to us, but we also need to be able to cook fast, so we often eat a lot of vegetables and pasta before we rush out the door. Graham's Minimax suggestions have helped to rework a lot of our favorites that aren't so healthy."

Time Estimate:
  Hands-on, 30 minutes
Serves 4

Chicken
1 teaspoon light olive oil with a dash of toasted sesame oil
4 (6-ounce) (150-g) boneless chicken breasts, skin on
1 bunch green onions, chopped
1 tablespoon mustard seed
1 teaspoon dried basil
3/4 cup de-alcoholized white wine
1/4 cup Dijon mustard
2 teaspoons cornstarch mixed with 4 teaspoons de-alcoholized white wine (slurry)
2 tablespoons strained yogurt (page 234)
2 cups cooked white rice

Vegetables
2 pounds (900 g) broccoli, rinsed
4 medium carrots, peeled and cut on the diagonal into 1/4-inch (0.75-cm) slices
1/4 teaspoon freshly ground sea salt

Garnish
2 teaspoons chopped fresh parsley
8 strips roasted red bell pepper from a jar

The chicken: Pour the oil into a large nonstick skillet over medium heat and brown the chicken breasts until golden, starting with the skin side down, about 2 minutes on each side. Remove from the pan, take off the skin, and set aside. Blot the skillet with paper towels to remove most of the fat, and fry the onions for 2 minutes. Add the mustard seed, basil, and wine and bring to a boil. Stir in the cooked chicken, cover, reduce the heat, and simmer for 5 minutes. Transfer the chicken to a warm platter and keep warm.

Over low heat, whisk the mustard into the pan juices. Remove from the heat, pour in the cornstarch slurry, return to the heat, and boil for 3 minutes. Pour a little of the sauce into the yogurt, mix well, then add all the yogurt to the sauce, stirring just until smooth and heated through. Keep warm on the lowest heat.

The vegetable: Cut off and discard the bottom 2 inches (5 cm) of thick broccoli stalk and peel the stalks up to the florets. Cut off the peeled stalks 1 inch (2.5 cm) below where the florets begin to branch out. Cut the stalks into 1/4-inch (0.75-cm) diagonal slices. Break apart the florets, leaving the stem on each.

Put 1 inch (2.5 cm) of water in a steamer pot and bring to a boil. Place the carrots in a steamer tray and steam for 6 minutes. Add the sliced broccoli stalks and florets, sprinkle with the salt, and steam for 2½ minutes longer.

To serve: Nestle the chicken breasts on a bed of rice. Ladle some sauce and the steamed broccoli and carrots on the side. Garnish with the parsley and roasted pepper strips.

Nutritional Profile per Serving: Calories—483; calories from fat—63; fat (gm)—7 or 11% daily value; saturated fat (gm)—2; sodium (mg)—493; cholesterol (mg)—87; carbohydrates (gm)—60; dietary fiber (gm)—7

✖ BREAST OF CHICKEN WITH CABERNET, ORANGE, AND GINGER SAUCE

This delicious dish by Chef David Day is a complex mix of flavors, but is basically a Minimax variation on the classic chicken breast cooked in wine, Coq au Vin. A comparison between the two recipes is quite interesting: instead of the classic's bacon fried in butter, David's complex sauce features bright notes of orange juice, fresh ginger, and thyme. Of course, the major reduction in fat comes from removing the chicken skin before serving. But simply using de-alcoholized wine resulted in big calorie savings. Then, to complete the picture, instead of the classic's accompaniment of butter-braised vegetables, David presents poached pears. A splendid example of reinventing the classic through the techniques of the future.

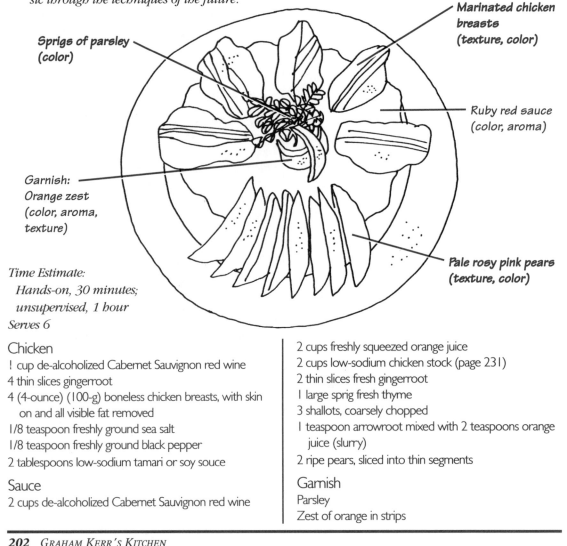

Sprigs of parsley
(color)

Marinated chicken
breasts
(texture, color)

Ruby red sauce
(color, aroma)

Garnish:
Orange zest
(color, aroma,
texture)

Pale rosy pink pears
(texture, color)

Time Estimate:
  Hands-on, 30 minutes;
  unsupervised, 1 hour
Serves 6

Chicken
1 cup de-alcoholized Cabernet Sauvignon red wine
4 thin slices gingerroot
4 (4-ounce) (100-g) boneless chicken breasts, with skin
  on and all visible fat removed
1/8 teaspoon freshly ground sea salt
1/8 teaspoon freshly ground black pepper
2 tablespoons low-sodium tamari or soy souce

Sauce
2 cups de-alcoholized Cabernet Sauvignon red wine

2 cups freshly squeezed orange juice
2 cups low-sodium chicken stock (page 231)
2 thin slices fresh gingerroot
1 large sprig fresh thyme
3 shallots, coarsely chopped
1 teaspoon arrowroot mixed with 2 teaspoons orange
  juice (slurry)
2 ripe pears, sliced into thin segments

Garnish
Parsley
Zest of orange in strips

This is a subject very close to home. I live on an island and have to drive about 30 miles to reach a good restaurant. How pleased I am that after that long drive I can eat at one of the best restaurants in Washington State: *David Day's* Wildflowers, in Mount Vernon.

David serves highly innovative and delicious food. For instance, this chicken breast recipe at his restaurant comes stuffed with a delicious mélange of tofu with figs, prunes, and apricots which have been marinated in orange juice and ginger.

David likes to cater to the interests of his two types of customers. "Some of my customers are here to celebrate, a birthday, or anniversary; they want an experience. Others are very interested in healthier choices, and I enjoy the challenge to create for them."

The chicken: Combine the red wine and ginger; place the chicken breasts, with skin on, in the marinade and refrigerate for at least 1 hour. Preheat the oven to 375°F (190°C). Remove the chicken from the marinade and pat dry. Sprinkle with the salt and pepper, place on a rack in a roasting pan, skin side up, and roast for 15 minutes. Brush the chicken with the tamari sauce and continue roasting for 5 minutes. Remove from the oven, let rest for 5 minutes, and remove the skin.

The sauce: While the chicken is roasting, pour the wine, orange juice, chicken stock, ginger, thyme, and shallots into a large saucepan. Bring to a boil and cook, uncovered, about 35 minutes, until the mixture is reduced to about 1 cup. Pour the sauce through a fine sieve into a smaller saucepan. Add the arrowroot slurry, return to the heat, and bring to a boil, stirring constantly. Add the pears and heat through.

To serve: Strain the pears from the sauce. Pool the sauce onto 4 plates. Carve each chicken breast into 4 or 5 slices, fan out onto the sauce, and garnish with the parsley. Fan the pear slices onto the plate and sprinkle with the orange zest.

Nutritional Profile per Serving			
	Classic	**Springboard**	**Daily Value**
Calories	726	176	
Calories from fat	288	27	
Fat (gm)	32	3	5%
Saturated fat (gm)	13	0.7	3%
Sodium (mg)	1301	345	14%
Cholesterol (mg)	159	38	13%
Carbohydrates (gm)	25	21	7%
Dietary fiber (gm)	4	2	8%
Classic compared: Coq au Vin			

24 PASTA

Naturally low in fat for all your cooking, enhanced with glistening, delicious, low-fat sauces and creative garnishes.

Much has been said and written about the Mediterranean diet and its apparent benefits. The question is, can we get a similar benefit where we live? Well, it's very hard to pinpoint one ingredient as the "magic bullet" of health. It isn't just the olive oil, or fresh fish, or red wine, or the fact that people walk more; it's all of the above working together, and much, much more.

However, if I were to pluck a single entrant out of the contest and modify its method of use, I'd take the hard durum semolina wheat flour from which pasta is made, and cut way back on the amount of oil used in many of its so-called classic preparations.

Not only is olive oil delicious; it's more stable than other monounsaturated oils and could contribute to increasing the good HDL cholesterol in the blood, but only to a point. I would suggest 4 to 6 tablespoons a day in a 2,500-calorie-a-day intake. After that, when added to other fats, it could easily break through the ceiling of 30 percent of daily calories from fat recommended as maximum intake for healthy folk.

The other change I'd make is to opt for the Rome-South selection that most Italians do, and take my hard durum semolina flour straight, without the eggs added by the Rome-North brigade. And while I'm at it, I would stop adding cream to Alfredo and carbonara sauces that never did start out that way, anyhow.

So now, what do you do?

Tips and Hints

Graham explains "eggless pasta" to some sharp critics

- Buy a good brand of pasta made without eggs. Read your pasta package cooking instructions and follow them closely, just cooking your pasta *al dente*, or "to the tooth." Never overcook pasta; a small cooking timer will help here.
- Use a large pot of vigorously boiling water. The water will boil quicker if you cover it. You can add a pinch of salt because most of it will leave with the straining. Add the pasta, stir well to keep the strands separate and from catching on the bottom. Cover until the pot reboils, then remove the lid to keep the water from boiling over, and cook according to package instructions.
- As soon as the pasta has finished cooking, strain into a colander over a large serving bowl, allowing the water to heat the bowl while you finish the sauce. Time this to occur just before you eat. You should never reheat pasta.
- Add a maximum of 1 tablespoon of arrowroot for each 1 cup of sauce to make it glisten. Pour the water from the now-warm bowl, add the sauce, then the pasta, and toss well. Garnish with up to 1 tablespoon of freshly grated Parmesan cheese, along with black pepper and fresh oregano to taste.

✖ LATIN AMERICAN PASTA SHELLS MARINARA

Judith Isaac, like so many of my new friends, is very fond of Italian and Mexican food. She also wants a dish that's reasonably fast. This is where the idea of the "extra meal" comes into its own. If you double or quadruple the marinara sauce now and freeze it in portion sizes, you can have a homemade meal later almost in a flash.

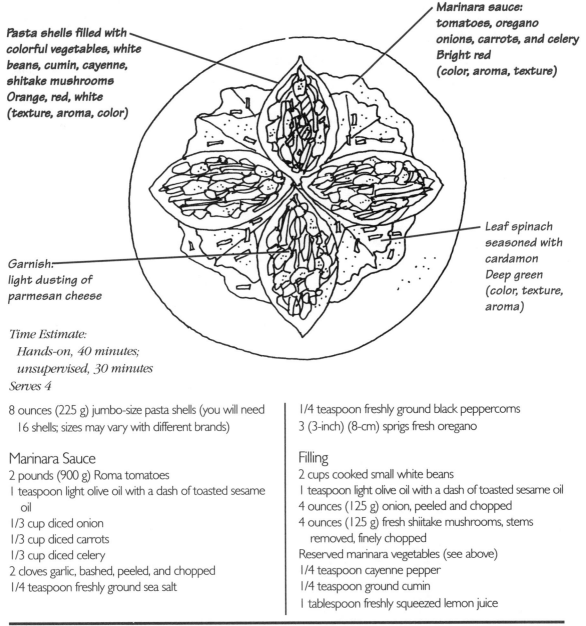

Pasta shells filled with colorful vegetables, white beans, cumin, cayenne, shitake mushrooms
Orange, red, white
(texture, aroma, color)

Marinara sauce: tomatoes, oregano onions, carrots, and celery
Bright red
(color, aroma, texture)

Leaf spinach seasoned with cardamon
Deep green
(color, texture, aroma)

Garnish:
light dusting of parmesan cheese

Time Estimate:
  Hands-on, 40 minutes;
  unsupervised, 30 minutes
Serves 4

8 ounces (225 g) jumbo-size pasta shells (you will need 16 shells; sizes may vary with different brands)

Marinara Sauce
2 pounds (900 g) Roma tomatoes
1 teaspoon light olive oil with a dash of toasted sesame oil
1/3 cup diced onion
1/3 cup diced carrots
1/3 cup diced celery
2 cloves garlic, bashed, peeled, and chopped
1/4 teaspoon freshly ground sea salt

1/4 teaspoon freshly ground black peppercorns
3 (3-inch) (8-cm) sprigs fresh oregano

Filling
2 cups cooked small white beans
1 teaspoon light olive oil with a dash of toasted sesame oil
4 ounces (125 g) onion, peeled and chopped
4 ounces (125 g) fresh shiitake mushrooms, stems removed, finely chopped
Reserved marinara vegetables (see above)
1/4 teaspoon cayenne pepper
1/4 teaspoon ground cumin
1 tablespoon freshly squeezed lemon juice

Vegetable

1 pound (450 g) fresh spinach, washed and stems removed

1/2 teaspoon ground cardamom

1/8 teaspoon freshly ground sea salt

2 tablespoons freshly squeezed lemon juice

1 teaspoon arrowroot mixed with 2 teaspoons water (slurry)

4 teaspoons freshly grated Parmesan cheese

Judy Isaac's daughter has prompted an experiment with vegetarian eating in their house that's resulting in the entire family eating less meat. But Judy discovered that many vegetarian cookbooks substitute high-fat foods like cheese or dairy products for meat. She found that it was a challenge to find something "quick to prepare that's not loaded with fat."

"That's why I like the filling in this recipe," says Judy. "It doesn't rely on the usual cheese filling for the shell, and I think the beans make it very hearty. We've tried this more than once and it's really a treat to find something everyone in the family likes.

"We just can't cook the way my grandma used to," Judy remembers. "Fried chicken with lots of Crisco is one example. My father died of heart disease and I'm sure he didn't eat right."

Judy tries consciously to aim for only 30 percent of her calories from fat. One of her favorite low-fat techniques for making creamy soups is to purée vegetables in her food processor and whisk them into the soup at the last minute. "I've also used powdered dried milk whisked in just before serving. It makes the soup look whiter and you think you're eating a cream soup when there's no cream at all. And no one knows it's powdered milk. If my family thought they were eating powdered milk, they might not!"

✕ Extra Meal

When you make the marinara sauce, make a double or triple recipe. Dip out 2 1/2 cups per recipe before straining. Freeze in quart-size resealable plastic bags. Use within 6 months.

Cook the pasta shells according to package directions until barely *al dente*. Drain and rinse in cold water.

The marinara sauce: Bring a medium saucepan of water to boil. Make a small incision with a knife in the stem end of each tomato and blanch them for 30 seconds. Drain and transfer to a bowl of ice water. Slip the skins off, place the tomatoes in a large sealable plastic bag, and press down gently until they squash somewhat; do not mash completely.

Pour the oil into a medium saucepan on medium heat and fry the onion, carrots, celery, and garlic for 5 minutes. Stir in the tomatoes, salt, pepper, and oregano; cover and cook for 15 minutes. Remove from the heat and strain, pressing the vegetables to extract the juices but do not crush. This should yield 2 cups of sauce. Reserve the pressed vegetables left in the sieve to use in the filling.

The filling: Purée 1½ cups of the beans in a food processor until creamy. Heat the oil in a large skillet on medium heat and fry the onion and mushrooms for 5 minutes. Stir in the puréed beans, reserved vegetables from the marinara sauce, and the remaining 1/2 cup of whole beans. Season with the cayenne, cumin, and lemon juice. Remove from the heat and set aside.

Assemble the shells: Preheat the oven to 350°F (180°C). Pour the marinara sauce into a 9 x 9-inch (23 x 23-cm) baking pan. Fill each cooked pasta shell with a heaping tablespoon of the filling and line them up in the pan. Bake uncovered for 30 minutes.

The vegetable: Just before the shells are finished baking, toss the spinach with the cardamom and salt. Pour the lemon juice into a high-sided skillet on medium heat and cook the spinach until just limp, about 3 minutes.

(continued)

To serve: Arrange a bed of spinach on each serving plate and top with 4 shells. Pour the sauce from the baking dish into a small saucepan, stir in the slurry, bring to a boil, and stir until thickened and clear, about 30 seconds. Pour the thickened sauce over the pasta and spinach. Garnish with a sprinkling of the Parmesan cheese.

Nutritional Profile per Serving			
	Classic	Springboard	Daily Value
Calories	624	464	
Calories from fat	369	45	
Fat (gm)	41	5	8%
Saturated fat (gm)	22	1	5%
Sodium (mg)	1190	333	14%
Cholesterol (mg)	183	2	0.06%
Carbohydrates (gm)	32	87	29%
Dietary fiber (gm)	3	12	48%
Classic compared: Baked Cannelloni with Spinach and Ricotta			

✖ ANGEL HAIR MARINARA

You can't go wrong with this recipe. Pick your favorite garnish for the delicate thin strands of angel hair pasta bathed in the delicious red marinara sauce. You'll be able to put it all together in minutes if you've made the marinara sauce ahead of time and have it frozen.

Time Estimate:
  Hands-on, 15 minutes
Serves 4

1 recipe Marinara Sauce (page 206)
8 ounces (225 g) angel hair pasta, cooked according to package directions

Garnish Variations
16 Little Neck clams, well scrubbed
1/2 cup pitted Greek olives, halved
16 medium shrimp, peeled and deveined
4 mushrooms, sliced
1/2 medium green bell pepper, seeded and cut into thin strips
8 artichoke heart quarters
1/2 cup freshly grated Parmesan cheese

   Heat the marinara sauce in a medium skillet. You can cook your favorite garnish in the hot sauce—the clams until they open, the shrimp until they're pink, the olives until they're warm, or the vegetables until they're tender.

To serve: Pour the sauce and garnish over the cooked pasta and garnish with a sprinkling of the freshly grated Parmesan cheese. Serve with French bread and a green salad tossed with low-fat dressing.

Nutritional Profile per Serving: Calories—526; calories from fat—63; fat (gm)—7 or 11% daily value; saturated fat (gm)—3; sodium (mg)—744; cholesterol (mg)—10; carbohydrates (gm)—94; dietary fiber (gm)—8

✖ Rigatoni Cavafiori Patty

Patty Sullivan Back's original recipe was a great low-fat creation, but the combination of the white sauce and cauliflower was just a whiter shade of pale. So I made only a slight variation. Patty's reaction: "The addition of the red bell pepper was an inspiration—it adds just a hint of sweetness and a wonderful color." Patricia lives in Missouri with her "husband of ten years and two beautiful but slightly neurotic cats." "I love to paint and to garden, and find these pursuits perfectly in tune with the creative urge necessary to be a good cook." And in Missouri you should be able to grow great red bell peppers for this dish.

Time Estimate:
  Hands-on, 35 minutes
Serves 2 for dinner, 4 as a side dish

Sauce

1 tablespoon light olive oil with a dash of toasted sesame oil
2 medium shallots, sliced thin
1 clove garlic, bashed, peeled, and chopped
10 large button mushrooms, sliced thin
1/2 red bell pepper, cored and cut into small strips
1 (6-ounce) (175-g) can evaporated skim milk
1 tablespoon chopped fresh basil
1 tablespoon chopped fresh cilantro
2 cups cauliflower florets, steamed
1/2 teaspoon freshly grated sea salt
1/4 cup freshly grated Parmesan cheese

8 ounces (225 g) uncooked rigatoni pasta
1 teaspoon freshly ground black pepper
4 large basil leaves

The sauce: Pour the oil into a large skillet on medium heat and fry the shallots and garlic for 2 minutes. Add the mushrooms and the peppers and fry for 1 minute. Stir in the milk and boil until reduced by one third, about 5 minutes. Stir in the basil, cilantro, cauliflower, and salt and cook for 1 minute. Remove from heat and fold in the cheese.

Cook the rigatoni according to package directions.

To serve: Place the rigatoni on individual plates, pour the sauce on top, sprinkle with the pepper, and garnish with the whole basil leaves.

Nutritional Profile per Serving (as a side dish): Calories—344; calories from fat—63; fat (gm)—7 or 11% daily value; saturated fat (gm)—2; sodium (mg)—452; cholesterol (mg)—7; carbohydrates (gm)—56; dietary fiber (gm)—4

✠ ANGEL HAIR PASTA WITH MUSHROOMS, ESCAROLE, AND CLAMS

"Tall, slim, with a grin" describes chef Peter Pryor exactly. But this dish made me smile: the combination of the pasta with escarole and clams keeps the fragile angel hair from clumping together. This is a pasta "light as a feather" but also quite satisfying.

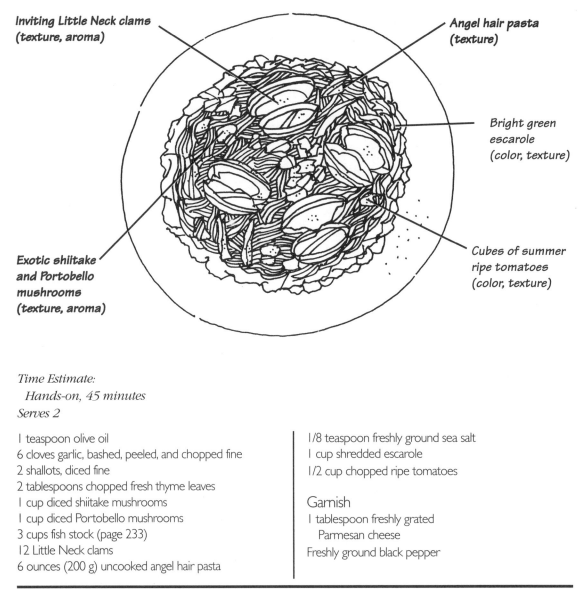

Inviting Little Neck clams
(texture, aroma)

Angel hair pasta
(texture)

Bright green escarole
(color, texture)

Exotic shiitake and Portobello mushrooms
(texture, aroma)

Cubes of summer ripe tomatoes
(color, texture)

Time Estimate:
  Hands-on, 45 minutes
Serves 2

1 teaspoon olive oil
6 cloves garlic, bashed, peeled, and chopped fine
2 shallots, diced fine
2 tablespoons chopped fresh thyme leaves
1 cup diced shiitake mushrooms
1 cup diced Portobello mushrooms
3 cups fish stock (page 233)
12 Little Neck clams
6 ounces (200 g) uncooked angel hair pasta

1/8 teaspoon freshly ground sea salt
1 cup shredded escarole
1/2 cup chopped ripe tomatoes

Garnish
1 tablespoon freshly grated
  Parmesan cheese
Freshly ground black pepper

Peter Pryor is the executive chef of Carolina's, which has two locations, one in Philadelphia and the other in Radnor, Pennsylvania. Carolina's features American cuisine with an emphasis on refined home-style cooking presented with a creative flair. The menu also features healthy and light selections. This is due, in part, to Peter's personal experiences.

"Over the past twenty years," explains Peter, "I have developed a healthy lifestyle for myself, including being a vegetarian for a time and living the philosophy of moderation."

Peter works with the Jefferson Hospital program "Dining with Heart" to develop low-fat selections at restaurants. Two examples of his creativity and conviction for me were a Peking-style pork loin with sweet and sour cabbage mixed with oriental vegetables, and a grilled loin of venison topped with a blackberry sauce and wild mushrooms.

Pour the oil into a large skillet on medium heat and fry the garlic, shallots, thyme, and mushrooms until the mushrooms are just cooked, about 4 minutes. Remove from the heat and set aside. In a separate medium saucepan, bring the fish stock to a simmer. Add the clams, cover, and cook until they open. Transfer the clams to a bowl, throwing away any unopened ones.

Bring the stock back to a boil in the medium saucepan, add the angel hair pasta, and cook until *al dente,* about 2 to 3 minutes. Drain into a large bowl, reserving the stock to use as a base for a fish soup.

In the large skillet, reheat the mushroom mixture. Add the escarole and tomatoes and mix well. Add the cooked pasta and clams and toss.

Serve on large dinner plates garnished with the Parmesan cheese. Season at the table with a little freshly ground black pepper.

Nutritional Profile per Serving			
	Classic	Springboard	Daily Value
Calories	1279	524	
Calories from fat	684	72	
Fat (gm)	76	8	12%
Saturated fat (gm)	46	2	10%
Sodium (mg)	1260	456	19%
Cholesterol (mg)	264	21	7%
Carbohydrates (gm)	103	87	29%
Dietary fiber (gm)	6	8	32%
Classic compared: Linguine with Porcini Cream Sauce			

CAKES

Baking soda, baking powder, and fruit purees, make the textural difference in great tasting low-fat cakes.

I have two great emotional needs in any cake: it must have a deep definite taste and it must be moist. This kind of cake allows me to have one *relatively small slice* and be satisfied. Light airy gâteaux have a way of sitting up on the cake stand, begging for an encore. From a nourishment point of view, I'd also like the cake to contain much more than empty sugar and flour calories. I'm also interested in cakes that can be heated and served with a hot sauce as a dessert on a cold winter's day.

To get good results with my recipes, you really must follow them exactly. After a while you'll learn how a recipe works best for you in the quantities you make. Jot down your findings and don't lose them.

The common link in my cakes is the use of baking

powder and baking soda, which produce bubbles of carbon dioxide when they come into contact with other ingredients in the batter, and cause the cake to rise. The important difference between the two is that baking soda causes large bubbles of carbon dioxide for a coarser-textured cake and baking powder makes tiny ones for a finer texture. By combining the two in just the right proportion, you get just the right texture.

In traditional cakes, oil and eggs are the major players that interact with baking powder and baking soda to provide the cake's texture. This is where I went to work: I immediately replaced whole eggs with liquid egg substitute. I cut the amount of butter in half and changed it to lower-saturated-fat oil. Then I replaced half of that amount of oil with fruit purée. At this point, I found it was necessary to double the spices and flavorings because there was so little fat left to carry around the flavors.

The frosting is the last fat trap in any cake. As you'll see in the following recipes, creamy strained yogurt became the basis of a delicious sauce that satisfies without extra fat.

The cakes that follow may not be exactly what you're used to; but as you'll discover, they have their own definite highlights.

Tips and Hints

Here's the secret to great low-fat moist cakes: baking powder and baking soda.

- Always substitute cake flour for all-purpose flour. It's made from a low-gluten (protein) flour and since it contains less protein, it takes less fat to tenderize it.
- I always try to slip in a little whole wheat flour for its incomparable nutritional addition. You will have to be cautious here because it will make the cake heavier and coarser. Start with 1/4 cup and see how it goes. Make sure you use whole wheat pastry flour, which, like cake flour, is made from low-gluten wheat.
- The equivalent amount of liquid egg substitute is a good substitute for high-fat whole eggs in moist fruit-filled cakes like carrot cake. However, in a drier, less fruity cake, you might need to leave in 1 or 2 egg yolks.

✖ CARROT CAKE

It seems that a recipe for carrot cake, moist and sweet, slathered in cream cheese frosting, takes up a slot in everyone's recipe file. Sally Fabro's recipe carried unusually high levels of sugar, eggs, oil, and cream cheese . . . could we springboard and achieve anywhere near the same levels of sweet-tooth satisfaction? Well, I liked the result so much I served it at my secretary Julie Carlson McIntosh's wedding. Now you be the judge!

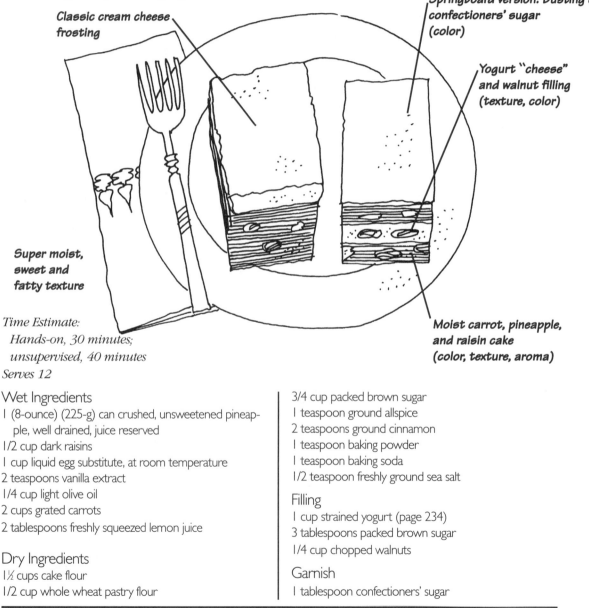

Classic cream cheese frosting

Springboard version: Dusting of confectioners' sugar (color)

Yogurt "cheese" and walnut filling (texture, color)

Super moist, sweet and fatty texture

Moist carrot, pineapple, and raisin cake (color, texture, aroma)

Time Estimate:
  Hands-on, 30 minutes;
  unsupervised, 40 minutes
Serves 12

Wet Ingredients
1 (8-ounce) (225-g) can crushed, unsweetened pineapple, well drained, juice reserved
1/2 cup dark raisins
1 cup liquid egg substitute, at room temperature
2 teaspoons vanilla extract
1/4 cup light olive oil
2 cups grated carrots
2 tablespoons freshly squeezed lemon juice

Dry Ingredients
1½ cups cake flour
1/2 cup whole wheat pastry flour

3/4 cup packed brown sugar
1 teaspoon ground allspice
2 teaspoons ground cinnamon
1 teaspoon baking powder
1 teaspoon baking soda
1/2 teaspoon freshly ground sea salt

Filling
1 cup strained yogurt (page 234)
3 tablespoons packed brown sugar
1/4 cup chopped walnuts

Garnish
1 tablespoon confectioners' sugar

The wet ingredients: Pour the reserved pineapple juice into a small saucepan and bring to a boil. Remove from the heat, stir in the raisins, and let them sit until plumped, about 15 minutes. Drain, discarding the pineapple juice.

Preheat the oven to 350°F (180°C). Grease and flour an 11 x 17-inch (28 x 43-cm) baking pan. In a large bowl, sift together all the dry ingredients. In a separate bowl, combine all the wet ingredients until mixed well. Slowly add the wet ingredients to the dry, stirring gently.

Pour the cake batter into the prepared pan and bake for 40 minutes or until a toothpick inserted in the center comes out clean. Remove from the oven and let sit for 15 minutes. Turn the cake out of the pan and onto a wire rack.

The filling: While the cake is cooling, mix the strained yogurt, brown sugar, and vanilla.

To assemble: Slice the cake horizontally into two even layers. Place one layer on a serving plate, spread with the filling and sprinkle with the walnuts. Cover with the second cake layer and garnish with a sprinkle of the confectioners' sugar.

Nutritional Profile per Serving			
	Classic	**Springboard**	**Daily Value**
Calories	740	249	
Calories from fat	423	54	
Fat (gm)	47	6	9%
Saturated fat (gm)	13	1	5%
Sodium (mg)	304	352	12%
Cholesterol (mg)	96	1	17%
Carbohydrates (gm)	75	42	14%
Dietary fiber (gm)	3	2	8%
Classic compared: Pineapple Carrot Cake with Cream Cheese Frosting			

STEAMED CARROT PUDDING

Would it be a Graham Kerr cookbook without a steamed pudding? Certainly not—this one's for the Queen! If you haven't tried one of my steamed puddings yet, it could be time to start a new tradition. It's easy; the ingredients are exactly the same as for the preceding carrot cake.

Incidentally, this pudding freezes well—as does the sauce. The sauce may separate slightly in thawing, but reconstitutes easily when pulsed in a blender.

Makes 2 puddings; each pudding serves 6

Wet Ingredients

1 (8-ounce) (225-g) can crushed, unsweetened pineapple, well drained, juice reserved
1/2 cup dark raisins
1 cup liquid egg substitute, at room temperature
2 teaspoons vanilla extract
1/4 cup light olive oil
2 cups grated carrots
2 tablespoons freshly squeezed lemon juice

Dry Ingredients

1½ cups cake flour
1/2 cup whole wheat pastry flour
3/4 cup packed brown sugar
1 teaspoon ground allspice
2 teaspoons ground cinnamon
1 teaspoon baking powder
1 teaspoon baking soda
1/2 teaspoon freshly ground sea salt

Sauce

1 cup strained yogurt (page 234)
3 tablespoons packed brown sugar
1 teaspoon vanilla extract
1/4 cup chopped walnuts
1/2 cup puréed steamed carrots

Garnish

Fresh mint leaves
Fresh cherries

The wet ingredients: Pour the reserved pineapple juice into a small saucepan and bring to a boil. Remove from the heat, stir in the raisins, and let them sit until plumped, about 15 minutes. Drain, discarding the pineapple juice.

In a large bowl, sift together all the dry ingredients. In a separate bowl, combine all the wet ingredients until mixed well. Slowly add the wet ingredients to the dry, stirring gently. Divide the combined batter into two equal parts.

Lightly oil two 5-cup capacity pudding bowls. Place two 4-quart (4-l) pots on the stove and fill each with about 1½ inches (4 cm) of water. Spoon the batter into the two pudding bowls and cover tightly with foil. Place each bowl in a saucepan and cover tightly with a lid. Slowly bring the water to a boil and simmer gently for 1 hour. Check the water level occasionally, making sure the pot doesn't get too dry.

The sauce: While the puddings are steaming, mix all the ingredients together and set aside. I like the textural crunch of the walnuts, but you may wish to leave them out. You can save them to sprinkle over the top as a garnish.

To serve: Remove the pudding bowls from the pans, cool slightly for 10 minutes, then unmold onto serving plates. Serve warm with the sauce spooned over the top and garnished with the mint and cherries.

Nutritional Profile per Serving: Calories—284; calories from fat—63; fat (gm)—7 or 11% daily value; saturated fat (gm)—1; sodium (mg)—291; cholesterol (mg)—1; carbohydrates (gm)—52; dietary fiber (gm)—3

❈ PUMPKIN BREAD

It was a plea for help: Page Le Blanc sent me her "favorite pumpkin bread recipe" asking if I "could do anything with it." I immediately went to work, substituting liquid egg substitute for the whole eggs, cutting the oil in half, and substituting low-fat raisins for nuts. My wish is that this lovely low-fat sweet bread will be a new favorite for Page and the many pumpkin fans of this world.

Time Estimate:
  Hands-on, 20 minutes;
  unsupervised, 1 hour
Serves 16

Dry Ingredients
1½ cups cake flour
1/4 teaspoon freshly ground sea salt
1 teaspoon baking soda
1/4 teaspoon grated nutmeg
1/2 teaspoon ground cinnamon
1/2 teaspoon ground allspice
1/2 teaspoon ground ginger

Wet Ingredients
1 cup canned pumpkin
1/4 cup light olive oil
1/2 cup liquid egg substitute
1 teaspoon vanilla extract
1/2 cup packed dark brown sugar
1/3 cup raisins

Preheat the oven to 350°F (180°C). Grease and flour a 9 x 5 x 3-inch (23 x 13 x 8-cm) loaf pan. Sift the dry ingredients together into a large mixing bowl. In a smaller bowl, combine the wet ingredients. Stir the wet ingredients into the dry until just mixed. Pour the batter into the prepared pan and bake for 50 minutes or until a toothpick inserted into the center comes out clean. Remove from the oven and let cool for 10 minutes before slicing into 16 (12-inch) (1.5-cm) pieces.

IS THERE LIFE AFTER HALLOWEEN?

Pumpkins aren't just for jack o'lanterns. The bright orange color tells you instantly that they're high in beta carotene and also contain lots of fiber. But fortunately you don't need to cook them from scratch to enjoy their taste and nutritional benefits. The canned pumpkin is a good-quality product: thicker and creamier than the meat cooked from fresh, and ready to use in all your recipes. Make sure you get pure pumpkin, and not a pie filling which is already mixed with sugar or spices.

Nutritional Profile per Serving: Calories—118; calories from fat—36; fat (gm)—4 or 6% daily value; saturated fat (gm)—1; sodium (mg)—104; cholesterol (mg)—0; carbohydrates (gm)—20; dietary fiber (gm)—1

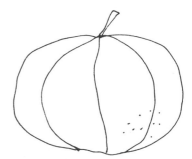

Cocoa Spice Cake

Culinary professional Howard Solganik is a very busy man. Could that be why this cake requires almost no work at all? It tastes chocolatey from the cocoa, is rich with color from the prunes and incredibly low in fat: a slice of the classic cake had a full 39 grams of fat, compared to the springboard's 4 grams!

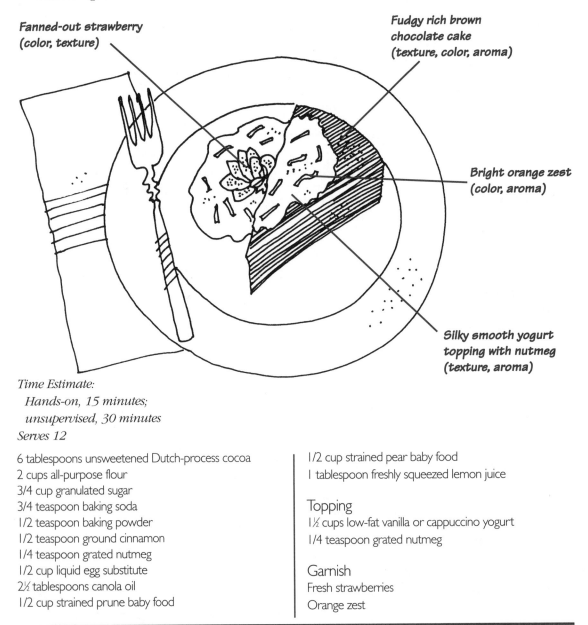

Fanned-out strawberry
(color, texture)
Fudgy rich brown
chocolate cake
(texture, color, aroma)
Bright orange zest
(color, aroma)
Silky smooth yogurt
topping with nutmeg
(texture, aroma)

Time Estimate:
Hands-on, 15 minutes;
unsupervised, 30 minutes
Serves 12

6 tablespoons unsweetened Dutch-process cocoa
2 cups all-purpose flour
3/4 cup granulated sugar
3/4 teaspoon baking soda
1/2 teaspoon baking powder
1/2 teaspoon ground cinnamon
1/4 teaspoon grated nutmeg
1/2 cup liquid egg substitute
2½ tablespoons canola oil
1/2 cup strained prune baby food
1/2 cup strained pear baby food
1 tablespoon freshly squeezed lemon juice

Topping
1½ cups low-fat vanilla or cappuccino yogurt
1/4 teaspoon grated nutmeg

Garnish
Fresh strawberries
Orange zest

Howard Solganik works hard developing the delicatessen foods we buy already prepared in our better supermarkets under the name Working Gourmet. He is founder and president of Solganik & Associates, a Dayton, Ohio–based food consulting firm that helps producers, suppliers, and retailers develop, market, and merchandise food products.

Among Howard's traditional delicatessen offerings tiptoe a few "nutritionally controlled" vegetarian dishes. In these dishes, Howard finds that the Mediterranean flavors are very "in," combined with low-fat cheese in layered dishes. His runaway success has been a Mexican lasagne layered with beans, tortillas, and reduced-fat cheese in a spicy tomato and bell pepper sauce.

A CAKE WITH POSSIBILITIES

Make this cake into an easy low-fat chocolate trifle. Cut it into squares and layer it in a large glass bowl with raspberry preserves and a cooled custard made from egg substitute, topped with low-fat vanilla yogurt. Refrigerate overnight so that all the flavors can blend together. Garnish with the fresh fruit of your choice, and perhaps the crunch of a little low-fat granola.

Preheat the oven to 350°F (180°C). Spray a 9-inch (27-cm) round cake pan with vegetable oil cooking spray. In a large bowl, combine the cocoa, flour, sugar, baking soda, baking powder, cinnamon, and nutmeg, whisking until completely mixed. Pour the egg substitute into a medium bowl and stir in the oil, strained fruit, and lemon juice. Stir the wet mixture into the dry ingredients. Spoon into the prepared baking pan and bake for 30 minutes. Remove from the oven and place on a rack to cool for 15 minutes. Then turn out of pan.

The topping: In a small bowl, mix the yogurt with the nutmeg.

To serve: Cut the cake into 12 wedges and serve each slice with 2 tablespoons of the topping, garnished with the fresh strawberries and sprinkled with the orange zest.

Nutritional Profile per Serving			
	Classic	**Springboard**	**Daily Value**
Calories	586	199	
Calories from fat	351	36	
Fat (gm)	39	4	6%
Saturated fat (gm)	21	1	4%
Sodium (mg)	132	110	5%
Cholesterol (mg)	141	2	1%
Carbohydrates (gm)	60	37	12%
Dietary fiber (gm)	5	2	8%
Classic compared: Austrian Chocolate Cake			

26 COCOA

Get the taste of chocolate without the fat for your desserts.

Recently a survey was conducted in which both men and women were asked what they would find hardest to give up. Listed among the top four were: alcohol, cigarettes, sex, and chocolate!

I'm a chocolate addict. Over twenty years of making changes, I've succeeded in doing two things: I refuse to take the key to the minibar refrigerator in my hotel room when I'm on the road—they all have slabs of ice-cold chocolate and there's nothing mini about *those* bars! Secondly, for baking I've switched to cocoa powder that has been "dutched." Cocoa powder is what's left after almost all the cocoa butter is removed (doubtless to be added to the mini bars). "Dutched"—for Dutch process—means that its acidity has been reduced. You still have the flavor and color of chocolate, but what's gone is that risky mouthroundfullness that comes hard on the heels of fat.

Now and again I'll use a few of the commercial chocolate chips; but mostly I find that cocoa balanced by a little brown sugar does a great job. What really surprised me was when I invited two very young ladies to conduct the ultimate taste test of my cocoa brownies against a real full-blooded all-American brownie . . . and they preferred the cocoa! (That brownie recipe can be found in my *Minimax Cookbook*.)

Tips and Hints

- Look for the words "Dutch process" on the cocoa label. Try a gourmet store for the best quality, asking for a brand imported from (yes, you guessed it) Holland.
- In baking, always mix the cocoa with a little water or milk to make a paste; otherwise it forms small hard lumps that never dissolve.

Graham discovers the chocolate "mini-bar" in his hotel room.

- When using dutched cocoa in baking, use baking powder to get a fine texture, because baking *soda* needs acidity to react and dutching produces alkalinity.
- Try using a few extra drops of vanilla or almond extract when you've got the whole mix ready. This adds another pleasing aroma as a sensual distraction.
- Try adding applesauce, prune, apricot, or pear purée to batters to replace some of the lost moisture and mouthfeel of fat.

✖ Cocoa Cookies and "Cream"

Every year something comes up that shouts Christmas! *and here it is again—a "chocolate" cookie that is a treat on its own, or elegantly presented as a chocolate, cream, and raspberry parfait. It was created for cookie lover Darryl Heine, who wanted a cookie alternative, and Suma-Kotrba, who loves chocolate.*

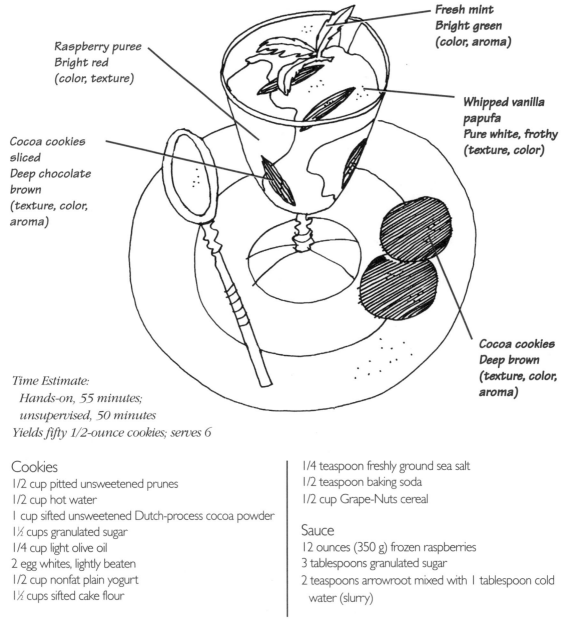

Fresh mint
Bright green
(color, aroma)

Raspberry puree
Bright red
(color, texture)

Whipped vanilla
papufa
Pure white, frothy
(texture, color)

Cocoa cookies
sliced
Deep chocolate
brown
(texture, color,
aroma)

Cocoa cookies
Deep brown
(texture, color,
aroma)

Time Estimate:
  Hands-on, 55 minutes;
  unsupervised, 50 minutes
Yields fifty 1/2-ounce cookies; serves 6

Cookies

1/2 cup pitted unsweetened prunes
1/2 cup hot water
1 cup sifted unsweetened Dutch-process cocoa powder
1½ cups granulated sugar
1/4 cup light olive oil
2 egg whites, lightly beaten
1/2 cup nonfat plain yogurt
1½ cups sifted cake flour

1/4 teaspoon freshly ground sea salt
1/2 teaspoon baking soda
1/2 cup Grape-Nuts cereal

Sauce

12 ounces (350 g) frozen raspberries
3 tablespoons granulated sugar
2 teaspoons arrowroot mixed with 1 tablespoon cold
  water (slurry)

Papufa

9 tablespoons instant nonfat dried milk powder

1/2 cup ice water

3 tablespoons superfine sugar

1 teaspoon light olive oil

1/4 teaspoon vanilla extract

1 envelope unflavored gelatin

3 tablespoons cold water

3 tablespoons boiling water

1 cup strained yogurt (page 57)

Garnish

Mint leaves

Soak the prunes in the water until plump and soft, about 15 minutes. Purée the prunes and their soaking liquid in a processor or blender until smooth, about 3 minutes. Add the cocoa and mix well.

Preheat the oven to 350°F (180°C). In a large mixing bowl combine the prune-cocoa mixture, sugar, oil, egg whites, and yogurt and stir well.

Sift the flour, salt, and baking soda into a medium-size bowl. Gently mix the prune-cocoa mixture into the dry ingredients with a rubber spatula. Fold in the Grape-Nuts.

Line one or two baking sheets with parchment paper. Spoon the dough into a large pastry bag with a large plain tip. Pipe 50 small cookies onto the parchment paper 1½ inches (4 cm) apart, or use 2 spoons if you haven't got a pastry bag. Bake for 12 minutes, then let cool on a wire rack.

Suma-Kotrba doesn't want her kids to cope with negative accumulated habits. "I grew up with a lot of fat in my diet and have had a lifelong problem being 20 to 30 pounds overweight. It took me 30 years before I knew how to cook healthy food. I don't want my kids to have that problem."

Of this recipe, she says, "None of my family is into prunes, and I was really hesitant to try the recipe. But I was really surprised: you don't taste them. They just make the cookies moist and chewy. I even liked the cookies plain with tea—they're almost like brownies, fudgy and chewy."

Now it simply must be said that Suma-Kotrba and I couldn't reach agreement on whether ot not to use Grape-Nuts. She likes cookies smooth, but I found the texture of the Grape-Nuts really great. So *please* if you like your cookies fudgelike 'n smooth . . . out with Grape-Nuts! That, after all, is the beauty of springboarding!

The sauce: Thaw the raspberries in a sieve over a bowl. When they've completely thawed, press through the sieve to yield about 3/4 cup raspberry juice/purée. Transfer to a small saucepan on low heat, add the sugar, and stir until completely dissolved. Bring to a boil, remove from the heat, stir in the arrowroot slurry, return to the heat, and boil until thickened and clear, about 30 seconds. Remove from the heat and let cool.

(continued)

WHIPPED CREAM BY ANY OTHER NAME?

Papufa is my invention to replace whipped cream. The name is an acronym for "physiologically active polyunsaturated fatty acid." It is totally saturated-fat-free and cholesterol-free.

The papufa: In a small mixing bowl, beat the dried milk and ice water with an electric beater for 5 minutes. Gradually beat in the sugar and oil. Add the vanilla and continue beating for 1 minute. In another small bowl, mix the gelatin with the cold water and let sit 3 minutes to soften. Stir in the boiling water until the gelatin is completely dissolved. In a large bowl, combine the milk mixture with the gelatin and strained yogurt.

To assemble: Take 2 cookies per serving and cut each one into 3 pieces. Start by pouring a small amount of the papufa in the bottom of a parfait glass and alternate layers of "cream" with the cookies and the raspberry sauce. Garnish with a mint leaf on top. This can be made several hours before serving and kept cool in the refrigerator.

Nutritional Profile per Serving			
	Classic	Springboard	Daily Value
Calories	480	278	
Calories from fat	378	36	
Fat (gm)	42	4	6%
Saturated fat (gm)	26	1	5%
Sodium (mg)	39	188	7%
Cholesterol (mg)	133	3	1%
Carbohydrates (gm)	28	53	18%
Dietary fiber (gm)	3	3	12%
Classic compared: Chocolate Trinity Parfait			

❖ CHOCOLATE COOKIE SANDWICHES

Gourmet frozen ice cream sandwiches are very popular. You can satisfy your sweet tooth and spend a lot less money by using the chocolate cookies from the preceding cocoa cookies and cream recipe to make your own delicious and low-fat ice cream sandwiches.

Time Estimate:
 Hands-on, 10 minutes
Serves 6

12 chocolate cookies (page 222)
6 teaspoons unsweetened raspberry jam
12 teaspoons strained low-fat vanilla yogurt (page 234)

Spread the bottom of one cookie with 1/2 teaspoon of the jam. Spread the bottom of another cookie with 2 teaspoons of the strained yogurt. Put the two together to make a delicious tea sandwich. Lay them flat in a freezer plastic bag, label, and date. Eat them thawed or frozen.

Nutritional Profile per Serving: Calories—98; calories from fat—18; fat (gm)—2 or 3% daily value; saturated fat (gm)—0.4; sodium (mg)—63; cholesterol (mg)—1; carbohydrates (gm)—20; dietary fiber (gm)—1

✖ New Black Bottom Cupcakes

Marykate Wilson remembers that "My mom was an excellent cook (all that high-fat stuff, you know!)." Then her husband, Don, had a small stroke at the age of 46 and they "were forced" to make changes in their eating and exercise habits. Now she and Don are "doing great and we can enjoy eating without feeling guilty." And these new cupcakes based on her recipe? They're "wonderful!!! Wonderful? They're fabulous!" Thank you for your enthusiasm, Marykate, just watch how many you eat. O.K.?

Time Estimate:
  Hands-on, 30 minutes;
  unsupervised, 20 minutes
Makes 18 cupcakes

Dry Ingredients
1½ cups cake flour
3/4 cup granulated sugar
1/4 cup unsweetened Dutch-process cocoa powder
1 teaspoon baking soda
1/4 teaspoon freshly ground sea salt
1/2 teaspoon baking powder

Wet Ingredients
1 cup water
2 tablespoons light olive oil
2 tablespoons prune purée (see sidebar)
1 tablespoon vinegar
1 teaspoon vanilla extract

Filling
2 tablespoons strained yogurt (page 234)
1 teaspoon cornstarch
1½ bananas, mashed (6 ounces or 175 g)
1/4 cup liquid egg substitute
2 tablespoons brown sugar
Pinch of freshly ground sea salt
3/4 cup crisped rice cereal
1/4 cup mini chocolate chips

Preheat the oven to 350°F (180°C). Place paper baking cups in cupcake baking trays for 18 cupcakes. Sift together the dry ingredients into a large mixing bowl. Combine the wet ingredients in a smaller mixing bowl. Stir the wet ingredients into the dry, gently and slowly, mixing well. Fill the prepared cupcake pans 1/2 full.

The filling: Mash the strained yogurt and cornstarch with the bananas and mix as well as you can. Add the rest of the ingredients and stir well. Drop about 2 teaspoons of the mixture into the center of each cupcake and top each one with a sprinkle of chocolate chips. Bake for 20 minutes.

Nutritional Profile per Serving: Calories—118; calories from fat—27; fat (gm)—3 or 5% daily value; saturated fat (gm)—1; sodium (mg)—264; cholesterol (mg)—0.06; carbohydrates (gm)—28; dietary fiber (gm)—1

THE POWER OF PRUNE PUREE

Prune purée provides such great moisture and color to your baking, you'll want to keep some on hand and use it often. Make a large batch from dried prunes, or you can buy the baby food jars of puréed prunes.

To make your own, soak 1/2 cup unsweetened pitted dried prunes in 1/2 cup hot water until plump and soft, about 15 minutes. Purée the prunes and their soaking liquid in a processor or blender until smooth, about 3 minutes. You should have about 1 cup. Transfer to an airtight container and keep refrigerated. Use as needed in baking recipes.

�֍ Frozen Cocoa Soufflé with Warm Raspberry Sauce

Chef Vincent Guerithault has whipped up one of the lightest soufflés I have ever tasted: the warm raspberry sauce gently melts the iced soufflé. And it's always useful to have a great dessert for which you can do the majority of the work the day before. Please note: if you are at risk for serious side effects from salmonella, you might want to replace the uncooked egg whites with meringue powder.

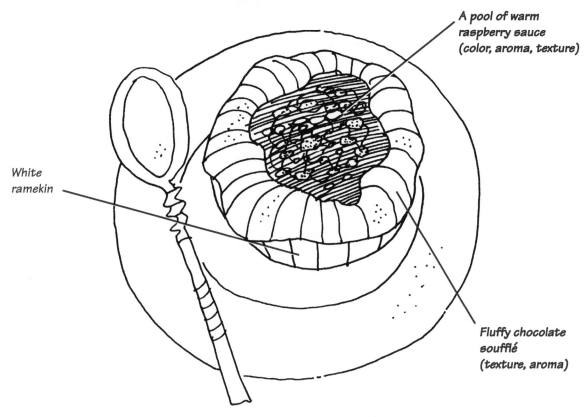

A pool of warm raspberry sauce (color, aroma, texture)

White ramekin

Fluffy chocolate soufflé (texture, aroma)

Time Estimate:
  Hands-on, the day before, 35 minutes;
  hands on, the day of serving, 10 minutes
Serves 6

8 ounces (250 g) low-fat yogurt, strained (page 234)
1/4 cup (25-g) unsweetened Dutch-process cocoa powder
8 egg whites or 5 tablespoons plus 1 teaspoon and 3/4 cup water
6 tablespoons (75 g) sugar

Raspberry Sauce
12 ounces (375 g) frozen raspberries
3 tablespoons sugar
2 teaspoons arrowroot mixed with 1 tablespoon cold water (slurry)

Whenever Treena and I visit our dear friends in Scottsdale, Arizona, we eat at **Vincent Guerithault's** restaurant, Vincent's on Camelback.

Vincent is a native of France who has made a breakthrough in combining the elegance of classic French cuisine with the rustic ingredients of the American Southwest. His use of cactus, jicame, cilantro, and chiles has been cited as one of the most exciting styles in the food industry today.

Vincent has joined me before in creating lighter, brighter cooking for my television shows. He takes a keen interest in what people really want to eat. "I have developed dishes to meet growing customer preferences for lower fat. People are definitely more aware of what they eat and are also more aware that they have options when dining out."

Vincent has also pioneered a most effective way of presenting his lighthearted fare on his menu, where several dishes, making up an entire meal, are printed together. This gives one an idea of how a complete evening's courses can be planned, literally from soup to nuts, without wondering if you are about to step on a fat-laden land mine.

The day before, wrap a strip of parchment paper or wax paper around the outside of 6 ramekins so that it extends about 1½ inches (4 cm) above the rim, creating a collar. Mix the yogurt with the cocoa powder. Whisk the egg whites until stiff, then very gradually fold the sugar into the egg whites. If you are using meringue powder, combine sugar, powder, and water in a bowl and beat to stiff peaks. Gently fold in the strained yogurt until the mixture is evenly combined. Spoon the mixture into the prepared ramekins, filling them nearly to the top of the collar. Freeze overnight.

The raspberry sauce: Just before serving, push the raspberries through a small metal sieve into a small saucepan. Add the sugar and arrowroot slurry and heat gradually, stirring constantly, until the mixture simmers and thickens slightly. Keep warm.

To serve: Remove the collars from the ramekins and scoop out a tablespoon of the soufflé with a sharp knife or melon baller. Pour some hot raspberry sauce into the crater and serve immediately.

SUPER SOUFFLÉS

Two tips: You'll get much more volume from the egg whites if you bring them to room temperature and then whisk them in a copper or stainless steel bowl. Then, when folding the egg whites into the yogurt mixture, pretend you are being filmed in slow motion; this will slow down your action and increase the chances of your presenting your guests with a light fluffy soufflé!

Nutritional Profile per Serving			
	Classic	**Springboard**	**Daily Value**
Calories	207	195	
Calories from fat	108	18	
Fat (gm)	12	2	3%
Saturated fat (gm)	6	1	5%
Sodium (mg)	262	132	6%
Cholesterol (mg)	122	5	2%
Carbohydrates (gm)	22	37	12%
Dietary fiber (gm)	1	3	12%
Classic compared: Chocolate Soufflé			

THE BASICS

BASIC CHICKEN, TURKEY, OR DUCK STOCK

Yields 4 cups

1 teaspoon light oil with a dash of toasted sesame oil
1 onion, peeled and chopped
1/2 cup coarsely chopped celery tops
1 cup coarsely chopped carrots
Carcass from a whole bird and any meat, fat, or skin scraps
1 bay leaf
2 sprigs fresh thyme
4 sprigs fresh parsley
6 black peppercorns
2 whole cloves

Pour the oil into a large stockpot over medium heat, add the onion, celery tops, and carrots and fry to release their volatile oils—about 5 minutes. Add the carcass and seasonings, cover with 8 cups water, bring to a boil, reduce the heat, and simmer for 2 to 4 hours, adding water if needed. Skim off any foam that rises to the surface. After 1 hour, add 1 cup cold water—this will force fat in the liquid to rise to the surface so you can remove it.

Strain; use with relative abandon.

The best way to get rid of excess fat is to chill the stock, let the fat rise to the top and harden, and then pick it off the top.

BASIC BEEF, LAMB, OR VEAL STOCK

Yields 4 cups

1 pound (450 gm) beef, lamb, or veal bones, fat trimmed off
1 teaspoon light olive oil with a dash of toasted sesame oil
1 onion, peeled and coarsely chopped
1/2 cup coarsely chopped celery tops
1 cup coarsely chopped carrots
1 bay leaf
2 sprigs fresh thyme
6 black peppercorns
2 whole cloves

Preheat the oven to 375°F (190°C). Place the beef, lamb, or veal bones in a roasting pan and cook until nicely browned—about 25 minutes. The browning produces a richer flavor and deeper color in the final stock.

Pour the oil into a large stockpot and fry the vegetables for 5 minutes, to release their volatile oils. Add the bones and seasonings, cover with 8 cups water, bring to a boil, reduce the heat, and simmer 4 to 8 hours, adding more water if necessary. Skim off any foam that rises to the surface. Strain and you've got a marvelous Minimax tool.

If you chill the stock in the refrigerator, the fat will harden on top and you will be able to pick it off.

QUICK BEEF STOCK IN A PRESSURE COOKER

Yields 4 cups

Same ingredients as for Basic Beef Stock, minus the carrots

Brown the bones in the oven as for Basic Beef Stock.

Pour the oil into a pressure cooker over medium heat and fry the onion and celery tops for 5 minutes. Add the browned bones and the seasonings, cover with 6 cups of water, fasten the lid, bring to steam, lower the heat, and cook for 40 minutes from the time when the cooker starts hissing.

Remove from the heat, leave the lid on, and let cool naturally—about 30 minutes. Strain; you will have about 4 cups of stock.

Note: Whenever you're using a pressure cooker, check your manufacturer's instruction book for maximum levels of liquids, etc.

BASIC HAM HOCK STOCK

Yields 6 cups

1 pound (450-gm) ham hock
1 bay leaf
3 whole cloves

In a pressure cooker, cover the ham hock with 2 quarts cold water, bring to a boil, remove from the heat, and drain, discarding the water. Put the ham hock back in the pressure cooker, add the bay leaf and cloves, pour in 2 quarts water, fasten the lid, and put over high heat. When the cooker starts hissing, turn the heat down to medium-low and let simmer 30 minutes. Carefully skim the fat off the hot soup or chill it thoroughly and pick the hardened fat off the top. Strain and have at it.

CLASSIC FISH OR SHRIMP STOCK

Yields 4 cups

1 teaspoon light olive oil with a dash of toasted sesame oil
1 onion, peeled and coarsely chopped
1/2 cup coarsely chopped celery tops
2 sprigs fresh thyme
1 bay leaf
1 pound fish bones (no heads) or shrimp shells (see Note)
6 black peppercorns
2 whole cloves

Pour the oil into a large saucepan and sauté the onion, celery tops, thyme, and bay leaf until the onion is translucent—about 5 minutes. To ensure a light-colored stock, be careful not to brown.

Add the fish bones or shrimp shells, peppercorns, and cloves, cover with 5 cups water, bring to a boil, reduce the heat, and simmer for 25 minutes. Strain through a fine-mesh sieve and cheesecloth.

Note: Salmon bones are too strong for fish stocks.

BASIC VEGETABLE STOCK

Yields 4 cups

1 teaspoon light oil with a dash of toasted sesame oil
1/2 cup coarsely chopped onion
2 cloves garlic, bashed and peeled
1/2 teaspoon freshly grated gingerroot
1/2 cup coarsely chopped carrot
1 cup coarsely chopped celery
1 cup coarsely chopped turnip
1/4 cup coarsely chopped leeks, white and light green parts only
3 sprigs fresh parsley
1/2 teaspoon black peppercorns

Pour the oil into a large stockpot over medium heat, add the onion and garlic, and sauté for 5 minutes. Add the rest of the ingredients, cover with 5 cups of water, bring to a boil, reduce the heat, and simmer for 30 minutes. Strain, and great flavor is at your fingertips.

Easy, Quick, Enhanced Canned Stocks

Canned stock (low-sodium if possible)
Bouquet garni

Pour the canned stock into a saucepan, add the appropriate bouquet garni, bring to a boil, reduce the heat, and simmer for 30 minutes. Strain and move forward, enhanced, of course.

Basic Bouquet Garni: For ease of operation, I suggest you use our basie "bunch of herbs": 1 bay leaf, 2 sprigs fresh thyme (1 teaspoon dried), 6 black peppercorns, 2 whole cloves, 3 sprigs parsley.

For poultry: Add a 4-inch branch (10 cm) of tarragon (2 teaspoons or 10 ml dried) or 6 sage leaves (1 teaspoon or 5 ml dried).

For fish: Use either a few small branches of fennel or of dill, incorporated into the basic bunch of herbs.

For beef: Use a few branches of marjoram or rosemary incorporated into the basic bunch of herbs.

I let my herb bunches go around twice when I use them to flavor a canned broth. In this case, I simply simmer for up to 20 minutes and then put the bunch of herbs into a sealable plastic bag and keep it deep-frozen until its next appearance. Do be sure to label it: a frozen herb bag could be a disappointing late-night microwave snack for twenty-first-century teenagers!

Remember: canned stocks are often loaded with sodium. Please check the label if you are sodium sensitive.

Basic Strained Yogurt

Yields 3/4 cup

1½ cups plain nonfat yogurt (354 ml), no gelatin added

Put the yogurt in a strainer over a bow—or you can use a coffee filter, piece of muslin, or a paper towel and place in a small sieve over a bowl. Cover and let it drain in the refrigerate for 5 hours or overnight. After 10 hours it becomes quite firm and the small lumps disappear, which makes it ideal for use in sauces. The liquid whey drains into the bowl, leaving you with a thick, creamy "yogurt cheese."

Index

✠